Microsoft®

online *travel*

D1450711

Ed Perkins

PUBLISHED BY
Microsoft Press
A Division of Microsoft Corporation
One Microsoft Way
Redmond, Washington 98052-6399

Library of Congress Cataloging-in-Publication Data
Perkins, Ed.
    Online Travel / Ed Perkins.
       p. cm.
    Includes index.
    ISBN 0-7356-1110-6
     1. Travel--Computer network resources--Directories.   2. Internet addresses--Directories.
   3. World Wide Web--Directories. I. Title.

    G155.A1 P377   2000
    025.06'91--dc21   00-042380

Printed and bound in the United States of America.

  3 4 5 6 7 8 9   QWTQWT   5 4 3 2 1 0

Distributed in Canada by Penguin Books Canada Limited.

A CIP catalogue record for this book is available from the British Library.

Microsoft Press books are available through booksellers and distributors worldwide. For further information about international editions, contact your local Microsoft Corporation office or contact Microsoft Press International directly at fax (425) 936-7329. Visit our Web site at mspress.microsoft.com. Send comments to *mspinput@microsoft.com*.

Acquisitions Editor: Christey Bahn
Project Editor: Kristen Weatherby

Contents

Chapter 3   **Winning the Airfare Game**   **37**

Acknowledgments

I would like to express my special thanks to my wife and partner, Eleanore, both for her editorial assistance and for her tolerance of those eternal on-line data-gathering sessions. I would also like to thank Kristen Weatherby, of Microsoft Press, for being the ideal editor: fixing what needed to be fixed, but not changing just for the sake of change.

Introduction

This is a travel book with an Internet focus, not an Internet book about travel. This distinction is not without a difference; it goes directly to the book's ongoing utility. Internet sites come and go, and even the ones that have been around a long time reinvent themselves with a speed that can startle even the most dedicated Web surfers. That's why a book that merely catalogs and describes Internet sites is obsolescent the day the author submits final manuscript.

But the basics of travel planning and buying don't change all that rapidly. So a book that focuses first on travel strategies, and then shows how representative Internet sites can help implement those strategies, can remain useful for several years or more. If you know how to use a travel site—what to ask, where to ask it, and how to ask it—you can effectively apply that knowledge even to sites that weren't out there when I completed the text of this book.

Target: Maximum Efficiency

My target audience is you travelers who want to use the Internet with maximum efficiency, both to plan trips and to purchase travel services at the lowest possible prices.

My aims are to help you:

- Decide exactly what information you need to plan a trip and determine which travel services you must purchase.

- Formulate the questions you need answered and the additional inputs you require from the Internet and other sources.

- Find the Internet sites that best answer those questions, provide those necessary inputs, and supply needed travel services at the lowest prices.

- Learn when the Internet has incomplete answers, potentially misleading answers, or even no answers at all, plus how to find the alternative non-Internet sources you need to consult.

I'm assuming that you already have a working base of travel experience, at least enough to know that you'll be buying one or more big-ticket travel services—airline tickets, accommodations, car rentals, tours, and cruises—either through the Internet or through some other channel. I target this book at those of you who are planning somewhat full vacations that require management of several details—and not at those of you whose idea of travel is "throw the kids in the SUV and head for the lake."

Some of you might already have used the Internet to plan trips, make reservations, and buy tickets—maybe successfully, maybe not. Others might not yet have seen any reason to use the Internet for solving travel problems. Either way, I'm assuming that you already know how to get on the Internet, search for sites of interest, and conduct online business—at least enough to handle the typical travel site. There's nothing in this book about modems, ISPs, browsers, or keyboarding, nor do I spell out in detail exactly what words to type into the various boxes and forms you'll encounter. If you need help at that level, consult one of the many good basic Internet reference books. I have only one technical recommendation: If you're serious about searching out all the Internet's travel possibilities, high-speed access will make your life a lot easier. Still, if you can't access at high speed, you can get the job done with a conventional phone-line modem.

Web Details

I show specific examples, using real Web sites accessible in the spring of 2000. But the overall approach does more than catalog existing sites: By organizing the information in terms of travel services rather than Web sites, it assures that you'll be able to use the book's lessons to explore new sites that weren't even up and running at the time I wrote the book.

Very little changes more rapidly than the design of a Web page, and what you see when you access any of the listed sites might be quite different than what I describe or what the book's graphics show. Still, I note which site features are helpful and which are not, even when change is likely. And presumably, if you see a change, it's for the better.

These days, the rashest statements an author can make start out "No Web sites provide…" Where I can't find something after I've tried diligently, I note that omission. But to say that it isn't there at all is foolish—when the real problem might well be that I wasn't clever enough to find it.

Using This Book

This book is organized around the way most travelers plan and buy travel services, not by type of Internet site. After a brief overview of how the Internet and travel planning fit together (Chapter 1), Chapter 2 discusses the most basic part of travel planning: deciding where to go and what to do. Many travelers who make these decisions without using the Internet might choose to skip this chapter. However, even if, say, you've decided to go to France, you might still want to search out details: What's going on in the cities you plan to visit, what's the weather likely to be, and such. Chapter 2 is where you'll find sites that can help you with those questions.

Subsequent chapters detail the specifics of various important travel purchases: air tickets, hotel accommodations, cruises, package tours, and the rest of the travel panoply. In each case, the book's presentations are organized around the kind of trip you're likely to take and the sites that provide the specific sort of tickets or other arrangements you need for different trips. And in each case, the book notes where you might have to check with non-Internet sources to find answers to your questions or to buy a specific travel service.

The final chapters deal with some of the more minor nuts and bolts of travel: buying a railpass, renting a car, currency conversions, travel insurance, travel scams, and—if things go bad on your trip—how and where to lodge an effective complaint. I end the book with a brief discussion on working with a travel agent, should you decide that you want some help in making your travel plans.

Each chapter begins with a "Quick Trip" section, which provides a brief summary of the information that appears in the chapter. You can refer to this section before you read a chapter to see if the chapter contains the information you need for your particular trip, or you can use it after you've read a chapter as a checklist for what you need to do next. I've also included two groups of sidebars:

- "Inside the System" sections try to convey a feel for the "whys" as well as the "whats" of travel. I know that not all of you will care, but some of you will—especially regarding airlines. Surveys show that many of you are justifiably stumped by what seems to be capricious pricing, and you're certainly disgusted by today's poor levels of service.

- "Ed's Notebook" sections record some of my individual opinions and conclusions, based on my own long-time observations of the travel industry and its many foibles. They're the book's "op-ed" pages.

When you've finished reading this book, I hope you feel both confident that you can successfully navigate the Internet to find the best deals for your trip, and aware of what to do when the Internet doesn't have the answers you need. If I've been successful, the only thing that remains for you is to have a great trip!

Let's go!

1 Internet Travel: The World on Your Desktop

Quick Trip Through Chapter 1

With its ability to match supply and demand on almost a real-time basis, the Internet is ideal for buying and selling travel: Suppliers can fine-tune prices and availabilities to meet changing market conditions, and consumers can shop around among hundreds of sources for the best prices—especially for last-minute services that might otherwise go unused.

But the Internet's strengths also entail weaknesses: You find so many suppliers, with so many options, that you might sometimes long for the advice and counsel of a knowledgable travel agent. Not everything you might want is online—yet. Also, the free-wheeling Internet is becoming a happy hunting ground for scamsters. If I've been at all successful in my efforts, this book should help you take maximum advantage of the Internet's strengths and overcome its weaknesses.

To help navigate the intricacies of the Web, I've classified sites in terms of their function in the overall process of providing travel information and enabling online purchase. In practice, however, you find a good deal of overlap.

Given that I wrote this book in the spring and summer of 2000, it's unlikely that the prices I quote will still be current at the time you're reading. Because of that, the prices I use serve primarily to illustrate the sorts of price structures you're likely to encounter, even though the actual numbers might vary.

f you're reading this book, you're probably one of the millions of people who use the Internet as their main information source. You might even be one of the increasing number of Americans who are turning to the Internet to buy all sorts of goods and services. But there's both good news and bad news about using the Internet to plan and buy your travel. The upside is that the Internet brings the world of travel to your fingertips, providing a wealth of information about everything ranging from how to find a cheap ticket to Orlando to how to arrange a sightseeing junket to Greenland. This overwhelming amount of information is also the downside: Without a guide through the mountains of material available on the Internet, you can easily end up lost or frustrated—or both. This book will serve as your guide and will lead you through the rocky terrain of navigating the travel information on the Internet as expertly as a Sherpa guiding you up Mt. Everest.

In this chapter, I introduce some terminology that I use throughout the book and introduce the types of sites you'll encounter as you explore the world of online travel. But first, I show why travel quickly became one of the Internet's early success stories.

Made for Each Other

The Internet and travel are a natural fit. The Internet provides quick access to almost limitless information about almost anywhere you're likely to want to go or about any activity that's likely to appeal to you. But the Internet's potential as a marketplace for travel services eclipses its potential as an information resource. Travel services are ideally suited to the sort of instant supply-demand matching that the Internet can provide:

- The Internet permits the equivalent of a real-time auction of travel services. Without changing list prices, suppliers can continually re-assign the quantities of rooms, seats, and cabins they allocate to each of their various list-price categories. As a consumer, you can buy when you find an attractive price; if you don't find a price you like, you can try another supplier or wait for a shift.

- The Internet allows suppliers to unload unsold seats, rooms, and cabins at last-minute prices without disturbing the normal marketplace. This ability has opened the door to new services available only through the Internet, most notably the Internet-only, short-notice weekend airfares and associated hotel deals.

- The Internet gives you immediate ownership of a travel service you have bought over the Internet. When you buy merchandise over the Internet, you have to wait for the product to be shipped—and possibly pay extra for delivery. But you don't have to wait for an e-ticket or for instant e-mail confirmation of your travel purchases.

Because the Internet is a cheap way for suppliers to sell travel services, consumer use of the Internet helps keep costs and prices under control. The big U.S. airlines averaged only about 10 percent of their ticket sales over the Internet in 1999, but Southwest sold 25 percent, and the British low-fare airline easyJet sold more than half of their tickets that way. Many others are targeting similar figures over the next few years. And where the airlines have led, other travel suppliers will likely follow.

Nobody's Perfect

But the story of travel on the Internet isn't all positive. If you want to buy travel online, you will still run into these barriers:

- Many of you still worry about giving out charge card numbers to an Internet site. Consumer resistance remains high even though the Federal Trade Commission (FTC) reports that misuse of charge card numbers on the Internet is not widespread, and even though Internet suppliers are vigilant about security precautions.

- Nobody polices the Internet for crooks and scamsters. While you might feel secure dealing with sites maintained by giant airlines and hotel chains, you might be somewhat less comfortable dealing with an intermediary agency you don't know. After all, a seller needs to be skillful to put up a great looking Web site, but not necessarily honest. Whereas newspapers and magazines generally require at least a minimum of information from anyone who wants to place a print ad, and radio and TV stations screen companies looking to air commercials, no agency performs any such function for Web sites. Consumers are therefore justifiably concerned.

- Some Internet sites require that you *register* before the site will do anything useful for you. Registering, in this case, means entering your name and e-mail address as a minimum; sometimes you even have to supply a charge card number. That's a real turnoff—like having someone stand at the entrance to a department store and demand that you swipe your charge card before he or she will let you through the door. Several important sites—including Expedia and United Airlines—have abandoned the onerous registration requirement. But, turnoff or no, all too many sites still demand it.

- For the most part, Internet sites don't offer personal interaction with a knowledgeable person—a feature any travel agent can offer. Sure, on some sites, you can e-mail a question, but that's no substitute for a person-to-person discussion.

Plan B Deficit is one example of what happens when there's no personal interaction: Nobody is available to suggest an alternative (a Plan B) if your normal choice doesn't work. Say you want to fly from the West Coast to Philadelphia. A "lowest fare" search engine might come up with a $600 round-trip fare as the best deal available. What the search engine can't tell you is that by flying to nearby Baltimore you can take advantage of a $200 sale-fare on Southwest. You can find similar situations all around the United States. Fares to and from Milwaukee—some 80 miles north of Chicago—are often much lower than those to Chicago O'Hare. Sites are starting to attack the Plan B Deficit with text messages such as "if the fares to your first choice airport seem high, try a nearby alternate airport," possibly with specific examples. Still, the Internet is not ever likely to provide Plan B suggestions as well as a knowledgeable person can.

Travel Agents: A Dying Breed?

Ill-informed observers of the travel scene are fond of pronouncing travel agents dead—killed off by the Internet. In fact, the whole "Internet versus travel agents" issue is what logicians call a false dichotomy. Most Internet travel sellers *are* travel agencies, performing their traditional role via electronic media rather than—or in addition to—storefront locations. Sure, the agency business will change. But travelers don't always want to be confined to dealing with a single supplier. And as long as at least some consumers need a knowledgeable person to assist them in making the right travel decisions, storefront agencies will be with us. (See the Endnote for more information on working with travel agencies.)

Seven Varieties of Sites

This book focuses on helping you use the Internet most efficiently. First, I examine your main options for getting information and buying travel services, and then I show you how to locate the resources you need on the Internet.

Throughout the book I show specific examples, using real Web sites accessible in the spring of 2000. But my approach does more than catalog existing sites: Because I organize the information in terms of travel services rather than Web sites, you'll be able to use the book's lessons to explore new sites that weren't even up and running at the time I wrote the book.

Overall, the book covers seven types of sites:

Gateway Sites

Gateway sites (or portals) consist mainly of links to other sites, organized so that you can quickly locate the sites you're trying to reach. You don't get much in the way of information from a gateway site, nor can you buy travel services there. But gateway sites save you a lot of time when you have an idea of the sort of site you want to reach but don't know an exact URL (or address).

Figure 1-1, on the next page, shows the home page of Tourism Offices Worldwide Directory (*www.towd.com*), a gateway site to destination areas. It shows two pull-down menus, one for foreign countries and the other for individual U.S. states. You scroll through either list until you get to the name of the place you're considering visiting. Click the name and the Search button, and the next screen shows you a list of official tourism organizations covering the destination you selected. Some of the individual list entries include links that allow you to go directly to a site; others just give telephone numbers, fax numbers, and street addresses.

Some gateway sites are designed to be used as home pages by travel enthusiasts. And some general-interest home pages provide the equivalent of gateway listings for key travel services: destinations, airlines, cruise lines, hotel chains, and such. Gateway sites can cover a very broad subject area, as in the Tourism Offices Worldwide site, or they can get very specific, as in a gateway to golf course sites. No matter what you call them, these pages can lead you very quickly into extended listings of individual sites for a variety of travel subjects.

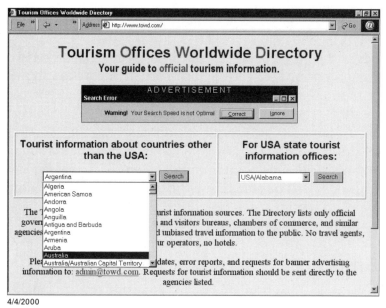

Figure 1-1. *The home page for the Tourism Offices Worldwide Directory links you to hundreds of destination sites.*

Single-Supplier Sites

Thousands of sites are run by companies that are trying to sell you their services on the Web. As you might expect, this category includes sites run by conventional travel suppliers: major and minor airlines, rental car companies, hotel chains, cruise lines, and such. It also includes some that aren't quite so obvious, such as International Currency Express, who wants to sell you foreign currency before you leave the United States. The home page of its site (*www.foreignmoney.com*) is pictured in Figure 1-2.

Some single-supplier home pages are simply portals, with dozens of individual pages you can scan for more specific information. Others however, include the most popular options directly on their home pages. More and more airline sites, for example, show boxes for requesting flights on their home pages.

Whether they are simple or complex, single-supplier sites share one critical feature: Everything you see is at list price. That doesn't mean you won't see an airline's "discount" fares or a hotel's "sale-priced" rooms, but it does mean you won't find much about the many "less-than-the-supplier's-asking-price" deals that are rife in the marketplace.

5/29/2000

Figure 1-2. *You can check rates and order currency online through International Currency Express.*

Agency Sites

Some of the most heavily visited travel sites are operated by travel agencies of one stripe or another—agencies that sell a broad range of travel services from a broad range of suppliers. Figure 1-3, on the next page, shows the home site for Expedia (*www.expedia.com*), the Web's most frequently visited travel site (at least according to some figures), which promotes virtually all travel services.

Every week, one or two more agency sites appear on the Internet. And every week, it seems that one of the big agency sites is acquired by someone else, modified, and given a new URL.

Many agency sites referenced in this book claim to offer "discount" prices, promise to find the "best" prices, or both. As I describe later, in the travel marketplace there are discounts and then there are discounts. Some discount prices are list prices for restricted or off-season services, and many agency sites search among only these list-price discounts. Other discount prices are actually below what the suppliers say they should be, and some agencies specialize in finding these below-list discounts. Unfortunately,

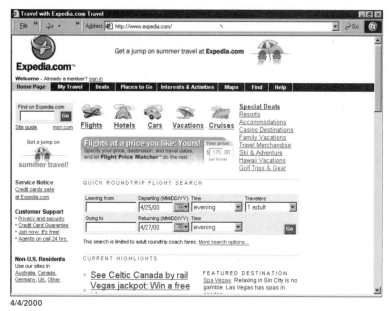

4/4/2000

Figure 1-3. *Expedia is a big agency site that features a wide range of services.*

agencies are all too frequently unclear about which they do. When a supplier touts discount prices, as with disarmament, "trust but verify."

Information Sites

Some of the most helpful sites don't sell anything. Instead, they provide useful information about a particular subject. They can be supported by individual companies as a public service or supported by sale of advertising. For example, FrequentFlier.com (*www.frequentflier.com*) is a commercial, advertising-supported site that compiles information on a wide range of frequent flyer programs. In contrast, an "unofficial history" site for the New York City subways (*www.nycsubway.org/maps/transit/*) offers transit maps from cities around the world, compiled by volunteer subway fans.

Government Sites

Government agencies are outstanding sources of useful information. Among the best known sources is the U.S. State Department's site for Consular Information sheets (*travel.state.gov/travel_warnings.html*), widely referenced as the most extensive available source of information on what's really going on, right now, in more than 100 countries.

Another U.S. Government site provides the latest cruise-ship sanitation scores; yet another lists countries not in compliance with current FAA standards for surveillance of aviation safety. Useful sites are also maintained by state and local governments in the United States, and by national and local foreign governments as well.

Consumer Sites

As you might expect, most consumer organizations maintain Internet sites. Consumers Union (publisher of *Consumer Reports* and *Consumer Reports Travel Letter*) maintains a site (*www.consumer.org*) where you can keep up to date on current consumer advocacy issues, including those that deal with travel. Unfortunately, you have to pay for full access to the organization's data bank and back-issue library.

Other self-styled consumer sites are more narrowly focused. Some are, in effect, online publications, supported by advertising. A case in point is *The Ticked-Off Traveler* (*www.ticked.com*), shown in Figure 1-4. Others are little more than organized gripe sites run by a single disgruntled former customer.

6/8/2000

Figure 1-4. *At* The Ticked-Off Traveler, *travel writers report on scams, problems, and frustrations.*

Travel Publication Sites

Several guidebook publishers and big-circulation travel publications host sites, such as Arthur Frommer's Budget Travel (*www.frommers.com*). For the most part, they give you free access to at least some of their recently printed content; some provide quite a bit more. Clearly, however, they're also selling books and subscriptions.

You can also find sites from more specialized publications. Among them are *Zagat* (*www.zagat.com*), guides for restaurant ratings, and the *Specialty Travel Index* (*www.spectrav.com*), which lists operators of special-interest tours.

About Prices

Discount might be the most abused word in the travel lexicon. Airlines routinely call any fare lower than full Coach-fare a "discount" fare, despite the facts that only about 2 percent of travelers actually pay that full fare; and the myriad other fares are official, list-price fares for tickets that entail one or more restrictions, so they're not the same as full-fare tickets. Similarly, hotels often tout their reduced weekend rates as "discount" rates, when a weekend night in a Business-class hotel is a very different (and less valuable) product than a midweek night.

In this book, I reserve the word *discount* to mean any service that is priced lower than the supplier says that service should cost. So a hotel's own weekend rate is not a discount rate, but a hotel broker's midweek rate is genuinely discounted.

Most agency sites promise discounts of one kind or another. It's easy to claim a discount, and quite another thing to deliver a genuine discount. I have often tried to distinguish between reduced list prices and true discounts, but you'll find, as you explore the Web, that it isn't always an easy call.

At any rate, in this book I direct you to sites where you're likely to find the lowest prices, without any guarantee that those prices are truly discounted. Certainly, prices change far too often for this or any other book to claim that some sites have better prices than others. As with so much in the travel marketplace, there's no substitute for comparison shopping.

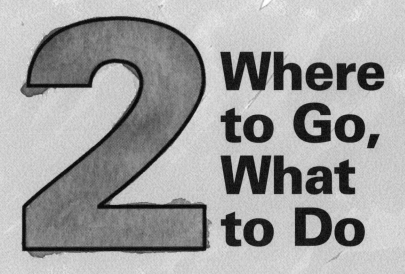

2 Where to Go, What to Do

Quick Trip Through Chapter 2

Once you've decided where to go (or what you'd like to do), the Internet can provide a wealth of supporting information:

- Destination sites for cities, regions, states, provinces, and countries provide lots of basic data. The better ones link you to other useful sites, and many are set up so that you can order brochures online.

- Some of the sites run by major natural resource agencies provide great information. I'm especially impressed by the National Park Service, state parks, and several private operators.

- Special-interest sites run the gamut from art museums to zoos, and online events calendars help you track activities you might want to pursue.

Finding sites you want is sometimes easy, sometimes not. It's easy when someone or something—a government agency, commercial enterprise, or an amateur hobbyist—has already compiled a gateway site with links to hundreds of individual sites. But you sometimes have to do a bit of detective work to find what you want, by checking destination or commercial sites you think might have links to what you're seeking. And if all else fails, general-purpose search engines can usually get the job done—but often at a price: You'll be forced to wade through lots of extraneous "hits."

Microsoft uses the phrase "Where do you want to go today?" as a metaphor for the entire world of computing. But when applied to researching travel on the Internet, you can take this question quite literally. You can find a wealth of information—some general, some incredibly detailed—for almost any place you'd consider visiting.

About the only question the Internet can't answer for you is where to start looking. Even a natural language search engine such as the one used on the Ask Jeeves site (*www.askjeeves.com*) won't be able to answer the question, "Where should I go on my next trip?" You must take the first stab at determining your destination based on your interests, your objectives, and your finances.

But once you've made your decision, the Internet can do much of the rest. Whatever mix of nature, nightlife, beaches, or cathedrals you're seeking, you'll find help on the Internet. In this chapter, I identify some of the better places to conduct your online search—and how to find the sites that aren't listed here.

I've organized destination sites into categories such as state sites, city sites, national sites, natural resource sites, and activity sites to make it easier for you to decide where to begin your information search. In practice, you'll find quite a bit of information overlap among sites in the various categories. Most state and city sites, for example, include events calendars, either internally or through links. These sites often also provide information on major attractions, the weather, hotels, and such.

HEADS UP

In this book, I focus mainly on the sites that are sponsored by governments and official tourist agencies. As you explore, you'll find many independent sites, with sponsors ranging from profit-making commercial organizations to volunteer student groups. Some of those independent sites might well be more useful than the official ones, but many have their own axes to grind. My advice? Check as many options as you can conveniently explore, but whenever you encounter a nonofficial site, be aware of its source. Read on.

What's in a Destination Site?

Every U.S. state, many multistate and intrastate regions, some foreign countries and regions, cities all over the world, park and natural resource systems, and private attractions maintain official Web sites. What sort of information do they provide?

- Almost all give a Web version of the destination's printed brochures, or at least highlights of the brochures. Most provide extensive color illustrations plus text descriptions, in addition to detailed sub-pages for natural features in the region, commercial attractions, accommodations, restaurants, and such. And most have provisions for you to request printed materials by postal mail.

- Beyond these basics, many destination sites include links to other sites that supplement the basic information: regional transit authority information, state and local park system guides, college and university overviews, individual private attraction details, and climate and weather data.

- Most provide an online means for you to request that the sponsor send printed brochures.

- Many official sites are also linked to agencies that sell air tickets, arrange hotel rooms, rent cars, and otherwise provide travel services. However, you might want to ignore those links while you're considering where to go and what to do. Destination sites are supported, in part, by advertisers, and any particular advertiser that sponsors the site you're viewing isn't necessarily going to offer you the best deal on whatever it's selling. Instead, use the subsequent chapters on airfares, accommodations, cruises, tours, and other travel services to decide which sites are likely to be the best places to buy.

How "Good" Is a Destination Site?

My personal system for rating destination Web sites is based on the answers to three questions:

1. Does the site provide enough information about the destination area's features and attractions to allow me to decide whether I want to visit?

2. Does it provide a reasonable number of links to other sites with additional useful information?

3. Is the information current, by Web standards—which usually means more current than any guidebook?

If I can answer "yes" to all three questions, the site is outstanding, and "yes" to any two probably means it's well worth a visit. By that test, a "good" destination site should give you enough information to decide whether you want to go to that destination. But no site I've seen provides the detail you need to plan a specific itinerary for a week's drive through a region or a week's stay in a big city. You still need a copy of a good sightseeing guidebook, best exemplified by the *Michelin Green* series but available in many other forms. And you need to look elsewhere on the Internet, or buy a different sort of guidebook, to decide where to stay and where to eat.

HEADS UP

No matter how attractive, a site has limited value if it isn't current. How do you tell if it is? Some sites display a "last updated" notice, often at the bottom of the home page. With others, you can sometimes check the dates of press releases or announcements of special prices or services. Most of the travel sites I visited while researching this book were up-to-date. However, I found one hotel site, early in 2000, that hadn't been updated since August 1999. Never assume that a site is current unless you can find some direct evidence.

The State of the States

If you're planning a sightseeing or recreational trip in the United States, chances are you're interested in visiting one or more entire states, or at least sizable regions of several states. That's why many of you will want to start out with one or more state sites.

To see how the system works, let's take a close look at the official sites for two states: California and Florida. Figure 2-1 shows the top part of the index page of the California Division of Tourism's Web site (*www.gocalif.ca.gov*), as it appeared in early 2000. The initial page on this site was a full-screen photo with almost no text; a simple click took you to this index page, the real home page. A quick exploration of this site shows some of its important strengths.

4/6/2000

Figure 2-1. *California's index page steers you to a wide range of options.*

The site provided several choices to help you learn more about California and its travel information. If you clicked the main buttons, you were taken to additional menus and maps, with information on hundreds of individual regions and communities. This made it easy to quickly zero in on topics that intrigued you. For example, if you clicked the Visitor's Guide button, you ended up at a page where you could click a region or type the name of a community in California; doing either, in turn, provided links to information on places to stay, things to do, and more information for that area.

True, some regions contained more information than others, and for some, the level of detail was less useful than a copy of the AAA guide. But on Web sites like this one, you can't give up easily. Often you can find more information by using a different search route. For example, on California's Visitor's Guide site, if you clicked a subregion and then clicked For More Information, you could scroll through a long list of local and regional Chambers of Commerce and Visitors Bureaus. Many of the Chambers of Commerce and Visitors Bureaus had sites that you could access from there. On those sites, you could find links to new sites with a wealth of details about the region's natural and commercial resources. Overall, California passed the "good site" test: You could really decide to visit there without having to buy any guidebooks, the site had lots of interesting links, and most of the information was current.

As a second example, consider the Florida site (*www.florida.com*). According to at least one Internet metering service, it's the most frequently visited of all state sites. But if you take a look at it, you'll wonder why. At least in its early-2000 form, it lacked some of the detail that the California site provided.

The "Attractions" page available through the "Search Florida" link divided the state into regions—three, in this case. If you looked at the Central Florida region, you were presented with a list of 27 private attractions, mainly centered on the Orlando/Disney tourist mega-complex.

Unfortunately, that list seemed to have been influenced by commercial considerations more than by visitor needs. Sure, Walt Disney World was listed, along with a link to its extensive Web site (*www.disneyworld.com*), as was Cypress Gardens (*www.cypressgardens.com*). However, although nearby Universal Studios Orlando was also listed (as Universal Studios Florida), there was no link to its site (*www.uescape.com*). If you wanted anything more than a brief paragraph with phone numbers and postal mail addresses, you had to use some other source to find it. Moreover, the Florida site had very few listings of non-commercial natural attractions, and city information was also weak. Click a city's name (only 27 on the drop menu), and all you found was a site that arranges accommodations—nothing about attractions or events, and no obvious links to that information.

I expect that the sites for both California and Florida have changed since I wrote this. However, I'm using these examples to illustrate a basic point about state sites: To take maximum advantage of the Internet's destination resources, you can't rely on a single site for all the information you might need. Instead, you have to regard the state's primary site as a starting point. You must move around in each state's site and follow any interesting-looking links you find—often a series of several such links. On good sites, you can find your way to links offering a wide variety of helpful information. On the other hand, some other sites leave you pretty much stuck with the meager menu that's available; for what's missing, you must turn to other sources.

City Sites for the Details

Do individual city sites do as well as states? Yes—in fact, they're usually better about details. Figure 2-2 shows part of the home page for San Francisco (*www.sfvisitor.org*), as of early 2000. As befits one of the nation's top visitor cities, the site was outstanding, with plenty of details on attractions, events, and local transportation. It had links to a hotel reservation service as well as to individual hotels, B&Bs, apartments, and other types of accommodation. You could easily plan a short San Francisco trip by using the information on this site (although a good guidebook would help even more).

4/6/2000

Figure 2-2. *The City by the Bay mounts a top-flight site with lots of detail.*

According to one Web metering measure, three of the nine most frequently visited destination sites deal with Las Vegas. Figure 2-3, on the next page, shows the top of the "Attractions" index page for the official Las Vegas Convention and Visitors Authority site (*www.lasvegas24hours.com*). It's quite comprehensive, with excellent search capability for entertainment, shows, and commercial attractions. However, as with some other sites, it's weak on natural features, public parks, and such. Two private Web sites—*www.lasvegas.com* and *www.vegas.com*—seem to cover about the same territory as the official site does. If anything, the private sites cover nearby natural features better.

HEADS UP

You can find other city sites either through one of the travel gateway sites or by using almost any search engine. For a list of some city sites to get you started, see the Appendix.

5/29/2000

Figure 2-3. *The site for Las Vegas has a heavy focus on attractions and activities.*

City sites aren't confined to the tourist mega-centers. You can find a decent Web site for just about any U.S. city that depends to a significant extent on tourism. As an example, even tiny Cave Junction, Oregon, population 1100, has a site (*www.cavejunction.com*) that describes the area's attractions and facilities, with links to a few of the most important ones.

Hundreds of National Sites, Worldwide

Well over 100 individual countries maintain Web sites. And, as you might expect, the quality of these sites varies tremendously. The big tourist countries' sites rival the best any U.S. state has to offer, while countries that attract fewer tourists might have only a page or two, often only in the native language. Here's an overview of the sites most likely to be of interest to U.S.-based travelers.

The Americas

Canada maintains an excellent national site (*www.travelcanada.ca*), with a good bit of detail and links to provincial and city sites. Figure 2-4 shows the initial search page, which provides several choices for further exploration of the site. Unfortunately, as with many similar sites in the United States, the official tourism site did not have links to the Canadian national park system, at least as of this writing. A private online publisher, World Web Technologies (*www.worldweb.com*), also maintains sites for Canada and several of its provinces and regions. The country is so large, however, that you might want to start off with the site for the individual province of greatest interest to you. See the Appendix for a list of the sites for all Canadian provinces and territories.

4/6/2000

Figure 2-4. *The Canadian Government Tourism site provides a comprehensive national overview.*

The Mexico Ministry of Tourism's national site (*www.mexico-travel.com*) provides extensive details about the country's many tourist destinations although, in early 2000, it was extremely slow to load even with a cable modem. Moreover, links to accommodations gave only the names and star ratings, with no descriptive material at all. You might find more helpful information on lodgings in Mexico by looking at some of the guidebook sites mentioned later in this chapter.

Central America, the Caribbean, and nearby islands are well represented on the Internet. For a complete list of their sites, see the Appendix.

Europe

Befitting its status as the top European destination for Americans, the United Kingdom has a large presence on the Internet. For starters, there's the official site of the British Tourist Authority (BTA at *www.travelbritain.org*), shown in Figure 2-5. It has just about everything you would expect in a comprehensive destination site—attractions, natural resources, transportation, accommodations, and all the other categories shown in the figure. It is also extremely useful in planning your trip in that it allows you to start your searches with a broad focus and narrow them down to something specific.

4/6/2000

Figure 2-5. *The British Tourist Authority shows how to do a good national site.*

Take Stonehenge as an example. You start out at "Attractions," where Stonehenge is prominently listed. Going to the Stonehenge section, you find a wealth of detail, including what it is, where it is, how to get there, when it's open, admission policies, parking, public transportation, and access for disabled travelers. Presumably, since you're interested in Stonehenge, you might like to visit other stone circles in Britain—so they're listed, too.

Such sequential narrowing of focus is typical of a good destination site. In fact, the best sites usually provide more than one pathway to a final piece of information—through a hierarchy, or directly from an index or site map. Similar paths can lead you to information for such diverse focuses as "Mature Travelers," "Students," and "Gay and Lesbian" travelers.

National sites also usually include links to specific regions and major cities. Sometimes they're extensive, sometimes not. Links on the BTA site, as of early 2000, included 14 English regions, most of which included further links to individual cities. Linked to the BTA or not, many main British cities do have their own sites. London's is *www.londontown.com*, a full-featured site with lots of detail about what to see and do. It also has a "message board" where travelers can post questions for others to answer. There's even a separate site for the Islington district of London (*www.discover-islington.co.uk*). Other major provincial cities have pages, as well; York's is *www.ytb.org.uk*.

France is the number two European destination for Americans. Figure 2-6, on the next page, shows the official site of the French Government Tourist Office (FGTO at *www.francetourism.com*). This site parallels the BTA site, with a wealth of detailed information. Unfortunately, as of early 2000, it lacked extensive links to major cities. If you wanted more about Lyon than the single paragraph the FGTO site provided, you had to use some other source to locate Destination Lyon, at *www.lyon-france.com*, or *www.ec-lyon.fr/tourisme*, a university-sponsored site with several pages of local detail.

What Other Travelers Say

Many of the Internet destination sites (as well as those devoted to airlines and other travel topics) include forums, where travelers can post their own recommendations, messages, requests, and such. Also, independent news groups available through e-mail services and Web sites such as *www.deja.com* have plenty of travel topics represented.

I know that many travelers enjoy these highly personal and often decidedly uncensored comments. In my experience, however, a surprisingly high proportion of the questions could easily be answered by a quick visit to a few of the Web sites mentioned in this book—or by a short call to a travel agent. If you enjoy ordinary travelers' comments, take a look, but you'll find far more oyster shells than pearls.

The official site for the French Government Tourist Office; Travel Information on France, the French West Indies, Tahiti,

Address http://www.francetourism.com/

5/29/2000

Figure 2-6. *The French Government Tourist Office official site is typical of a good national site.*

Germany's site (*www.germany-tourism.de*) is one of Europe's best. Its home page is one of the most detailed you'll ever see. Although, as of early 2000, the site didn't link to the major cities, it included more detailed city information than the British or French sites (although the omission of Heidelberg was puzzling). It certainly passes the "good site" test. Also worth visiting are Europe's other main official national sites; you can find their URLs in the Appendix.

The Rest of the World

Most other important tourist destinations elsewhere in the world also have sites; many are listed in this book's Appendix. Australia's official site (*www.aussie.net.au*) is good, but in early 2000, a private site (*www.anzac.com /aust/aust.htm*) had better links to individual provinces.

Egypt's site (*www.touregypt.net*) provides an exceptionally detailed list of individual cities, towns, and oases you might want to visit. Hong Kong's site (*www.hkta.org*) is especially good on hotels and transport. Even an area as remote as far eastern Siberia has a private site (*www.iaito.com*). And you can check what's going on in Greenland at *www.greenland-guide.gl* or in Vanuatu at *www.vanuatu.net.vu*.

A Walk in the Park

Destinations aren't necessarily defined—or confined—by national or municipal boundaries. For some trips, your best handle on a destination is a park system or other resource agency.

For an outdoor or sightseeing vacation in the United States, for example, you might well want to start with the U.S. National Park Service (*www.nps.gov*). You can search for parks by name, by state, or by a theme (although a theme search is likely to generate far too many hits to be useful for vacation planning). You can download maps. And you can find out about admission policies, how to get reservations at in-park facilities, and a host of other information. The U.S. Department of Agriculture Forest Service maintains a similar site (*www.fs.fed.us/links/forests.shtml*) where you can access individual parks by name or geographic location. Parks Canada also maintains a site (*parkscanada.pch.gc.ca*) that parallels the site for the U.S. National Park Service. You can search the site by region, park name, or keyword. For each park, the site provides a description, at least one graphic, and a list of available resources, facilities, and accommodations; associated fees are included when applicable.

You can generally find state park pages by starting either at the state site or the state tourism site. Some state home pages have direct links to the park system; on others, you have to type "State Parks" in a site search engine. A list of useful state park and other resource agency sites can be found in the Appendix.

Countless private and charitable organizations are involved in natural resource planning and operation, and many of them operate Web sites. One of the most comprehensive is the National Parks Conservation Association—a private, nonprofit organization with a site (*www.npca.org*) featuring extensive resource data. For others, try using such keywords as "parks" or "conservancy" in a search engine.

You can also use the Internet to locate sites related to extremely narrow resource interests. For example, the "Speleo Link Page" (*hum.amu.edu.pl/~sgp/spec/links.html*—please note that *www* is not part of the URL) includes links to almost 1000 sites related to caves and underground exploration all around the world. (As an example of the worldwide nature of the Internet, that site, in both Polish and English, is maintained by the Association of Polish Geomorphologists, in Poznan.) Creative use of search engines will lead you to many similar sites, in just about any field of interest you can name.

Attractions, Too

Major commercial visitor attractions around the world maintain active sites. Walt Disney World and Universal Studios Orlando were mentioned earlier. You can reach other Disney attractions, including Disneyland Anaheim, Disneyland Paris, and Disneyland Japan, through the corporate Disney home page at *disney.go.com*. The other big Universal Studios park, in Hollywood, can be accessed from *www.universalstudios.com*. The master site for Six Flags (*www.sixflags.com*) links you to any of the chain's theme parks and water parks across the country—abetted by animated Loony Tunes characters. These and other theme park sites typically cover all the basics you need to know in planning a visit: major park features, hours of operation, admission charges, parking, and available tour packages.

For something more intellectual, the world's major museums operate outstanding Web sites. Examples range from the Getty in Los Angeles (*www.getty.edu/museum/*), Chicago's Art Institute (*www.artic.edu*; see Figure 2-7 for the museum's index page to permanent collections), and New York's Metropolitan Museum of Art (*www.metmuseum.org*), to the British Museum (*www.thebritishmuseum.ac.uk*) and also the Louvre (*www.louvre.fr /louvrea.htm*). Hundreds of lesser-known but excellent museums throughout the world also maintain sites. As with theme parks, museum sites typically provide the information you'll need to plan a visit: what's on display, including current touring exhibits; hours of operation; ticket prices; and available guided tours and packages.

Sports fans might like a preview of what they can see at the Pro Football Hall of Fame (*www.profootballhof.com*) in Canton, Ohio; the National Baseball Hall of Fame and Museum (*www.baseballhalloffame.org*) in Cooperstown, New York; or Hooptown, USA, the Basketball Hall of Fame (*www.hooptown.com*) in Springfield, Massachusetts. And did you know there's a College Football Hall of Fame (*www.collegefootball.org*) in South Bend, Indiana? These attractions' sites tell you what you need to know about a visit; most also have links to sites for individual teams and other related activities.

5/29/2000

Figure 2-7. *The Art Institute of Chicago is a top museum site featuring current and coming exhibits.*

While theme parks, major museums, and sports halls of fame are among the country's most visible attractions, they certainly aren't the only ones with Web sites. For example, if you're interested in taking a tour of the factory where Boeing builds its 747, 767, and 777 jumbo jets, you can get all the details at *www.boeing.com/companyoffices/aboutus/tours/*. You can locate other such sites either through a gateway site or through links on the site of the city in which each venue is located.

What's Playing?

Theaters, concert halls, sports arenas, stadiums, and other multi-purpose venues often maintain sites that provide a complete schedule of events, prices and ticket information, seating diagrams, and transportation information; many also provide for online ticket buying. In addition to listings under multipurpose venue sites, information on theatrical and musical performances is usually found on sites sponsored by the program. Opera fans can check out schedules, prices, and availability for the Chicago's Lyric Opera (*www.lyricopera.org*), La Scala (*lascala.milano.it*), and dozens of other companies, as well as opera sites for performances in such remote places as Derry, New Hampshire (*www.newww.com/org/operafest/*) and Juneau, Alaska (*www.juneau.com/opera/*). Similarly, the country's main classical orchestras maintain sites with schedules, prices, and ticket information.

Interested in the theater? Sites that list performances and schedules, provide critical reviews from various sources, and sell tickets to Broadway and West End theaters—as well to others theaters around the world—are abundant. Check out Playbill On-Line (*www.playbill.com*), Theatre Direct International (*www.theatredirect.com*), Applause Theatre & Entertainment Service (*www.applause-tickets.com*), and Keith Prowse (*www.keithprowse.com*). Most of those sites also sell theater tours and hotel accommodations in New York and London. Individual theaters, too, often maintain Web sites. The Appendix lists other online ticket sources for a variety of events.

Download a Mini-Guidebook...

Several major publishers of travel guidebooks maintain sites on which at least some of their regular content is available at no cost. The main advantage to a guidebook's site is that it can incorporate recommendations and critical judgments, rather than the canned enthusiasm you get from official brochures and publicity releases.

Another big advantage to online guidebooks is that you can download and print just the information you need—in effect, develop your own mini-guide. It's a lot easier, neater, and less expensive than the low-tech approach travelers used to use: buying a thick printed guide and then tearing out only the pages you want to take along on your trip. Several sites also provide maps you can similarly download. But the sites do want to sell you the printed books, too, so they don't include all of their books' details.

The redoubtable Arthur Frommer maintains a site (*www.frommers.com*) with extensive excerpts from both his guidebook series and his highly successful new *Budget Travel* magazine. Arguably the most comprehensive travel publication site on the Internet (at least as of early 2000), it provides an amazing amount of detail on hundreds of cities and areas, worldwide. Frommer is especially good for attractions—you first select the type of attraction that interests you, and then select from an extended list of individual attractions. Clicking each attraction takes you to a detailed description. Of course the hotels, restaurants, and transportation guidelines are there, too. You can narrow your search—and the size of the resulting printout—by a variety of parameters, such as price range; location; or cuisine. Or check off everything and download a not-so-mini-guide, still tailored to your immediate requirements.

The site for *Fodor's* guides (*www.fodors.com*) also permits you to assemble a quite respectable "mini-guide" to any of several dozen principal destination cities, with detailed entries about hotels, restaurants, transportation, and things to see. The results are comparable to what you might extract from a printed guide, although *Fodor's* mini-guides are generally better about hotels and restaurants than about sightseeing and attractions.

The "Planning Center" portion of *Fodor's* site provides copious background information on travel, with lots of links to related sites. But there's a good bit of unique material, too. For example, *Fodor's* has assembled what amounts to a separate, small textbook on travel photography (see Figure 2-8 for a portion of the table of contents). It's amazingly thorough; check out, for example, the material on polarizing filters.

The *Lonely Planet* guidebook folks also have a site; you can find it at *www.lonelyplanet.com*. It's especially good on attractions, sightseeing, and internal transportation. Similarly, the site for the *Rough Guides* series (*travel.roughguides.com*) provides a wealth of destination information that you can access from the home page either by country or by a list of "featured" cities.

5/29/2000

Figure 2-8. *The "Cameras" section of* Fodor's *site gives a lesson on polarizing filters.*

The student-oriented *Let's Go* guides also have a site, at *www.letsgo.com*. However, the main focus is on selling books, with only limited access to material (press the cryptically labeled YellowJacket button to see what's available).

...Or a Magazine Story

Travel magazines, like their guidebook brethren, maintain sites, too. And like the guidebook sites, their primary objective is to sell subscriptions, although their sites do provide a good sampling of recent and archived editorial materials. A search in early 2000 located sites for 101 individual travel magazines. Most are fairly narrow in focus, but the four large general-interest travel magazines all have sites (as does Arthur Frommer's new magazine, mentioned earlier):

- Condé Nast maintains the *Concierge* site (*www.concierge.com*), which combines excerpts from its *Condé Nast Traveler* magazine with a variety of other travel information. Much of the destination coverage from the magazine suffers from Condé Nast's usual problem: concentration on expensive—even extravagant—hotels and restaurants of interest to travelers in the, perhaps, top 1 percent of income brackets, with the attendant neglect of the more modest places where real-world travelers eat and sleep. Still, reference material on destinations is supplied by Fodor's, and is therefore reliable and useful.

- The National Geographic Society's site (*www.nationalgeographic.com*) permits you to peruse its library and view current stories from both *National Geographic* and *National Geographic Traveler*. The site also has lots of links to other travel resources, ranging from currency conversion to photography.

- *Travel and Leisure*'s site (*www.pathfinder.com/travel/*) is billed as "Time Warner's exhaustive guide to all travel matters," but the actual content (as of early 2000) was a little less grandiose: excerpts from recent publications, plus extensive links to other sites.

- *Travel Holiday*'s site (*www.travelholiday.com*) provides a sizable backlog of current and prior articles, along with the usual assortment of travel tips; it also includes travel links.

There's even an online-only travel magazine. The *Web Surfer Travel Journal* (*go.to/wstj*) is an idiosyncratic and personal effort by author Dan K. Phillips to provide an outlet for his own ideas and a forum for the comments of his readers.

Do I Need an Umbrella?

At some point, you'll need to know what sort of weather to expect at your destination. Most state, city, and national sites include general data on climate—average, peak, and low temperatures; monthly rainfall/snowfall patterns; average number of sunny days; and such. This data can give you a general idea of what sort of clothing you'll need.

A few days before your departure, you can also get a detailed weather forecast. Again, many destination sites have links to such forecasts, as do home page Weather buttons. These sources also include predictions about likely delays at your origin, destination, and intermediate hub airports.

If you want more detail, The Weather Channel (*www.weather.com*) is a good place to start. You can get seven-day forecasts for localities throughout the U.S. cities, which you can search for by city name, zip code, or state. You can also get shorter-term forecasts for hundreds of cities around the world: Click first on the region, then the country, and then select from a list of cities. Figure 2-9 shows a three-day forecast for London. The site also has specialized forecasts for driving, skiing, and golf (although the site's detail on skiing, for example, includes fewer links than the specialized ski site, GoSki, mentioned later in this chapter).

Figure 2-9. *A leading site provides a three-day forecast for London.*

USA Today's weather site (*www.usatoday.com/weather/wfront.htm*) is quite similar, again offering a mix of local and international data. Its London forecast is for four days, rather than the Weather Channel's three. Its "Almanac" section provides year-round climate data for hundreds of U.S. cities, in an easily searchable format. Intellicast (*www.intellicast.com*) is similarly arranged.

AccuWeather (*www.accuweather.com*) is yet another comprehensive weather site, with lots of detail about weather all around the world. Its London site gives a five-day forecast. That's part of the regular stuff; you can also sign up for a "premium" service, which costs $39.95 a year, that will send you automatic e-mail messages about general weather conditions in places of special interest.

Travel with a Focus

Five decades of traveling have taught me many lessons, but none more important than this: Travel is best when a trip has a focus. No, I don't mean a business trip; I'm talking about some specific personal reason to visit somewhere. Whether for self-improvement, education, or tracking a special interest, having a specific objective in mind adds a great deal of zest to a trip—and a feeling of real accomplishment when you get back home.

The range of possibilities is almost endless. Last year, I organized a seminar series on focused travel, and I invited a diverse group of tour operators to illustrate the spectrum of choices:

- One runs overseas language schools, mainly in Europe.

- Another conducts tours to some of the most significant mystical sites in India and Nepal, for travelers interested in enriching the spiritual sides of their lives.

- A husband-and-wife team takes wine lovers to tour famed vineyards and wineries in France and in Chile.

- Still another takes faith-based groups to Israel, with either a Jewish or a Christian focus, depending on the group.

- Two take travelers to explore the wilderness—one in the Pacific Northwest, the other in the remote wetlands of Brazil.

- An expatriate European organizes bicycle tours of Europe and New Zealand—the travelers ride, while a truck hauls their baggage.

Live Weather Images (*www.weatherimages.org*) displays a long list of links to a variety of weather sites—temperature forecasts, cloud forecasts, satellite images, infrared images, and such. Although not strictly weather, the site also links to seismic data.

I can't really offer criteria for choosing among these weather site options—it's a matter of personal preference. Each gives you more information than you probably wanted to know about weather and climate.

Through the Gateways

If you're searching for a site, but don't have a URL, you can often locate the site through a gateway site. In Chapter 1, I defined a gateway site as one that contains lists of, and links to, a group of related sites, and little

Travel with a Focus (*continued*)

Other options? You can sign up to help archaeologists on their digs. You can help a land-management agency build or maintain hiking trails. Senior travelers are offered a wealth of educational and self-help options through Elderhostel (*www.elderhostel.org*), which combines a solid week of learning experience with low-cost dormitory accommodations. For a more complete listing of operators that run focused tours, look to the *Specialty Travel Index*; its Web site (*www.spectrav.com*) has a database you can search by activity, interest, or geographic location.

Focused travel doesn't mean you have to take a tour package; you can focus an independent trip, too. A few years ago, when my wife, Eleanore, was on a design committee, we spent a week in France visiting and photographing architecturally interesting churches—from the famed le Corbusier, Matisse, and Plateau d'Assy chapels to unheralded but attractive parish churches. We're also opera freaks, so on our next trip to Italy, we plan on an itinerary that traces the life and works of Verdi.

Travel needn't be limited to checking off the blockbuster sights listed in all the guidebooks. Instead, on your next trip think about pursuing a coherent idea or theme. Chances are you'll have more fun—and add something new to your life, as well.

or nothing else. Some gateway sites are commercial, some are operated by governments, while still others are maintained by educational organizations or volunteers.

Tourist Offices Worldwide Directory (TOWD, at *www.towd.com*) is one of the most comprehensive (and frequently linked) destination gateway sites available. A portion of its home page is shown as an example of gateway sites in Figure 1-1 in Chapter 1. Once you're at the site, you can search for information about both U.S. states and foreign countries.

Most of the state pages have entries for the state and its major subregions and cities. However, with TOWD, as with any other site, you will sometimes encounter a work in progress. In early 2000, for example, on TOWD's Massachusetts page, the only entry for Boston information was for a tourism office in Brazil. Boston actually has two sites—the Convention and Visitors Bureau (*www.bostonusa.com*) and *boston.com*, an independent site run by the *Boston Globe* newspaper. The state site has links to both, but neither made TOWD's index (although they might be there by the time you read this). Similarly, although some contact information about Philadelphia's Convention and Visitors Bureau (*www.pcvb.org*) is listed for Pennsylvania, its URL is not.

Equally useful—and with links to far more ancillary information—is the Rec.Travel Library (*www.travel-library.com*). For detailed destination information, you go through a sequence of pages, ultimately reaching a regional page with links to general information, accommodations, and tour operators and travel agents. The site also provides links to selected "Travelogue" articles from a variety of sources.

Even more useful are the links to individual countries, which you can also select from Rec. Travel Library's home page. Country links are organized in the same way as regional links; they also include links to "Travelogue" articles and reports. Figure 2-10 shows part of a typical country page; Egypt is the example.

While both TOWD and Rec.Travel Library are quite extensive, in early 2000, neither had all of the official sites discussed earlier in this chapter. If you don't find what you're seeking on one site, try others.

Although not limited to travel, the multipurpose site About.com (*www.about.com*) contains an excellent set of destination links for both U.S. and international trips. Just click the "Travel" link on the home page to go to the main travel page, which lists links to dozens of destinations. Like

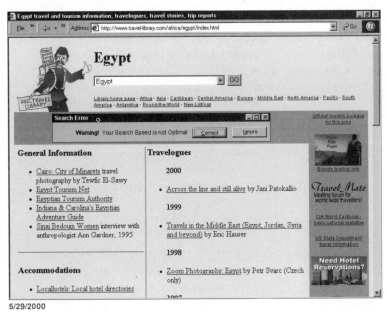

Figure 2-10. *The entry for Egypt illustrates this site's wealth of detail.*

Rec.Travel Library, the pages for individual destinations contain numerous sub-links to individual communities, special-interest sites, and resource agencies, plus additional links to recent feature articles in travel magazines. Because it has such a comprehensive compilation of links, many dedicated travelers have undoubtedly adopted About.com as their home page.

Tapped Into Travel (*www.tappedintotravel.com*) is still another gateway site option, with outstanding detail on U.S. cities—including many smaller ones. Listings even include movie schedules. However, as was the case with many sites, a test in early 2000 showed that information was often incomplete. For example, although the page for Ashland, Oregon included local movies, it failed to list performances by the Oregon Shakespeare Festival—easily the most important visitor event in all of Southern Oregon, let alone Ashland.

These last four sites are general-interest travel gateways, although the latter three do contain links to special-interest areas. You can find other gateway sites dedicated to much narrower interests, focused either on location or on activity. A few examples are shown in Table 2-1 on the following page.

Site and URL	Description
Global Golf Guide *www.globalgolfguide.com*	Contains links to golf resorts and golf-tour packages. The site allows you to search golf courses of the world by name or locale (it lists 44 courses in Scotland). You can even find out about tee times at a few courses.
GoSki *www.goski.com*	Contains detailed information about ski areas worldwide, including location, vertical lift, numbers and types of lifts, days and hours of operation, lift ticket fees, and such. Many areas also include current snow status reports.
TennisOnline.com *www.tennisonline.com*	Contains detailed information about professional and amateur players, upcoming tournaments, and equipment.
FishSearch.com *www.fishsearch.com*	Contains links related to the world of fishing. It provides an exhaustive gateway site for fisherpersons and is brought to you by the FishingLife.com network.
CuisineNet *www.cuisinenet.com*	Contains links to a reputed "more than 10,000" restaurant sites in 16 large U.S. cities. As with many such sites, however, listings are far from complete—the Kansas City pages didn't even mention Arthur Bryant's, arguably the nation's most famous barbecue joint.
Tim Melango's Directory of Amusement Park and Roller Coaster Links *www.users.sgi.net* */~rollocst/amuse.html*	Contains links to over 100 official park sites in the United States, to overseas park sites, and to additional "fan" sites. It is an interesting example of a private site maintained by an enthusiast (as opposed to the more common commercial sites).

Table 2-1. *Many gateway sites are focused on location or activity.*

Other gateway sites you might find useful are listed in the Appendix.

Finally, most of the big agency sites, such as Expedia and Travelocity (see Chapter 3), also contain extensive information on major destinations, as well as links to destination sites. To that extent, they also serve as gateway sites.

Home Pages and Search Engines

The distinction between gateway sites and home pages is hazy. The MSN home page (*www.msn.com*) has entries for both "City Guides" and "Travel." A click on "City Guides" takes you to a menu of close to 100 major U.S. visitor destinations. Each city sub-site, in turn, contains extensive information—what to see, what to do, maps, weather, and the usual commercial links. Yahoo's home page (*www.yahoo.com*) does much the same as MSN's home page.

The Excite home page (*www.excite.com*) also has the expected "Travel" link, with the claim that you can "Search over 5000 destinations." When you explored its travel directory in early 2000, you often found yourself connected seamlessly to one of the separate gateway sites mentioned earlier. For example, a search for "Skiing" led you to the GoSki site. Similarly, the "Destinations" area of Netscape's (*www.netscape.com*) "Travel" section linked you seamlessly to the Travelocity database.

Search engines should be your last resort for locating a site that isn't listed in this (or some other) book or on a gateway site. Most of them do a great job; use your favorite(s) as you normally do. If you've used them at all, however, chances are you've seen the two big problems:

- All too often, even a fairly tight keyword search generates tens of thousands of hits. Sifting through all the possibilities can take hours.

- Even when you find a site you want, bookmarking that site and managing it as a favorite can be cumbersome. When a search engine locates a page, the URL you see at the top of your screen is often a complex mess that incorporates the engine's search parameters. (It might even be too long to view or copy.) If you bookmark that site, you will forever return via the search engine you used the first time. And you'll have a tough time trying to copy the URL to text or an e-mail message. It's better to use the site's own URL for a bookmark. If the real URL isn't obvious, you can often extract it from an e-mail address on a "Contact Us" (or similar) page.

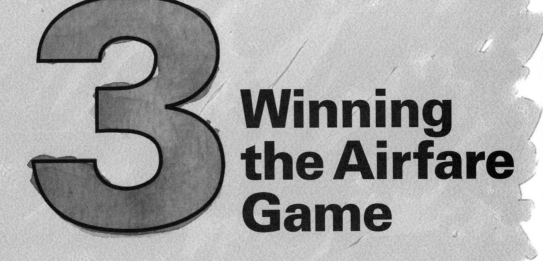

3 Winning the Airfare Game

Quick Trip Through Chapter 3

Here are four steps that should lead you to the lowest airfare—at least most of the time:

1. Start at the site of any airline that flies where you're heading—they're the only places you'll find Internet-only deals (Web specials). Special deal or no, the airlines' lowest official asking price is the benchmark against which to compare all other options. Don't forget low-fare and charter airlines in this step.

2. Next, try one of the big agency sites such as Expedia or Travelocity, where you can compare airline deals and maybe find some better prices.

3. Check with a real discounter (consolidator)—an agency that can often undercut published fares by hundreds of dollars—especially for overseas trips. Or if you're really flexible, check out such arcane options as a courier ticket or a "hitch."

4. If you're willing to accept the possibility of a less-than-desirable flight itinerary, make your final stop at a name-your-price reverse auction site. The danger here is that if you "win," you're locked into that deal—no more shopping!

Depending on the trip, you might want to bypass some of the early steps and go right to the low-fare airlines and discounters. You can also use the Web to get flight information, check your frequent flyer account, and do other miscellaneous chores.

T he American traveling public is obsessed with airfares. Never mind that, on many trips, you'll pay more for hotel accommodations than for your flights. Whenever I appear on a radio or TV call-in show, it seems the first question—and most of the later ones, too—is about airfares. Why the tunnel vision? Two possible answers:

- Travelers believe that all airlines provide essentially the same quality of product. When the products are the same, price is paramount.

- Travelers believe that the airlines are ripping off anyone who pays even a few dollars more than the lowest possible fare.

Although neither of these beliefs is strictly true, each contains enough truth to shape many travelers' views of the airline marketplace.

The major airlines' pricing schemes are complex and confusing for a reason. The complexity of the system actually works to the advantage of consumers—at least most consumers, most of the time. By knowing how

Inside the System: Who's Who Among the Airlines

In this book, I frequently refer to the "giant U.S. airlines." These are American, Continental, Delta, Northwest, TWA, United, and US Airways. Together, they account for some 75 percent of the domestic U.S. air travel. They generally make important pricing moves in lockstep; their favorite form of long-range planning is "me, too." Two smaller airlines—Alaska and America West—usually follow the giants' lead in both pricing and product. Midwest Express and startup Legend also follow the giant airlines on fares (except that they might sit out the fare sales), but they offer a sharply superior Coach product. Air Canada to play the system, you can often buy a ticket for any sort of trip at the bottom price, or at least avoid paying top dollar. The purpose of this chapter is to show you how to use the Internet to find these best deals—and to point out the few cases where the Internet isn't yet able to deliver what you need.

"Low-fare airlines" form a different and distinct group. Southwest is by far the largest; although it's actually larger than TWA, it's not in the giant group because it goes its own way in pricing and product. Southwest and the other, much smaller U.S. low-fare airlines generally charge prices that are below what the giant airlines would charge, absent low-fare competition. However, where they do compete, the giant airlines often match prices with the low-fare airlines. Also, most low-fare airlines offer only Coach service. Although still small compared with the international giants, low-fare airlines are becoming a major factor within Europe and, more recently, Australia. A few others also fly across the Atlantic.

Basically, what you pay for an airline ticket is determined by the timing of your trip—how far ahead you plan it, how long you stay at your destination, and how much flexibility you have in dates, days, and hours of travel. Go where and when the airlines want to sell unused seats and you get a great deal; go where you want, when you want, and you might pay top dollar. I've organized this chapter to highlight the impact of trip timing on what you pay—and how best to buy tickets.

Inside the System:
Who's Who Among the Airlines *(continued)*

(which absorbed Canadian Airlines International but was still operating separately in mid-2000) sometimes follows its U.S. equivalents, sometimes not.

Similarly, by "giant international airlines" I mean the familiar major airlines based in the main economically advanced nations of Europe, Asia, South America, and Australasia. Among the dozens of airlines that fit this category are Air France, British Airways, Cathay Pacific, Lufthansa, Qantas, and Singapore. As with their U.S. counterparts, they usually move in lockstep on matters of pricing and product, as do most smaller international airlines.

Here's one caveat: I wrote the bulk of this chapter to follow the current market view that low fares trump whatever quality differences might exist among various airlines' Coach/Economy service. Increasingly, that view might be incorrect, at least for some travelers. Unfortunately, the Internet isn't yet able to provide meaningful data on many of the real differences in quality that exist among airlines. Only a minority of airlines post their seating dimensions on their Web sites, for example, and none posts the information (available in trade publications) on their per-passenger food and beverage expenses.

No matter what sort of trip you plan, no one source of tickets is consistently lowest-priced, on or off the Internet. You must always shop around among several different possibilities—and the more flexible you are, the more shopping you should do. Look at a search for the best price on an airline ticket as something of a treasure hunt or one of those video games that reward you for solving a series of clues. And if you don't have time to do all that shopping yourself, you can go to an Internet-savvy travel agent who keeps on top of the deals—and who will locate, for a modest fee, the best deal for you.

The Easy Trips: Buy in Advance, Stay Saturday

The giant airlines—both domestic and foreign—all follow the same basic pricing principle: They establish very high "full-fare" prices for Coach/Economy seats that carry no restrictions. They figure that business travelers will pay top dollar to be able to buy a peak-time seat on short notice and to be able to switch tickets to different flights at any time. Airlines sell seats they don't fill with business travelers to vacation travelers for sharply reduced prices—well under half the full-fare prices—with restrictions that discourage business travelers from using them.

Undoubtedly, most of you, most of the time, can comply with the airlines' conditions for their cheapest tickets: Buy your ticket in advance—up to 21 days ahead—and stay at your destination at least over a Saturday night, but no more than 30 days. Depending on the route, the advance-purchase period ranges from 21 days to just 1 day, with 21, 14, and 7 days the most common. Similarly, the minimum stay can vary from just 1 day to a full week, but Saturday night and one week are the norms.

Also, these cheapest tickets are typically "nonrefundable," meaning you can't turn them in for a cash refund if your plans change. However, most cheap tickets are "reusable," in that you can retain their cash value and apply that value to a future ticket, less a stiff exchange charge of $75 to $150 per ticket (and often the difference between the original fare and the new ticket price).

HEADS UP

If you do use an old ticket toward a new flight, you must pay whatever the fare is at the time you book the new flight; you can't lock in your original fare.

As noted, the main idea behind these restrictions is to make them impractical or unattractive to business travelers. That's why restrictions are typically less stringent on tickets to destinations that cater heavily to vacation travelers, such as Las Vegas and Honolulu, than on tickets to destinations with a lot of business travel.

On Sale by a Giant Airline

The first place to check for almost any air ticket is to see what the giant airlines are asking. You need that information for three reasons:

- A list-price ticket on a giant airline might be the best deal you can find.

- Some of the lowest giant airline fares are available only through airline Internet sites and not through independent sites.

- A giant airline's best deal is the benchmark against which you measure all other alternatives.

Tracking the Promotions

"You can't sell it unless it's on sale" is a current axiom in department store merchandising. It also seems to apply to the giant airlines when they're trying to sell tickets to vacation travelers. And it's why the giant airlines have held so many airfare "sales" over the last half-dozen years—about every six weeks, on average. During such sales, fares drop as much as 50 percent below what the airlines say are their cheapest regular list-price fares.

The purchase window when you can buy sale-priced tickets is usually short—a week or two—but the reduced prices apply to flights over a period of several months. Sale fares carry the usual giant airline restrictions: advance purchase, minimum and maximum stay, and nonrefundability.

The big plus to these giant airline sale fares is that you can use them to travel practically anywhere. When one giant airline announces a sale, the others almost always match it within 24 hours. Since the giant airlines cover so much of the United States, one of their sales immediately becomes a national event. About the only travelers left out are those who fly to or from small cities with limited airline service: They often find their sale prices are well above those available at nearby larger cities.

Sales are almost always confined to Coach/Economy travel. Only rarely do you find a promotion involving Business or First Class. If you ever see one, it's almost always for intercontinental trips—virtually never for domestic flights.

HEADS UP

You might think that airfare sales would be hotbeds of "bait and switch" tactics, but they aren't. In a true bait and switch promotion, the seller is really trying to get you to pay more for a supposedly better product. The airlines don't do that: They genuinely want to sell at least some of their seats at the advertised sale prices. What's more, to keep them honest, the U.S. Department of Transportation requires that the airlines allocate a reasonable number of seats (generally 10 percent) to any sale price. Of course, sale seats are limited, as the ads take care to note; airlines often run out of their sale-priced inventory in a matter of days.

Whenever you can find one, a giant airline sale fare is a strong candidate to be your best available deal. To avoid missing out on a sale, you can sign up on several sites for weekly e-mail notification of all special deals from your home airport. You can also ask your travel agent to alert you any time a sale is announced. If you can't find a sale fare—and if you have enough lead-time—your best strategy might well be to wait a few days or weeks for the next sale to break. Chances are, one will.

Some sales, moreover, are available only on the Internet. An airline's Web site might be the only place some sales are listed, or Internet prices might be lower than other published fares. Many Internet-only fares are strictly limited to a few routes and a few dates; these don't fall into the "easy trip" category at all. Others do apply systemwide, however, with the same purchase windows and flight dates as regular sale fares. Such Internet-only sales are usually noted on each airline's home page.

Where to Ask, Part 1: Airline Sites

An obvious place to start looking for a sale fare is on the Web sites of whichever giant airlines fly to your planned destination. All of the giant U.S. and international airlines have sites. And although their "looks" might vary greatly, they work in about the same way. They all have a box, either on the home page or within the site, where you can enter the destinations and dates of your proposed trip. All have a search engine that automatically provides the best fare and schedule for your trip. Some travel writers have recommended that you bypass airline sites and go directly to one of the agency or consolidator sites (discussed later in this chapter). That's not a good idea: You might miss a deal that isn't available anywhere else. Also, the airline sites will give you the airlines' official asking price for a trip you're considering. That's an essential benchmark for price comparisons against the other alternatives.

The Appendix contains URLs (current as of early 2000) for all giant and smaller U.S. airlines and giant international airlines. You can find the Web sites for other airlines—U.S. regional and commuter airlines and smaller international airlines—through several gateway sites. The following are among the best of these gateway sites:

- Wheels Up (*www.pathcom.com/~fshska/*) is arguably the most useful gateway site. It has a complete, worldwide airline directory you can access alphabetically either by region, or by the two-letter/number codes used in computer reservation systems (CRSs) and on tickets. The site also contains links to worldwide airports. Figure 3-1 on the next page shows a typical page of alphabetical airline listings from this site.

3/31/2000

Figure 3-1. *Wheels Up provides a very useful worldwide airline directory.*

- Airlines of the Web (*www.flyaow.com/airlines.htm*) is also good, although many of its listings refer to AOL sites rather than directly to the airlines' sites.

- Airlines.com (*www.airlines.com*) isn't as comprehensive as the other two, but it's fine if you aren't looking for one of the smaller, more obscure airlines.

As with any gateway site, these three can sometimes fall a bit behind the Internet's rapid pace of change. Overall, however, it's hard to think of an airline you couldn't locate through at least one of them.

If you're a typical traveler, you're asking for some combination of the lowest fare and the best schedule. Often the same fare structure applies to any schedule (as long as seats are available). But some airlines charge less for undesirable connecting flights than for nonstops. And fares might be lower for off-hour flights than for flights at preferred times.

Most sites give you a choice between a lowest-fare search and a schedule search early in the procedure. Just follow the site's instructions. However, for anything but the lowest fare—as well as to ask about such special deals as infants' or seniors' discounts—you often have to bypass the quick-entry mode and instead enter into a full or extended search.

Airline site search engines typically require that you provide dates and times before they display a fare. You can't tell if you could get a lower fare by changing your travel dates. Finding the lowest fare on one of these sites can be painstaking: You must check on all feasible flight dates to make sure you're getting the best deal.

The best of the sites shortcut that process. They give you the option of finding the lowest fare first and then locating schedules where you can apply that fare. That process is far easier than one driven only by itineraries.

Let's take United as an example. Figure 3-2 shows United's home page. Note the Quick Fare Finder box, filled out for a sample trip. After you complete this search, you'll notice that United shows the fare component associated with each optional schedule. In effect, at that point, you can select either the lowest-fare or best-schedule option. Many other airlines provide the same information.

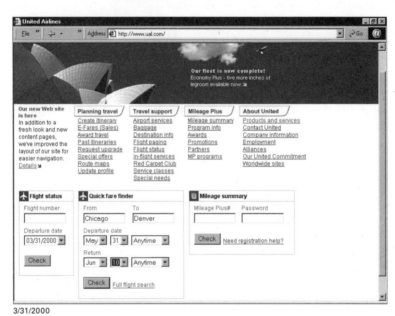

3/31/2000

Figure 3-2. *The United Airlines Quick Finder rapidly comes up with basic fare information.*

International trips work much the same way. Figure 3-3 on the next page shows the "booking" page of the British Airways site with a sample trip entered. But on the British Airways site, unlike United's, you're choosing blind. There's no way of telling whether the fare for alternative schedules might be lower than the one for the schedule you selected—except by testing all of the possibilities individually, a tedious process on routes with lots of flights.

British Airways

Address | https://www.british-airways.com/flightSelling/starUm.jhtml | Go

> If you have a Membership Number/Username and PIN/Password, please complete the boxes below to save time while booking.

Membership No./Username

00000

PIN/Password

Plan Your Trip

Leaving from (city or airport)

Chicago

Departing on

30 | May

Going to (city or airport)

London

Returning on

8 | June

Type of Flight/Class

Economy (Lowest)

Adults

1

Children (2-11yrs)

0

Infants (under 2yrs)

0

Select Flights
go on to step 2

3/31/2000

Figure 3-3. *On British Airways' site, you don't know the fare until you select an itinerary.*

Both the United Airlines and British Airways sites ask you to register, but neither requires it if all you want is a quick schedule or fare check. However, you must register before you can buy tickets online.

Most other giant airlines' sites operate in much the same way. The process can take anywhere from two to five or six screens, but the end result is always the same: You pick dates, flights, and your class of service, and the site delivers schedules and fares.

"Nyah, Nyah" Airfares

Occasionally, airlines seem to trade fare cuts the way squabbling schoolboys trade insults or punches. Airline A, for example, might get mad at airline B and slash children's fares to one of airline B's vacation strongholds. Airline B might indignantly retaliate by cutting fares to one of airline A's hubs. Those cuts don't last long, and they might not be advertised much—if at all; sometimes only travel agents and airfare hobbyists find out in time to take advantage.

Of course, those fares are available on the airlines' Internet sites for the short times they're available at all. But the best way to find them is to check out the Best Fares site (discussed later in this chapter). Editor Tom Parsons has a big staff dedicated to ferreting out details like these.

What You Risk

You face several risks in relying just on airline sites:

- Unless you already have a good feel for which airlines fly where, you might have to search through a half-dozen or more sites before you find even one airline that has a reasonable schedule for the route you're considering. At best, that process is tedious; at worst, you never get to some airlines you really should check.

- Many airline sites won't display other airlines' flights at all, and even the best might bias their results in favor of their sponsoring airlines' own flights. Sometimes that doesn't matter much, but it matters a lot when a site steers you to connecting flights on the sponsor airline for a trip where a competitor offers a nonstop flight.

- As of early 2000, not all of the giant U.S. airlines' sites could handle *open-jaw excursion tickets*. These tickets allow you to fly from your home city to one destination and return from another. They let you avoid tedious (and expensive) backtracking when you want to travel overland in your destination area. Take, for example, a trip to Europe on which you want to visit London, Paris, Geneva, Milan, and Rome. The easiest way to make that trip would be to fly from your home city to London, take trains between the European cities, and fly home from Rome. By using that open jaw, you'd cut the extra time and cost of doubling back to London for your return flight. Typically an open-jaw ticket costs half the round-trip to each destination.

- Most airline sites couldn't (as of early 2000) yet handle some senior fares, infant fares, and some kinds of frequent flyer trips. For these, you must still call the airline (see the "Frequent Flyer" section later in this chapter).

Where to Ask, Part 2: Agency Sites

The big online travel agencies all trumpet their ability to find you the lowest airfare. Since they search all airlines, they avoid the biases and omissions that are built into most airline sites. In fact, some experts recommend that you forget about individual airline sites and just start with an agency site. However, as I stated earlier, you will sometimes miss out on an airline's special deal if you take this route. I think it's best to check individual airlines sites *and* agency sites.

As of early 2000, the two largest agency Web sites were Expedia (*www.expedia.com*) and Travelocity (*www.travelocity.com*). Expedia was then somewhat larger, but Travelocity was in the process of acquiring another of the top agency sites, Preview Travel (*www.previewtravel.com*), and the merged site might well become larger than Expedia. Other agency sites are listed in the Appendix. As with airline sites, you probably want to check for either the lowest fare or the best schedule. Agency sites can generally accommodate you either way—just follow the directions on the home page. Expedia illustrates how a good agency site works. As with many airline sites, Expedia starts out with an itinerary box on its home page. Figure 3-4 shows the entry portion of that page—obviously, it looks a lot like the United and British Airways sites pictured earlier.

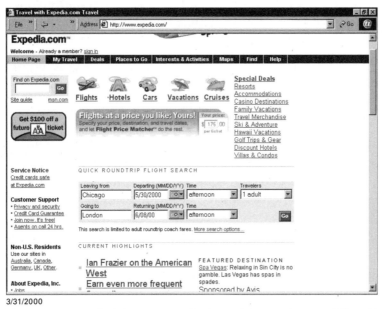

3/31/2000

Figure 3-4. *Expedia's home page asks for an itinerary, just as airline sites do.*

The differences between agency sites like Expedia and airline sites like United and British Airways show up in the results. When you search for a particular itinerary, Expedia shows you several flights that provide the lowest fares. So far, that's pretty much like an airline site. But Expedia gives you additional choices. If you click the Fare Compare button on the first results page, you see a new display that shows the lowest available fares for the route you've selected, on any airline and on any flights (Figure 3-5). The difference is that the Fare Compare search isn't constrained by the specific itinerary you entered. It notes, for example, if you can get a lower fare on a different airline by limiting your visit to five days rather than seven. For many travelers, knowing that information would result in a significant cut in total travel costs.

3/31/2000

Figure 3-5. *But you won't find anything like Expedia's Fare Compare on an airline site.*

A different search branch provides still different results. On the home page, if you click More Search Options instead of the Go button, you can confine the search to direct flights, a single airline (if you want to maximize your frequent flyer earnings), or both. You can't confine your search to nonstop flights, but if you ask for only direct (no change of plane) flights, the nonstops are included among them. You can quickly tell which are nonstop flights and which are not. That, too, is a very useful option for anyone who hates connecting flights.

The search results don't indicate specifically which fares are "sale" fares. But you can easily tell. The sale fares typically have a relatively short-term "you must buy by" date and a limited period during which you can fly; these restrictions are clearly indicated on the Fare Compare listings. You can also locate that information by clicking Details And Purchase Options opposite each itinerary on the Results page.

Agency sites have other great features as well. If you sign up for the service, they can automatically send you e-mail notifications whenever there's a sale on flights from your home city. They can also quote hotel rates, car rental rates, vacation packages, and other travel services (see other chapters for details).

What You Risk

You face several risks in relying just on agency sites:

- Although most agency sites claim to offer "lowest" airfares or even "discounts," some rely entirely on searching fares and schedules available in the large computer reservation systems, such as Amadeus, Sabre, and Worldspan, that travel agencies and corporate travel offices use. Airlines and fares that aren't in the CRSs therefore don't get considered in the searches—and several low-fare and charter airlines are not included in the CRSs. Also, some Internet-only fares are left out of the CRS data banks. And the CRS computers don't list discounted consolidator fares at all.

- Agency sites typically don't show the type of airplane used on each flight, while airline sites typically do. That information is important to travelers who favor wide-body planes, for example, or those who want to avoid extra-cramped 737s or 757s on long-haul flights.

- Agency sites generally can handle the simple 10 percent senior discount, but they can't handle a question like "What is the lowest fare that I can upgrade using frequent flyer mileage?"

Fly a Low-Fare Airline

Any time a low-fare airline flies where you're heading, chances are its lowest fares will always be as low as—or lower than—the best deal the giant airlines have to offer. That's why you should always check out a low-fare airline option, unless you already know that you'll find no low-fare airlines on your route.

HEADS UP

The following section includes a few charter airlines that sell seats directly to the public, as opposed to selling only through tour operators—a distinction that means little to consumers (see "Charters: Still Around, Still Cheap" later in this chapter).

  Online Travel

Southwest—and Southwest Wannabes

Southwest is the 800-pound gorilla of low-fare airlines. Its fare policies differ sharply from those of the giant airlines. Unrestricted full fares are much less than the giant airlines charge on similar routes. Although Southwest's cheapest tickets require round-trip and 21-day advance purchase, the minimum stay is usually no more than one night.

Like its giant competitors, Southwest often runs sales. The giant airlines almost always match Southwest's fares whenever it starts to fly one of their routes. As a result, Southwest has had a huge impact on the airline marketplace—so profound that three giant airlines established separate "airline within an airline" operations to compete in low-fare markets: Delta Express, Shuttle by United, and Metrojet (US Airways). "If you can't beat 'em, join 'em" is alive and well as an airline strategy.

Smaller low-fare airlines follow a variety of pricing policies. Most share the principle that their highest fares are lower than giant airline fares on comparable routes. Beyond that, however, you find important differences. Several low-fare airlines, including American Trans Air (ATA), use "capacity control" pricing. They impose no special restrictions on any ticket—not even round-trip. They simply allocate varying numbers of seats on each flight to different fare "buckets." They start selling the cheapest seats first; when the cheapest bucket is exhausted, they start tapping the next-higher price bucket. As with the giant airlines, the cheap seats sell out early. But the number of days in advance you must buy isn't fixed at, say, 21 or 14 days; instead, it depends on how fast the seats sell.

Others use more complex pricing. For example, AirTran has up to six Coach prices on most flights—three different advance-purchase periods, with separate peak and off-peak levels for each.

Unfortunately, none of the Web sites except Southwest's clearly states those pricing policies. Knowing the specific pricing rules would be a great help to some travelers. As it is, you have to ferret out the pricing by testing different options.

Where to Ask

As in the case of giant airlines, the two places you search for flights and fares on low-fare airlines are the airlines' own sites and the agency sites. Low-fare airlines operating in North America (in early 2000) include AirTran, ATA, Canada 3000, Frontier, Jet Blue (new in 2000), National (new in 1999), Pan Am (the third incarnation of the name, new in 1999), Pro Air, Royal Aviation (Canada), Southwest, Spirit, Sun Country, Vanguard, and Westjet (Canada); their Web sites are listed in the Appendix.

Several low-fare airlines fly the Atlantic: Air Europa (Spain), Canada 3000, Citybird (Belgium), Corsair (France), LTU International Airways (Germany), Martinair (Netherlands), and Royal Aviation (Canada); their URLs are listed in the Appendix. Most of them started out as charter airlines (see "Charters: Still Around, Still Cheap" later in this chapter), a few still are charters, and all still operate the way charters do. Based in Europe for the most part, they serve only a few U.S. or Canadian gateway cities and only one or two cities in their home country. They seldom fly more than three times a week on any one route, and just once a week on some. And they sell out a large portion of their capacity to wholesale tour operators.

A few low-fare airlines (also listed in the Appendix) have started to fly within Europe. As of early 2000, several low-fare airlines had announced plans to fly within Australia, but none had yet started. No low-fare airlines cross the Pacific or fly to South America.

Agency sites that search among the giant airlines also include many (but not all) of the low-fare airlines. The biggest exception is, unfortunately, the most important: Southwest. Since Southwest does not fully participate

Inside the System:
Did Deregulation Work?

Airline deregulation, accomplished in 1978, was supposed to usher in an era of intense competition in the marketplace—a competition that was assumed to result in lower fares. And, with some important qualifications, that's just what happened. Adjusted for inflation, today's sale fares and other cheap tickets are the lowest they've ever been. On that basis, deregulation was—and remains—a smashing success.

The other promise of deregulation was a marketplace with many competitors, offering a spectrum of prices and product quality, much as the hotel market does today. Sadly, that didn't happen. Although deregulation encouraged hundreds of investors and operators to start new low-fare airlines, only a handful survived the fierce, selective fare matching and other heavy-handed responses by the giant airlines. The in the CRSs, the standard search engines used in Expedia, Travelocity, and several others do not include Southwest.

By all means, check agency sites when you're looking for a ticket on a low-fare airline. But also make sure you try the airline sites, too, in case the agency site doesn't include the airline you're considering.

Since many low-fare airlines are small, the first question you have to ask is whether they fly where you're heading. Their sites provide destination and route information. Otherwise, you ask the same questions as with a giant airline: Specify either a preferred schedule or the lowest fare.

Southwest's Web site works much the same way as the giant airlines' sites do. The initial reservation page includes the familiar entry boxes used for an itinerary search. However, Southwest's fare display (Figure 3-6 on the next page) is more useful than the fare displays of most other airlines: On a single screen, you see schedules at the time of day you requested, all of the fares Southwest offers on the specified route, and which of those fares are available on each flight. The giant airlines could learn a lot from this site.

The Web sites of smaller low-fare airlines are generally somewhat simpler than those of the giant airlines or of Southwest. However, several share the Southwest advantage: You can request a complete breakdown of fares without first entering a specific itinerary. The site for LTU International Airways is especially comprehensive.

Inside the System:
Did Deregulation Work? *(continued)*

academics who fostered deregulation claimed that airline markets would be easily "contestable" by startup airlines, but it didn't turn out that way.

Still, enough low-fare airlines have survived to add a reasonable degree of competition and innovation to the marketplace. Southwest, the largest survivor by far, started out before the 1978 deregulation: Originally flying entirely within Texas, it escaped Federal rate and route regulation. Instead, it was regulated—barely—only by the state, which basically allowed it to fly where it pleased and charge what it pleased. Southwest flourished under that benign umbrella: When deregulation arrived, Southwest was big and strong enough to challenge the giants on flights beyond Texas. Now, Southwest carries more passengers and flies more passenger-miles than TWA, the smallest of the giant airlines.

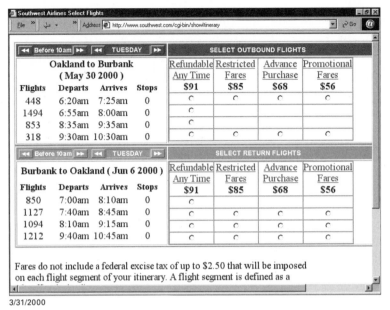

The screenshot shows a Southwest Airlines Select Flights window.

Oakland to Burbank (May 30 2000)				Refundable Any Time $91	Restricted Fares $85	Advance Purchase $68	Promotional Fares $56
Flights	Departs	Arrives	Stops				
448	6:20am	7:25am	0	○	○	○	○
1494	6:55am	8:00am	0	○			
853	8:35am	9:35am	0	○			
318	9:30am	10:30am	0	○	○	○	○

Burbank to Oakland (Jun 6 2000)				Refundable Any Time $91	Restricted Fares $85	Advance Purchase $68	Promotional Fares $56
Flights	Departs	Arrives	Stops				
850	7:00am	8:10am	0	○			
1127	7:40am	8:45am	0	○	○	○	○
1094	8:10am	9:15am	0	○	○	○	○
1212	9:40am	10:45am	0	○	○	○	○

Fares do not include a federal excise tax of up to $2.50 that will be imposed on each flight segment of your itinerary. A flight segment is defined as a

3/31/2000

Figure 3-6. *On the Southwest Airlines site, one page shows both schedules and fares.*

What You Risk

The risks you run using a low-fare airline's site are pretty much the same ones you risk with the giant airlines' sites. As to the risks of flying a low-fare airline, I've seen no valid data to suggest your chances of an accident are any greater on a low-fare airline than on any other. On a small low-fare airline, you'll probably face a bigger hassle if your flight is cancelled than you would on a giant airline, since the low-fare airline usually has fewer alternative flights to your destination and fewer available substitute aircraft or crew.

Charters: Still Around, Still Cheap

Through the 1970s, taking a charter flight was about the only way you could beat the giant airlines' often-high asking prices. Since then, however, the importance of charters has declined sharply. But the few that operate can still offer some good deals.

This section covers only those charter seats that are sold through wholesale tour operators. Charter airlines that sell seats directly to the public are grouped with low-fare airlines in the preceding section.

Mostly for Tours

The factors that characterize a charter flight are primarily legal. On a charter, your contract is with a tour operator, not an airline, and the operator is financially responsible for your trip. The operator charters planes and crews from one or more airlines, and the airlines actually operate the flights.

When things go well, you seldom notice that distinction. But when a problem arises, it's the tour operator that must find a solution. If the airline performing the charter runs into difficulties, the operator is responsible for finding a substitute airline. When travelers have been left stranded at a destination, it's usually because a tour operator failed and couldn't pay any airline for the return trip.

Some charter trips are flown by specialist charter airlines that don't sell tickets to the public under their own names at all. The reservation computers don't list their fares and schedules, and you can get seats only through tour operators. However, some ordinary airlines fly charter trips— ATA is big in charters as well as scheduled services. And charter tour operators sometimes buy big blocks of seats on individual flights of giant airlines and low-fare airlines.

Seats on charter flights are often cheaper than seats on a scheduled airline. Even when a scheduled airline seems to have a price advantage, it might offer only a few seats at the come-on fare. But most charters sell all their seats at the same low price. A charter seat might be your only low-fare alternative when the giant airlines sell out their allotments of seats at lowball, promotional prices.

Charters can also be more convenient: You occasionally find a non-stop charter on a route that other airlines serve only with connections. Also, charter tickets usually aren't as restricted as the cheapest tickets on an ordinary airline—the minimum advance-purchase period usually depends only on how long it takes to complete the paperwork, and the minimum stay depends only on how often the charter airline flies a particular route, rather than on arbitrary rules. That advantage is often a particular appeal of domestic charters.

Price and convenience aside, charters are generally less desirable than flights on other airlines for some of the following reasons:

- Most charter airlines have relatively few planes, and they're scheduled tightly. Consequently, flights might arrive or depart at odd hours. And any significant delay of a single flight can throw a charter airline's schedule out of whack for days.

- Since charter airlines and tour operators don't have agreements with other airlines to exchange tickets, baggage, and passengers, most other airlines won't accept a charter airline's ticket in the event of a cancellation or a major delay. In those cases, if the tour operator doesn't find a substitute airline, you wait until the charter airline gets its planes flying again.

- Seating on charter airlines isn't always worse than on a giant or low-fare airline, but it's hardly ever better. Moreover, most charter flights operate close to full: One of the reasons charters are relatively cheap is that close to 100 percent of the seats on each flight are sold, rather than the 70 percent or so you find on scheduled airlines.

- Charter airlines normally subcontract check-in, boarding, and baggage claim services to other airlines or to airports. Many apparently skimp on budgets for these services, resulting in long check-in lines and harried counter service.

- You might have trouble getting a refund if you have to cancel a charter flight, and your ticket might not be as easily exchangeable (reuseable, usually for a fee) as a ticket on another airline—in fact, it might not be exchangeable at all. If you're considering a charter ticket that isn't exchangeable, you can protect your payment with trip-interruption insurance, at a cost of $4 to $6 per $100 of coverage.

"Charter" doesn't automatically mean "cheap." Upscale tour operators run some programs using chartered Concordes or all-First-Class planes that can cost more than $50,000 per person.

Where to Ask

Wholesale tour operators focus primarily on selling complete tour packages, combining air transportation, hotel accommodations, and sightseeing. To provide airlift for these programs, they commit to buying bulk seats from airlines. Some operators sell a few of these air seats to the public without any other tour components.

Wholesale tour operators are generally geared up to sell through travel agencies (including Web-based agencies). However, some sell directly to the public, as well. The URLs for leading tour-operators' Web sites where you can buy charter airline seats are listed in the Appendix.

HEADS UP

The line of distinction between tour operators that sell charter seats, and consolidators, is thin to invisible. See the "Consolidator Tickets for Real Discounts" section for more detailed information.

As with low-fare airlines, your first job is to find out where the tour operator's charters fly. Typically, you have far fewer origin-destination choices than with a large scheduled airline. Many operators focus on just one destination country or region.

Once you find an operator that sells air-only charters (as opposed to entire tour packages) to your destination, checking the airfare is straightforward. Other than dates of travel, you usually have no options to complicate matters.

Navigating a tour operator's site is usually simple. Since tour operators emphasize complete package tours, you search their sites for an "air only" or "airfares" menu choice. Figure 3-7 shows a typical airfare page (in this case, Vacationland), listing some of the discount tickets available. The option for airfares (and hotels) is clearly indicated.

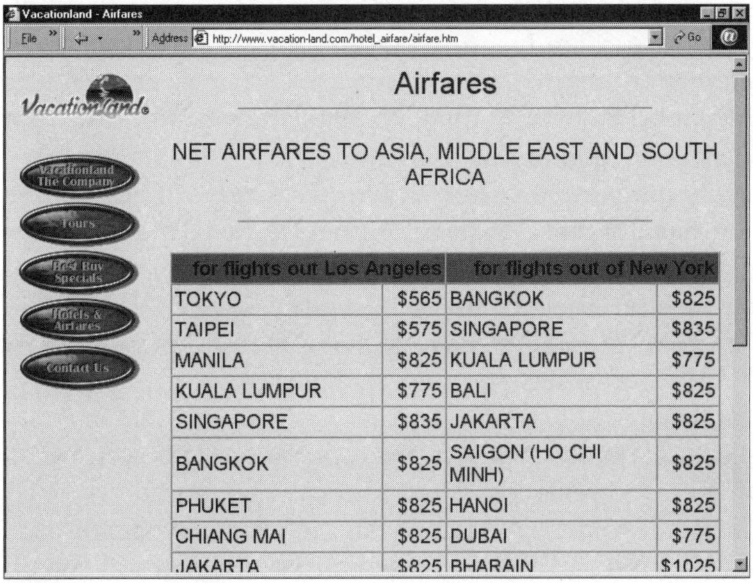

3/31/2000

Figure 3-7. *Tour operators like Vacationland often sell at well below list price.*

The Vacationland Web site (and some other operators') notes when Business and First Class seats are available on a particular flight. In most cases, these fares are not shown; instead, you're encouraged to call or e-mail for a quote.

What You Risk

As noted, some of the biggest tour operators sell tours and charter seats only through retail travel agencies. They require a travel agent's sign-in before showing any pricing information. So unless you inquire through a travel agency, you're unlikely ever to find out about some operators' charter flight programs.

Consolidator Tickets for Real Discounts

Consolidators sell tickets at real discounts—prices below those the airlines say the tickets should cost. Consolidator tickets are especially attractive for trips to Asia, where even the lowest list-price fares are relatively high and you seldom see a sale. Discount tickets are also a good bet for travel to Europe in peak season, as well as for other international trips.

Bucket Shops Move Uptown

What the airlines call "discount" tickets really aren't: They're list-price tickets with restrictions. Sure, they cost less than full-fare Coach. But full-fare is a phony benchmark; only a tiny percent of the U.S. tickets really sell at full-fare (almost entirely to business travelers). As long as a ticket sells at a price openly published by an airline, it isn't discounted—it just has a lower price and different conditions than a full-fare Coach ticket.

The only truly discounted airline tickets are those you buy from a consolidator. Consolidators are the airlines' outlet stores. They obtain tickets from the airlines at less than the published fares; mark them up as much as they can; and then sell them to the public, either directly or through other retail travel agents. Since they're priced at less than airlines say tickets should cost, consolidator tickets are true discount tickets.

Ticket discounting used to be illegal in the United States and in many other countries. Consolidators labored in shady obscurity: They were called "bucket shops." Now, however, most economically advanced countries have either legalized discounting (Australia and much of Europe) or have declared they won't enforce archaic anti-discounting laws that still remain on the books (the United States). Either way, consolidators have moved uptown to become an integral part of the system airlines use to distribute tickets.

The result of this movement is a thriving off-price marketplace, but one that lacks the order of the list-price market. Although consolidators can often cut your airfare costs substantially, you encounter some risks you don't face with list-price tickets. By all means check consolidators, but by all means check carefully.

If you shop carefully, you can often shave hundreds of dollars off your airfare by buying a consolidator airline ticket. The extent of your discount depends on where you're going and when:

- You're likely to find the largest reductions on flights to Asia. Trans-Pacific airlines apparently prefer to keep list prices relatively high and serve price-conscious travelers through consolidators. The result is significant consolidator discounts all year round.

- Reductions to Europe are seasonal. The best deals are in the summer, when advertised fares are high. In winter, the airlines' sale fares are often no higher than the best deals consolidators offer. Even in summer, fare wars sometimes reduce the difference between consolidator fares and advertised fares to minimal levels.

- For domestic trips, consolidator tickets don't consistently beat the lowest advertised fares by much. The best consolidator deals are often on tickets for trips that can't meet the restrictions placed on the cheapest regular tickets. However, some consolidators can shave about 20 percent off the price of any TWA ticket—even during a fare sale.

Though the consolidator market focuses on Coach/Economy tickets, some airlines also discount Business and First Class tickets. The reduction, however, is seldom more than 50 percent. And Business and First Class fares are so high—especially to Europe—that even at half price, a premium flight is well out of reach for most vacation travelers.

Be wary about any Business or First Class discount promotion. Some agencies that advertise big Business and First Class discounts are actually coupon brokers that buy frequent-flyer awards for resale (see "…And Not-So-Legal Coupons" later in this chapter). But a coupon-based ticket is a far cry from a discounted ticket. Flying on a purchased award or upgrade violates airline rules: Airlines won't honor your ticket if they catch you—and they do check.

Where to Ask

Quite a few consolidators maintain Web sites. Figure 3-8, on the next page, shows the home page for Economy Travel (*www.economytravel.com*), with a box that highlights a few sample deals. Menu choices lead you to additional listings, depending on your destination.

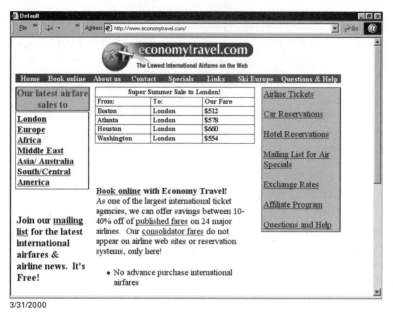

Figure 3-8. *Economy Travel is a typical consolidator that discounts airfares substantially.*

Unfortunately, not all consolidators provide either fare displays or an immediate search result. Some just claim "great discounts," invite you to send an e-mail message or call with a specific request, and promise to respond within a day or two. Obviously, that sort of operation negates much of the value of the Internet; it's no more useful than a newspaper ad. The Appendix lists separately the sites that do provide immediate fares and those that don't.

Several gateway sites include links to agencies that at least claim to be discounters:

- Shoestring Travel (*www.stratpub.com*)

- TISS.com (*www.tiss.com*)

- Travel @ Smilin' Jack's (*smilinjack.com/travel.htm*)

- Web Travel Secrets (*www.web-travel-secrets.com*)

One of the Web's most interesting gateway sites is European Travel Network (ETN at *www.etn.nl* or *www.discountairfares.com*). Based in Amsterdam, ETN is an international network of discount travel agencies, tour operators, and hotels; it also runs a membership-based discount club for travelers. The site includes a large number of links to various travel sites; it's especially helpful in locating discount agencies overseas. Links cover every imaginable travel topic, including companion matching for singles.

The site also has links for such tangential topics as "Christian poetry" and "printing at wholesale prices."

As with other sites, searching for a discount ticket is usually straightforward: Follow the site's instructions.

Several of the listed sites still require that you register your name, e-mail address, and password before you get to the good stuff. A few even ask for charge card data, but these fields are usually not required.

Don't be fooled by claims about "best discount fares," and such. These days, with so many different list-price variations, it's difficult to separate the truly discounted from the merely promotional. So forget about comparisons with list prices, which might well be phony. Concentrate on the price and the restrictions.

HEADS UP

How can you separate true consolidator sites from those that just locate the best list-price deals? One keyword is "published" fares—a search limited to published fares automatically excludes consolidator deals. And if a site bases its searches on the Amadeus, Sabre, or Worldspan search engines, they're confined to published fares. Another warning: While many consolidator sites accept charge cards, some hike the price by 3 to 5 percent if you pay by charge card. Since banks don't allow merchants to assess a surcharge for charge card sales, discounters evade the rules by claiming their posted prices are "net, after a 3 percent cash discount," or similar. However the notice is couched, you'll pay extra if you buy over the Web rather than mail a check.

What You Risk

The biggest risk you run with a consolidator ticket is the buying process itself. Contrary to what you read in much of the travel press, consolidators don't buy seats in bulk and then resell them to travelers. Although consolidators must promise to buy a specified number of tickets from an airline, they don't actually pay for these tickets until consumers pay *them*, in full. And during that gap—between the time you pay the consolidator for a ticket and the consolidator pays the airline—a lot of problems can arise. Among them: slow ticket delivery, failure to procure a firm reservation, and—in the worst cases—using your money to pay off outstanding bills from earlier travelers.

That's why I (along with most other writers) recommend that you buy with a charge card, so you can avail yourself of the chargeback laws that protect card users. It's also a good reason to deal with a consolidator in or near your home city, if you can, so you can keep track of the process and haul the agency into small claims court if you have a problem.

Another hidden risk hasn't been as well publicized: You never really know how much markup you pay. Occasionally, a travel agent will sell you a consolidator ticket for only a little less than the airline's advertised fare and pocket a large markup instead of passing most of the difference along to you. Don't ever buy a consolidator ticket without first learning all you can about the current ticket prices for your trip.

Still More Places to Look

Online auctions are starting to handle air tickets. They work the old-fashioned way: A seller establishes an initial price, which buyers then bid up to a final selling price. Since airfares on most auctions are bundled with land packages, I discuss them in Chapter 6.

You can also check for possible deals at a reverse auction, such as those run by Priceline.com (*www.priceline.com*) and Expedia. However, these services are more likely to cut the costs for trips that don't conform to the usual restrictions (see "Bids in Reverse" later in this chapter) than for conventional trips.

A few shop-your-request sites handle travel. On these sites, you describe the service or product you want to buy, and interested sellers are supposed to respond with their best offers. Although the idea sounds intriguing, as of early 2000, there doesn't seem to have been much action on airfares.

Short Trips, No Saturdays

If you can't stay at your destination over a Saturday night, the giant airlines will usually charge you two to four times as much as if you could stay (at least for most destinations). It isn't that these airlines have it in for vacation travelers who don't want to stay a weekend, nor do they have a stake in filling up weekend hotel rooms. The reason, of course, is that business travelers hate to stay out over a Saturday night—hate it so much they'll pay extra for tickets that permit them to return home when they want. Short-trip vacation travelers are—like the dolphins caught in tuna nets—hapless victims of a snare targeted at others.

Fortunately, as a short-stay vacation traveler, you aren't completely captive to the giant airlines' pricing strategy. You do have some options.

Low-Fare Airlines

As noted earlier, several of the low-fare airlines don't require a Saturday night stay as a condition of their lowest fares:

- Southwest generally requires only a one-night stay—hardly a hardship for most vacation trips.

- Even the lowest fares on AirTran, American Trans Air, and PanAm are available one-way, so length of stay doesn't apply.

- The transatlantic low-fare airlines typically don't require a minimum stay, either. However, their flights are infrequent enough that you face a de facto minimum stay of several days to a full week.

Other low-fare airlines do require a Saturday night stay on their cheapest tickets. Even if you can't use their best deals, however, their unrestricted fares are usually a lot lower than those of the giant airlines. Always check a low-fare airline when you can't conform to the giant airlines' restrictions. See the previous section for details on where to ask and how to ask for flight and fare information.

Consolidators

Similarly, many consolidator tickets don't impose the usual advance-purchase and Saturday-night-stay limits (although they might have some less stringent requirements). Always check the consolidator marketplace before you pay a giant airline's asking price for an unrestricted ticket.

Name-Your-Price Tickets

One of the latest developments in travel buying—the reverse auction—is especially attractive to travelers who can't meet the typical restrictions imposed by the giant airlines. You might pay more than you'd pay for the cheapest restricted ticket, but you'll often pay a lot less than the giant airlines' asking prices for the cheapest ticket that your itinerary permits.

Bids in Reverse

Here's the idea: You set a price you're willing to pay, and then you wait to see if some airline accepts it. Before you submit your bid, you must enter a charge card number. If your bid is accepted, you automatically buy the ticket—you can't hold the deal open while you look for anything better. You don't have much control over the ticket you buy. You must buy a round-trip; one-way trips are not available. You can bid only for Coach seats—no Business or First Class. You can specify only the days you want to travel, not the hours; you agree to leave any time after 6 A.M. and arrive any time before midnight. You aren't forced to use an overnight red-eye, but as an option to increase your odds, you can accept one. You have no say in which airline you fly, although the participating airlines are mainly the giants. You must agree to make at least one stop (possibly changing planes); you can improve your odds by accepting two stops. Your ticket is completely nonrefundable and nontransferable: If you don't take the flight, your money is totally gone. You don't earn any frequent flyer mileage and you can't use frequent flyer mileage or vouchers to upgrade.

If these restrictions sound draconian, there's a reason. They substitute for the more usual advance-purchase and Saturday-night-stay restrictions that the giant airlines impose on their other cheap tickets, and they're supposed to be equally good at discouraging use by business travelers. The benefit for you is that these restrictions are instead of, rather than in addition to, the usual ones. So you can ask for a cheap ticket without the usual minimum stay requirement, and you can ask for it right up to a day or so before flight time.

Two reverse auctions were operating on the Internet in early 2000 (and don't be surprised to see a few other sites adopt the feature by late 2000):

- Priceline.com originated the idea and is still probably the biggest player. The promoter originally faced opposition from all the giant airlines and had a tough time finding any seats to sell. But last year several of the giant U.S. airlines suddenly decided Priceline was a good idea after all, and signed up for the program.

- Expedia operates a system similar to Priceline.

The bidding process is straightforward. Take Priceline as an example. Figure 3-9 shows the home page with the by-now familiar itinerary box, filled in for a trip from San Francisco to Boston. From this page, you go to a page on which you can extend your options by selecting multiple airports (or additional connections); and finally, you reach the page with the all-important box where you fill in your bid. After doing that, you enter a charge card number and click the Submit button.

Priceline notifies you within 1 hour for a domestic trip (Expedia promises 15 minutes), and 24 hours for an international trip, if an airline accepts your bid. If so, you've bought the ticket, with almost no recourse. If your bid is refused, you can re-bid immediately, but you must make at least one change in the itinerary.

4/1/2000

Figure 3-9. *Here's where you enter your itinerary on Priceline.com.*

The San Francisco to Boston itinerary display illustrates an interesting aspect to Priceline's system. You can increase your odds of success, the agency says, by accepting more than one airport in your destination area. For additional airport choices, you'd expect a request for San Francisco to include Oakland and San Jose, which are both inside the same Bay Area metropolitan concentration. But adding Providence, Rhode Island and Manchester, New Hampshire to the Boston request isn't as obvious; both are separate metro areas some distance from Boston, and neither are in Massachusetts. It's a good idea to include these cities, however, since both have smaller airports that cater more heavily to low-fare airlines than Boston does.

The biggest question, of course, is not how to make a bid, but how much to bid. Here, travel writers don't seem to agree. Some suggest that you should use Priceline for any sort of ticket, even when you can buy a sale fare on a giant airline. The clear implication is that some airlines accept bids below their lowest advertised prices—they're just cutting their already low prices a bit more.

Jay Walker, who originated the Priceline idea, didn't see it that way, at least early on. He told me that Priceline should provide restrictions that replace the usual Saturday night stay and extended advance purchase, not add to them. Thus, Priceline wasn't designed to undercut the lowest advertised prices. Instead, it was designed to help travelers who couldn't use one of the lowest-priced tickets because of the usual restrictions—when the only alternative would normally be a very expensive ticket. His early advice was that you forget about undercutting the cheapest fares and use Priceline to undercut more expensive, less restricted fares. By that logic, a correct bid would be $25 or more above the cheapest advertised fare, or at least $25 below the lowest fare available for any given itinerary. Expedia suggests that you bid 20 to 25 percent under the lowest fare you can find some other way—and that staying at your destination over a Saturday night will increase the odds of an airline accepting your bid.

Overall, you could certainly consider a reverse auction on any ticket—provided you're willing to accept the obvious disadvantages. But most of you are probably ahead of the game if you stick with a sale fare or low-fare airline when you can get one. Reserve the reverse auction for when your only alternative is a more expensive ticket.

Inside the System:
How "Bidding" Really Works

Much of the publicity about Priceline and other reverse auctions implies that some accountant in a carrel actually considers and makes an individual decision on each bid. That's not really how it works. Instead, each participating airline establishes a separate fare "bucket" for auction seats: They allocate seats on some flights for sale through auctions and establish a minimum auction price. The computerized auction systems simply check each bid against the airlines' auction seat databases. Airlines accept bids over the minimum as long as seats are available; they reject all bids under the auction-price floor and bids for days with no available auction seats.

The auction systems are also free to buy tickets in other ways. If you bid more than the price of a sale ticket, the auction site sells you the sale ticket and pockets the difference. Sometimes the auctions buy consolidator tickets. You never really know.

What You Risk

Buying a ticket through a reverse auction puts you at risk in three important ways:

- Your ticket has no residual value if you have to change your plans.

- You might wind up with an inconvenient itinerary.

- You lose all frequent flyer benefits.

If none of these risks bothers you, you might as well visit a reverse auction as your last stop when buying any ticket—last because you can't back away from a successful bid. However, finding a good schedule and earning frequent flyer benefits are probably worth anywhere from $25 to $100 on any given trip. Before you decide to try an auction, put a dollar value on these benefits, and set your auction price accordingly. And if there's any chance you won't catch your flight, protect your payment with trip-cancellation insurance.

Back-to-Back

Unfortunately, on all too many routes, you can't find either a low-fare airline or a consolidator ticket. If your only choice is a giant airline, you might be stuck with a very expensive, unrestricted ticket. As an example of just how overpriced these tickets are, in the winter of 1999, a one-day, round-trip ticket from Seattle to Medford, Oregon—about 350 miles each way—cost more than a restricted round-trip ticket from Seattle to London.

To avoid such ludicrously high, unrestricted fares, quite a few travelers have taken to buying "back to back" tickets when they don't want to stay over a Saturday night. That means they buy two round-trip tickets: one from their home city to their destination and back, with a return flight after the first Saturday; the second from their destination city to their home city and back, again with a return after the first Saturday. They then use the "going" portion of the first ticket to get to their destination and the "going" portion of the second ticket to fly back home. They don't show up for either of the return flights and simply discard the return tickets. Even better, if they want, they can schedule the return flights to make two round-trips, both without a Saturday stay—as long as they complete both round-trips within a month.

Needless to say, the airlines don't much like "back-to-back" tickets. With several airlines, back-to-back tickets violate specific provisions of the contract boilerplate that passengers accept when they buy tickets. Moreover, airlines claim that if you use a back-to-back ticket, they have a right to bill you the difference between what you should have paid and what you actually paid. Before this year, airlines hadn't targeted many individual travelers for enforcement, and had instead targeted travel agents that issued back-to-back tickets. But trade reports indicate that at least some airlines are starting to track individual travelers and challenge them when they try to use back-to-back tickets.

The upshot: Deciding the ethics of back-to-back travel is up to you. Sure, it violates airline rules, but you really don't have much say about the inclusion of these rules in your ticket. One rule is clear, however: If you decide to buy back-to-back tickets, don't tell either an airline reservationist or a travel agent what you're doing. Where possible, book the two round-trips on two separate airlines.

Let's Go—Right Now

Arguably the Internet's biggest impact on airline markets is in last-minute travel. Prior to the Internet, the only last-minute ticket you could buy was at the full, unrestricted fare.

The Internet's ability to bring buyers and sellers together has opened up a whole new range of options. For you as a consumer, it means low-cost travel without the usual restrictions (but with some new ones in their place). For airlines, it means yet another way to fill up seats that would otherwise go empty, sold in ways that prevent business travelers from buying them.

Weekend Internet Specials

Low, short-notice, weekend fares were the giant airlines' first important Internet innovation. Each Wednesday, they announce special very low fares for travel the following weekend. Typically, you start your trip on Saturday and return the following Sunday or Monday (sometimes extended to Tuesday). The fares are usually limited to a few dozen routes each week—and usually a different list each week. Most airlines have tie-ins with hotel chains for reduced-price rooms in the cities with that week's low airfares; a few airlines also have tie-ins with car-rental deals.

Originally, you had to sign up for a weekly e-mail notice, but most airlines now give you the choice of receiving an e-mail message or checking a listing on their Web sites. As with most promotional fares, seats are limited and might not be available on all flights.

Some giant airlines offer similar international deals, typically with a bit more flexibility. Even so, you have very little notice and can stay only a few days. Short trips to Europe are often available and might be to your liking. As someone once noted, however, "If you like jet lag, you'll love a weekend trip to Europe."

Several airlines—most notably Southwest—have extended the short-notice concept to give both a longer advance notice and a longer travel window. In fact, the distinction between short-notice trips and Internet-only airfare sales has become quite hazy.

For weekly routes and fares, check the Web sites of any airlines that serve your home community. Follow the onscreen instructions if you want weekly e-mail bulletins.

If you're too busy to check out each giant airline's Web site separately, several agency sites will send you an e-mail message listing all the short-term fares from your home city. Figure 3-10 shows part of such a message, from Smarter Living (*www.smarterliving.com*), sent to travelers who live in or near Portland, Oregon.

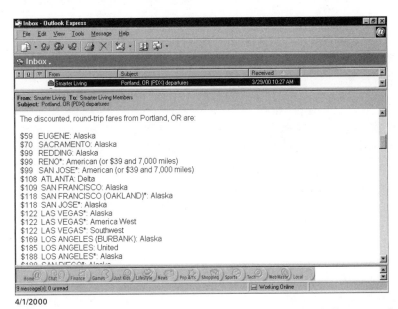

4/1/2000

Figure 3-10. *The agency site Smarter Living notifies you of all Internet deals from your local airport.*

Other Last-Minute Specials

Several agency and auction sites offer last-minute travel deals. However, for the most part, those sites emphasize air-land packages more than airfares only. Of those that do offer airfares, by far the largest number are misleading promotions offering free or cheap air tickets, but only when you buy hotel accommodations from the same supplier. See Chapter 8 for additional details.

Best Fares (*www.bestfares.com*) is an agency that sells a mix of consolidator and sale fares for both domestic and international travel, including last-minute deals. Figure 3-11 shows a portion of the Best Fares site with quite a few last-minute deals, often labeled "you snooze, you lose." Best Fares is also the Web's best source of information on coupon and merchandising promotions that involve airline tickets.

ED'S NOTEBOOK

Cheap Standby? Forget It

It never ceases to amaze me how some travelers never forget a deal, no matter how long it has been absent from the marketplace. Standby is a prime example. I still hear people talk about "heading out to the airport for a cheap standby seat."

Cheap standby has been gone for more than 20 years. Its heyday was when Sir Freddie Laker's Skytrain introduced low standby fares from the United States to London, which were matched by Laker's giant competitors. But when Laker folded, standby went away almost immediately.

These days, you have only one opportunity to stand by at a low fare: If you already have a low-fare ticket, most giant airlines will allow you to stand by for other flights on the same day as your originally ticketed return flight. If you get to the airport early, you might be able to catch an earlier flight; if you miss your original flight, you can try to catch a later one. Beyond that, cheap standby is dead.

5/29/2000

Figure 3-11. *Best Fares arranges lots of last-minute deals.*

The Ways Less Traveled

Most of you will undoubtedly be able to buy the tickets you need using one of the approaches mentioned previously. However, a few travelers have special requirements that might require some additional searching.

The One-Way Ticket Thicket

Many of the better airfare deals are confined to round-trip or open-jaw itineraries. But once in a while you might need a one-way ticket: You might, for example, fly to meet someone and drive back together. Whatever the reason, the system doesn't make it easy to buy inexpensive one-way tickets.

The first place to check is with a low-fare airline. As noted, several of them impose no round-trip requirement on even their cheapest tickets. You might have to buy up to 21 days ahead, but you can buy one-way for half the round-trip cost.

Next, look at consolidators. Typically, they sell one-way tickets for a little more than half the round-trip price—certainly much less than you'd pay on a giant airline.

One-way travelers who can't find a low-fare airline or a consolidator ticket face a real quandary. The giant airline one-way fares, which are usually unrestricted, are often more than double the fares of the least expensive round-trips. That's why many one-way travelers buy a round-trip and don't show up for the return flight. In effect, they use half of a back-to-back ticket (see "Back-to-Back"). As with the more usual back-to-back tickets, that system violates airline rules—which might or might not bother the travelers who use it.

Multistop Marathons

Occasionally you might want to schedule an air trip that takes you to several cities before you return home. Within the United States, you usually have two choices.

First, you can often book a multistop trip at excursion fares, provided you stay at the most distant point over a Saturday night and comply with the regular advance-purchase restrictions. You generally pay one-half the excursion round-trip for each leg of your flight. Some Web sites seem to be able to handle such trips, but it's still tough to find the best deal. Here's another case where a good travel agent is probably a wiser choice.

When you can't do a multistop trip that way—because it involves different airlines or the airlines can't accept your itinerary—you might find it easier to buy several out-and-back round trips from your home city. Yes, it's a lot of extra flying, but think of all that extra frequent flyer mileage!

In many foreign areas, you have a third choice: a visitor ticket or airpass that provides extended, multistop air travel at reduced cost. Visitor tickets are available for most of Western Europe, Australia, New Zealand, India, Japan, Thailand, Malaysia, Argentina, Brazil, Chile, and Peru. Most visitor tickets are sold by the major airlines based in the area; I didn't see any airline sites that included such visitor tickets, although I might have missed one or two.

One visitor ticket, however, has its own Web site. Fortunately, it's one if the best. Europe by Air (*www.europebyair.com*) is a consortium of some 16 different airlines, most of them small. You can travel on any nonstop flight for $99, with a minimum of three flights. The big weakness of most visitor tickets is that you typically must fly through a hub to get to your destination, which counts as two flights (or twice the $99 fare). But with its 16 different airlines, Europe by Air can offer more direct flights than its competitors.

Escaping the Cattle Car

Question: What do you call the combination of ultra-tight seating, lousy food, and indifferent service?

Answer: "Coach" in the United States; "Economy" everywhere else.

Travelers in the rear of the airplane might pay widely different fares, but they all get the same little seats, with service to match. If you want a comfortable seat, adequate legroom, and really good service, you have to pay from 5 to 20 times the price of a Coach ticket for a seat in Business or First Class. These are the general rules, worldwide, but there are a few exceptions. As a leisure traveler, you can occasionally escape the cattle car without taking out a second mortgage.

Really Good Coach

One—and only one—U.S. airline has a consistent track record of providing comfortable seats and good service at Coach fares: Midwest Express (*www.midwestexpress.com*), a small airline that flies from hubs in Milwaukee and Omaha to major business centers around the country. The airline has one-class seating: four seats in each row—two on either side of the aisle—with no middle seats in DC9s and MD80s. Midwest Express also spends about twice as much on food and beverages, per passenger, than the giant airlines. Its Coach Class is as close as you can come to First Class without paying extra.

Fares on Midwest Express are the same as those on the giant airlines. However, it often sits on the sidelines during fare wars, and it allocates fewer seats to its cheapest fares than most other airlines do. But it does sell

---

HEADS UP

Early in 2000, American Airlines announced it was taking a few rows of Coach seats out of each cabin and spacing out all of the remaining rows by several inches. Its new Coach product will certainly be a big improvement over its prior standard—and far better than competitors offer. However, the seats will be as narrow as before, so American's improved Coach really doesn't qualify as true Premium Coach. Still, at equivalent fares, American should now be a clear choice over any competitor (other than Midwest Express). But keep your eyes on those competitors to see how they might respond. American expects to finish converting its domestic planes by the end of 2000 and its overseas planes by sometime in 2001.

---

low-priced excursions. Any time you can find a good schedule and a good fare on Midwest Express, take it; you'll never do any better.

In early 2000, three startup airlines were planning to emulate the Midwest Express formula of superior service at Coach prices. Legend Air got off the ground in April, flying from a base at Dallas/Love Field to Las Vegas, Los Angeles, and Washington/Dulles. It provides the same four-across seating in DC9s as Midwest Express, with more than a foot of additional legroom. As of summer, competitors were challenging it both in the marketplace and in court, and it's far too early to determine if the airline will survive. Cardinal and Crystal, the other two startup airlines, were still trying to arrange financing as of this writing.

Premium Coach/Economy

A few giant international airlines offer two levels of Economy service: Standard and Premium. Typically, Premium seats are an inch or two wider than in Standard Economy, with an extra 6 to 8 inches of legroom; cabin service is also above Standard Economy levels. It's not as opulent as Business Class, but for leisure travelers who just want relief from ultra-cramped Economy, it's good enough.

By far the best Premium Economy deal is on EVA's trans-Pacific flights from the United States to Taipei. You can upgrade even a cheap Economy ticket for about $350 round-trip. Although a significant amount of money, that's not beyond the reach of many leisure travelers. And apparently it's working: EVA's newest 747 has more Premium seats than Standard Economy seats.

Virgin Atlantic's Premium Economy is similar to EVA's—except for the price. Unfortunately, Virgin charges up to 10 times its cheapest Economy fare for a roomy seat in Premium. Clearly, Virgin's product is for business travelers, not vacationers.

United introduced a separate Economy Plus Class last year. It removed a few rows of seats from each cabin, as American did. However, United added all the extra legroom to a few rows in the front of the cabin, leaving most seats as bad as before. Who gets those roomy seats? Business travelers on full-fare tickets or high-ranking members of United's frequent flyer program. Leisure travelers aren't likely to see any benefit whatsoever.

Low-Fare Business/First Class

Several low-fare airlines offer what they call Business or First Class. Here in the United States, you can find (relatively) cheap premium class seats on AirTran, National, and Pro Air. You pay as much as double the airlines' cheapest Coach fares, but much less than half of what you'd pay on a giant airline.

Low-fare international airlines CityBird, Corsair, LTU, Martinair, and Royal Aviation (Canada) all offer Business Class options to Europe. As with the domestic airlines, the ticket prices are at least double the lowest Economy fares, but less than one-third of the giant airlines' asking prices. Their seating and cabin service aren't as opulent as in Business Class on a giant airline, but they're far better than regular Economy.

Inexpensive Upgrades

Every once in a while, one of the giant airlines will allow leisure travelers to upgrade to Business Class for a reasonable price. El Al has often offered upgrades to travelers to Israel; last year, Olympic had a good upgrade deal to Greece.

Travelers interested in comfortable flights often use frequent flyer credit for upgrades rather than free trips. Typically, you need 20,000 to 30,000 miles for a domestic upgrade and 40,000 to 50,000 to Europe. And airlines are extremely stingy in the number of Business Class seats they allocate to frequent flyer upgrades.

The Long Way Around

Round-the-world (RTW) has been a small but important niche in the airfare market for years. It started out in the 1960s as a promotional gimmick, when Pan American (the original incarnation) initially pioneered single-plane multistop round-the-world flights. Then, the going price was $999 for a standby in Economy. At the time, no other airline flew all the way around the world, so all of the giant U.S. airlines hooked up with one or two European or Pacific Basin partners to offer competitive tickets.

The basic idea is still the same. For a fixed price, you can stop off as often as schedules and routes permit, as long as you keep going in the same direction and don't backtrack. Originally, it was a great way to hit some of the world's top tourist centers, as long as you had enough time to spend a few days at each important stop.

The original Pan American is long gone, but its RTW legacy lives on, although at higher prices; Economy now starts at around $2,500. However, the official RTW ticket, especially in Economy, has lost much of its appeal because of the following:

- With all the various promotional and discount fares available, you can buy round-trips from the United States to South Asia (which is half way around the world) via either the Atlantic or the Pacific for well under the official RTW fare.

- With the advent of long-range jets, it's hard to find flights that stop in enough places for a good RTW trip. On Pan American's original route, you could start from the West Coast of the United States; stop in Hawaii, Tokyo, Hong Kong, Singapore, Bangkok, Delhi, Teheran or Athens, and London or Frankfurt; and then fly back to the United States. Now however, most flights from the United States to Southeast Asia operate nonstop across the Pacific; and flights from Tokyo, Hong Kong, Singapore, and Bangkok to Europe operate nonstop across central Asia.

In place of official RTW tickets, a few clever agencies arrange their own RTW itineraries, using discounted tickets from as many airlines as required. The number of stops can be considerably greater than on any official RTW ticket. Figure 3-12 shows a typical page of an RTW option from AirTreks.com (*www.airtreks.com*), one of the big players in the RTW market.

4/1/2000

Figure 3-12. *You can fly around the world for as little as $1,000.*

Prices in the spring of 2000 started at just under $1,000—far less than the official ticket. However, these very cheap RTWs usually provided only two stops outside the United States, such as the New York-Bangkok-London-New York itinerary shown. Unless you really enjoy jet lag, that's not much of a trip. But when you moved up to $1,500 and above, you had lots of choices.

Agencies that specialize in RTW usually sell Circle Pacific (CP), as well: the same sort of deal for trips that visit East Asia, Southeast Asia, the South Pacific, and South America. As with RTW, CP trips assembled out of individual discount tickets usually undersell the airlines' official CP rates.

Other agencies offer similar itineraries; most will bid on a trip to destinations you specify. These agency URLs are listed in the Appendix.

Overall, these improvised RTW and CP tickets are not only cheaper than the airlines' official RTW tickets, but they also provide a much better choice of stops. Official RTW and CP tickets are good deals in only one case: when you want to fly in Business or First Class. The typical RTW Business Class fares start at around $4,500 to $5,000, more than $1,000 below the price of a Business Class round-trip ticket from Boston or New York to London. If you're thinking about a premium-class ticket to Europe anyhow, you can go or return via Tokyo, Bangkok, or Singapore and pay a lot less than you'd pay for a regular round-trip—appealing, but practical only if you have business in Asia or the time and inclination to take a couple of weeks off for an RTW vacation.

You have to call an airline for an official RTW or CP ticket. The only airline site I found with RTW fares displayed was Singapore Airline's, and it didn't show the current RTW ticket on the Star Alliance (of which it is a part).

Carry the Mail—Somebody Else's

If you travel by yourself, if you can travel on short notice, and if you'd like to visit one of the world's major cities, consider signing on as a courier. You pay less than the airlines' asking lowest prices—sometimes just a few dollars off the asking price, sometimes more than 50 percent.

You sign on for courier trips through a courier agency that specializes in arranging courier travel for shipping companies, not directly with a shipping company such as DHL or Federal Express. The fare is set by the agency, at a price determined by supply and demand. Fares are almost always below the lowest advertised fares, but sometimes not by much: During giant airlines' sales, courier agencies are hard-pressed to beat advertised fares. The best courier deals are last-minute openings, when you might have only a few days or even hours to accept, but these don't come along very often; you usually have to develop a track record of reliability before you'll be offered a really good deal.

Since courier tickets go one at a time, a couple can't travel together unless one buys a ticket or they travel on different days. Many don't earn frequent flyer credit, and you probably can't use your mileage to upgrade a courier ticket. The shipper might take up your entire baggage allowance, leaving you with just your carry-on luggage for your whole trip. And your return date might be fixed, as little as one week after arrival.

If you're interested, four membership programs maintain online databases on courier travel. You must pay an annual fee for full access. As an example of what's offered, Figure 3-13 shows the Air Courier Association's (*www.aircourier.org*) sample courier-flight page for European trips.

Inside the System: Courier Travel—How It Really Is

If your idea of courier travel is sitting in a First Class cabin, handcuffed to a briefcase, worrying what to do if that notorious enemy agent spots you, think again. Today's couriers sit in Economy with nothing more to protect than a baggage claim check. The shipping companies don't want you at all; they merely want your baggage allowance. As a courier, all you do is meet an agent of the shipper (probably at an airport), receive the shipment, and check it in as you check in for your flight. At your destination, you claim the shipment (or give your claim check to another shipping agent) and go on your way. You might have to sign up for a return trip, or you might be free to set your own return schedule.

Couriers go where high-priority documents and parcels go—from major U.S. cities to major cities in Europe, Asia, South America, and Australia. That means New York to London or Frankfurt, Miami to Sao Paulo or Santiago, San Francisco to Tokyo or Sydney. You won't find any courier opportunities leaving from, say, San Antonio or Buffalo, or trips to Glasgow or Bali. And paying for a separate ticket to a gateway airport might well wipe out the advantage of a courier fare.

But the most important fact about courier travel is this: Only about 100 courier seats leave the United States each day. While 100 a day might seem like a large number, seats are distributed among all major U.S. gateway cities and all foreign destinations—it's a tiny fraction of the total traffic on any individual route. That means seats to popular places sell out early—and courier companies don't have to pay a heavy subsidy.

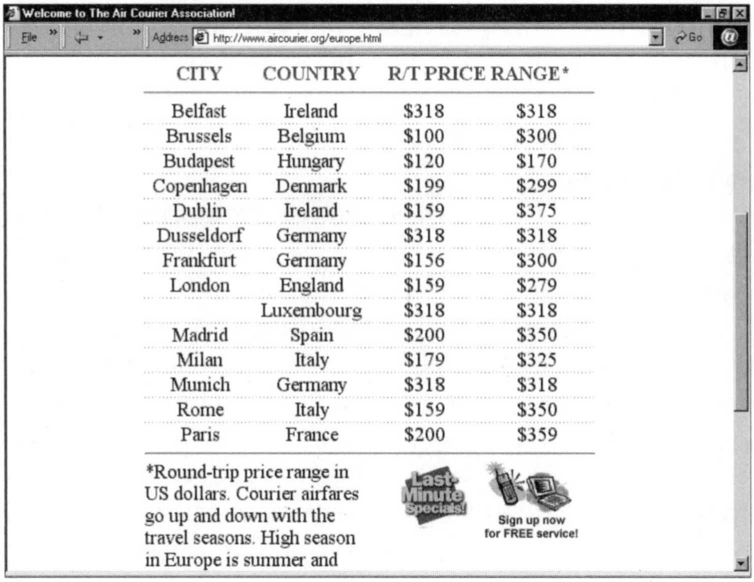

CITY	COUNTRY	R/T PRICE RANGE*	
Belfast	Ireland	$318	$318
Brussels	Belgium	$100	$300
Budapest	Hungary	$120	$170
Copenhagen	Denmark	$199	$299
Dublin	Ireland	$159	$375
Dusseldorf	Germany	$318	$318
Frankfurt	Germany	$156	$300
London	England	$159	$279
	Luxembourg	$318	$318
Madrid	Spain	$200	$350
Milan	Italy	$179	$325
Munich	Germany	$318	$318
Rome	Italy	$159	$350
Paris	France	$200	$359

*Round-trip price range in US dollars. Courier airfares go up and down with the travel seasons. High season in Europe is summer and

Last Minute Specials!

Sign up now for FREE service!

4/1/2000

Figure 3-13. *Air Courier Association shows courier fares that can beat even the discounters.*

The other three sites are Global Courier Travel (*www.couriertravel.org*), International Association of Air Travel Couriers (*www.courier.org*), and Worldwide Courier Association (*www.massiveweb.com*).

You don't need to join any association to fly as a courier. In fact, the associations can't arrange for any courier trips; all the associations provide is a convenient database. If you prefer to contact individual courier agencies, Beat the Monkey (*www.beatthemonkey.com*) sells a directory of them. These days, the rule is "don't buy a courier ticket until you've checked out the lowest available discount or promotional fare." And as with any supposed travel "deal," courier travel isn't always the cheapest you can find.

Hitch a Flight

If you're really flexible, you can "hitch" a flight to Europe or Hawaii through Airhitch (*www.airhitch.org*). In the summer of 2000, the round-trip peak season hitch fare to Europe from the East Coast was roughly half the price of a giant airline's sale-price ticket. Flights were consistently available from the East Coast and Florida, and were often available from other areas.

Airhitch requires that you be flexible—about travel dates, airline, schedule, and even destination city. Here's how the hitch operates to Europe (Hawaii works about the same way): First, you register and prepay for the flight, specifying your U.S. departure city, three acceptable major gateway cities in Europe, and a "date range" of five or more days. Airhitch gives you a "call-in date," typically the Wednesday before the start of your date range. When you call, the Airhitch office gives you a list of upcoming flights and its estimate of your odds of getting a seat on each. For any flight that you like, you go to the airport a few hours before departure, and an Airhitch representative handles the boarding.

Airhitch is more or less operating a standby system for a group of airlines—mainly charter and low-fare airlines. The airlines notify Airhitch of any unsold seats a week or so before departure, and Airhitch agrees to sell some or all of them. You won't know what airline you're on until you get your flight assignment. Airhitch claims a high rate of success in getting travelers to their preferred destinations. If no flight meets your needs, you can extend your date range, or Airhitch might be able to get you a confirmed seat at a somewhat higher price. As Airhitch notes, you don't have to be a student to use the service, but "it helps to think and travel like one."

An affiliate of Airhitch, Sunhitch (same Web site), sells inexpensive one-week round-trips to beach destinations in the Caribbean and Mexico. You can state a destination preference, but the only guarantee is a good beach.

Obviously, Airhitch works best for travelers who live in or near one of the major U.S. gateway cities for flights to Europe (especially Boston, New York/Newark, Washington/Baltimore, Orlando, Miami, Chicago, Los Angeles, and Oakland); and for travelers who are either traveling by railpass or driving through several European countries and don't particularly care where they start their trips.

From other U.S. cities, you can, of course, drive or find a low-fare airline to one of the big gateway cities. But buying a separate ticket from your home city to New York or Oakland, say, can add hundreds of dollars to your total cost. And you have the added expense of staying in that gateway city for up to five days. If you can get a good discount, a consolidator ticket from your home city straight through to your final destination might be a better bet. Check the alternatives before you commit to Airhitch.

If the hitch system is too iffy for you, Airhitch also arranges low-fare "target flight" tickets—essentially consolidator deals—with firm routes, dates, and seat reservations.

Not Just Tickets

Beyond buying travel, you can do lots of other airline business on the Web. Here's just some of what the Internet has to offer.

Frequent Flyer

Earning and using frequent flyer awards is as important to some travelers as finding low fares or convenient schedules. The Internet offers these travelers plenty of opportunities to pursue their obsession.

All the major U.S. airlines—and most big international airlines—let you track your frequent flyer account on their Web sites. On most, you can request award tickets and upgrades. Also, airline sites have started to publish data on how to use frequent flyer awards, but the numbers are too scanty to be useful to travelers trying to book a frequent flyer trip.

Several independent sites are dedicated to frequent flyer matters, including summaries of current bonuses, program comparisons, questions and answers, and reports from users. Undoubtedly the leading site is WebFlyer (*www.webflyer.com*). It's run by Randy Peterson, publisher of *Inside Flyer* and widely acclaimed as the "guru" of frequent flyer programs. It lists more than you probably want to know about frequent flyer programs and awards. There's even a page with frequent flyer cartoons and jokes.

Another site, MaxMiles (*www.maxmiles.com*) features much of the same material. It also provides an automatic tracking and summary of all your frequent flyer accounts.

Legal Coupons...

Airlines often issue coupons or vouchers that you can use to cut a percentage or a dollar amount off the advertised price of an air ticket. Some are premiums from frequent flyer programs, some are included as bill-stuffers for banks and other institutions, some are tied into promotions with various retail stores, and some are bound into guidebooks and discount books of one sort or another. Airlines give some to travelers as compensation for being bumped off a flight or otherwise inconvenienced. However issued, many of these coupons are available to anyone, and even "bump" coupons and other vouchers issued to individual travelers are transferable. Some coupons and vouchers are good for a percentage or amount off any ticket, others are limited to Coach/Economy tickets, and some exclude trips to and from the issuing line's major hubs. (And the airlines claim they don't mistreat travelers who live in those hubs!)

Some online agencies specialize in finding coupons and vouchers, and using them to cut the prices of tickets they sell. One such site is Discount Air Brokers (*www.discountairbrokers.com*), which also sells a mix of consolidator and other off-price tickets. It's just one more stop on a comprehensive search for the best deal.

...And Not-So-Legal Coupons

If you're involved with frequent flyer stuff at all, you surely know that buying and selling awards is against the policies of all airlines. Moreover, airlines actively try to run the "coupon brokers" out of the marketplace and have generally been successful in their lawsuits against the brokers. Airlines also refuse to honor award-based tickets and upgrades they believe to have been bought, and they cancel accrued mileage in the accounts of travelers they believe have sold credit.

Nevertheless, coupon brokers manage to stay in business, one way or another. The system is simple: If you decide to sell mileage, you list your miles with a broker and agree to request an award when the broker notifies you. If you decide to buy an award, you first make a deal with a broker, and then the broker notifies a seller to request an award for a ticket or upgrade from an airline, issued in your name. The broker sells you that award for about twice what it paid the seller. Contrary to some reports, you don't have to fly under the seller's name. But you do violate airline rules.

Brokers deal almost exclusively in Business and First Class tickets and upgrades; using mileage for Coach/Economy tickets doesn't make economic sense. Neither I nor any other reputable source of travel information can recommend that you use a coupon broker, either to buy or sell. If you want to run the risk, however, you can do it on the Internet; you can find a handful of coupon brokers with Web sites.

More to the point: Some agencies that promise really big discounts on Business and First Class air tickets actually use purchased awards without making it clear to their customers that coupons are involved. If you're thinking about such a ticket, always ask if it is based on an award. Unless you're willing to take a big chance, forget about the discount and the agent that is pushing it.

Scanning the Seats

Most airline sites include "seat maps" that show the locations and numbers of all seats on each type of aircraft they fly. They're useful for locating seats with extra legroom, such as those in exit rows and bulkhead seats, as well as undesirable seats with limited recline. If the pages aren't readily apparent on a home-page menu, enter "seat maps" or "fleet" into a site's search program.

As part of their response to pressures for improved passengers' rights, last year the big U.S. airlines agreed to publish data on seat dimensions. In response, American, Continental, Delta, Midwest Express, Northwest, Southwest, United, and US Airways added seat dimension data to their seat maps. As of early 2000, American Trans Air, Midway, Spirit, and TWA didn't list dimensions, nor did any of the giant foreign airlines. AirTran, Alaska, America West, Frontier, Sun Country, and Vanguard didn't even publish seat maps, let alone seat dimensions.

Expedia and Travelocity include seat maps—and selection—as part of their booking process. However, you can't view the seat maps until you're buying, which is not useful to travelers who want to select flights at least in part for roomier seats.

A few years ago, you'd have been hard-pressed to notice much difference in seat space among the big airlines. Now that seat space is becoming more of an issue among travelers, comparative seating dimensions are more important. If you treasure every extra inch of space you can get, those online compilations can help you select a flight.

How Late This Time?

Most big airline sites provide online flight information. You enter a flight number and date, and the site shows when the flight arrived or will arrive. Figure 3-14 on the next page shows the flight information screen on Delta's site, which is typical. If you can't easily locate the flight status page on an individual airline site, Expedia, Travelocity, and other agency and gateway sites can retrieve flight status data from a large number of airlines.

Of course, the GIGO (garbage in, garbage out) concept applies to flight data at least as much as to any other input stream. With all of today's technology, you'll still find the expected inaccuracies. So, whether you're flying out yourself or meeting someone coming in, the oldest advice remains valid: Never head for the airport until you've checked the flight status.

6/20/2000

Figure 3-14. *You can often check flight information on airlines' Web sites.*

Beware: Airfare-Shopping Pitfalls

Your biggest risk in buying airline tickets online is failure to find the best deal. Once you've located what looks to be a good price, you won't encounter many pitfalls.

The biggest sticker shock you're likely to experience is the extent to which taxes and fees pad your final price. Airlines and online agencies are perfectly within their legal rights to exclude those figures from their initial fare displays, and they do add them in before they present a bottom-line total. However, the amount—up to $90 on an international ticket—can be staggering.

Always watch out for extra fees and charges that some sites tack on to the nominal price. Some, for example, include conventional delivery in the posted prices, while others add up to $20 a ticket for "postage and handling." You also find occasional "service" and other fees that not only add to your total cost but also distort your comparisons.

Before you buy a heavily discounted ticket, make sure you know all the restrictions and limitations. Especially on overseas flights, some of these tickets might be totally nonrefundable and nonreusable—if you cancel, you've lost your entire payment. Avoid these when you can; when you can't, buy cancellation insurance (see Chapter 7).

No matter how attractive the price, never buy a ticket or upgrade issued against some other traveler's frequent flyer program. Airlines actively police what they believe to be abuse of those programs, and the cost reduction isn't worth the risk.

A Place to Stay

Quick Trip Through Chapter 4

Careful Internet shopping can lop many hundreds of dollars off your accommodation costs. I suggest checking these places out first:

- The Web sites of most big hotel chains offer occasional promotional rates, either chainwide or at individual locations.

- Internet hotel discounters often cut prices substantially—sometimes more than 50 percent—in major cities around the world, mainly in midpriced to high-priced hotels.

- A reverse auction (name-your-price program) can work for hotel rates as well as for airline fares—maybe even better—but make it the last stop on your search.

With all of these, keep in mind that off-peak prices are generally much lower than peak-time prices—but the off-peak product is different, too.

The Internet can also help if you're more interested in a special type of accommodation than in a discount at a conventional hotel. Thousands of bed & breakfasts (B&Bs) have Web sites or are listed on directory sites, and the Internet is a great way to locate and book a vacation rental.

I t's not the airfares that will break your budget this year, it's the hotel bills." That's been my mantra for several years, and it will likely remain so for quite a few more. Travelers who fixate on airfares and ignore their accommodation costs will ultimately pay a stiff penalty for their tunnel vision.

You don't have to look far for examples. During much of the winter of 1999 and the early spring of 2000, you could fly round-trip from the United States to London—even from the West Coast—for less than the asking price for one night's lodging in the Dorchester or one of London's other famous hotels. Clearly, lodging costs deserve at least as much attention as airfares—maybe more—especially when you head for an expensive destination.

The accommodation marketplace is very different from that in which the airlines operate:

- Location doesn't matter much with airlines. True, the destination city's location often impacts fares, but you don't have to decide if you want a beachfront airport, or one near a golf course. Many cities have just one airport, and even the largest metro areas give you only a few airport options. Not so with hotels: You find them scattered throughout metro areas, in small towns, and along Interstates and other major highways. Even a difference of a few blocks in proximity to your ultimate destination—city center, beach, theater, or relatives' house—can be very important when you choose where to stay.

- When you fly, you have only two or three real product choices. And to move up to a roomier seat and a better meal service costs you from 4 to 20 times more than the airlines' rock-bottom economy products. Hotel suppliers, on the other hand, offer you a broad range of price and quality, extending in small increments from a minimal budget product to a money-is-no-object one. If you want something a little better than the hotel industry's rock-bottom economy options, you move up a step, pay a little more, and get a slightly better room. In that respect, the hotel marketplace is much more user-friendly than that of the airlines.

For the reasons I just described, most travelers don't approach hotels with the same price-is-everything paradigm they apply to airline tickets. Sure, if you've decided to stay in a big-city hotel, price is critical: The published asking prices (*rack rates*, in hotel-ese) can be very high, and discounts are widely available. While the full-price-to-discount range is narrower than the range you find among airlines, it's big enough to warrant some real effort to buy at the bottom of the price range, not the top. Fortunately, you'll find plenty of discounters on the Internet.

Where Senior Starts at 50

Most hotel-chain Web sites allow you to ask for senior deals, although, with some, you must call either the chain's nationwide reservation system or the individual hotel for a senior rate. At many hotel chains, you're eligible for senior rates starting at the relatively young age of 50. That's because 50 is the minimum age for membership in AARP (American Association of Retired Persons; *www.aarp.org*, $8 per year), and AARP insists that any benefit offered be available to all qualified members.

AARP has official deals with more than three dozen hotel chains. Specific chains and their discount percentages can be found on the "Member Services & Discounts" page of the AARP Web site; other chains unofficially honor AARP cards, as well. And many others offer their own senior deals, although the minimum age might be higher than 50.

Rather than hook up with AARP, Hilton runs its own senior club, Senior HHonors (*www.hilton.com/hhonors/seniors/*). The minimum age is 60, but if one spouse qualifies, the other can be any age. Deals are quite good, often exceeding 50 percent off, but you have to pay to belong—$55 the first year, $40 for annual renewals. Once you have your Senior HHonors ID number, Hilton's Web site will automatically include special senior deals that might be available at each hotel. Days Inn (*www.daysinn.com*) also operates its own senior club, September Days Club; $15 for one year to $50 for five years.

But you might well prefer a budget motel, bed & breakfast, or vacation rental to a big-city hotel, even if you don't get much of a discount—or any discount at all. The Internet can be a big help in locating that sort of accommodation, too.

On Sale from a Hotel

As is the case with airlines, the best place to start looking for a hotel deal is the hotel chains' own Web sites. Just about any chain you can name operates a site; the Appendix lists more than 100 of them. Again, as is the case with airlines, even if a chain's best advertised deal isn't your best bet, it's the benchmark against which you measure other possible deals.

Big hotels and hotel chains typically have more than one published list price for any given location, on any given date. At a minimum, you'll find rack rate and regular corporate rate. The corporate rate is typically around 10 percent below rack rate, and usually all you need to get it is to present some sort of business card. No matter that you show up in shorts

Inside the System:
Where First Class Isn't the Top

If you've ever checked into a hotel described as "First Class" and wondered whether it was really one of the city's best hotels, you're in good company. Many travelers, used to the airlines' terminology, conclude that First Class represents the highest category the hotel industry can offer.

It doesn't. The hotel rating system in widest use these days (the Official Hotel Guide, or OHG) places First Class in the middle of its rating spectrum:

Deluxe	Superior Deluxe
	Deluxe
	Moderate Deluxe
First Class	Superior First Class
	First Class
	Limited-Service First Class
	Moderate First Class
Tourist	Superior Tourist
	Tourist
	Moderate Tourist

and an aloha shirt, with three kids in tow, you can still qualify for that corporate price. Most hotel Web sites show corporate rates.

Hotels also frequently run sales and short-term promotions. Rates range from a few percentage points below rack rate to a really big cut. These rates, too, are often shown on the chains' Web sites. In some cases, promotional rates will come up automatically when you check prices and availability. In others, you must click a button for promotions or deals.

An example of a hotel sale offer is shown on the next page in Figure 4-1, which shows an Internet-only promotion from Outrigger Hotels (*www.outrigger.com*). If you book through the Web site, you can get up to 30 percent off rack rates at most Outrigger properties. You'll find similar displays from other major chains—some for Internet-only deals, others that are available through multiple sources.

Obviously, hotels don't post all their rates on their Web sites. Most big chains offer additional sets of rates that are individually negotiated with some of their better corporate customers—rates that are well below the published corporate rates.

Inside the System:
Where First Class Isn't the Top *(continued)*

Here's what OHG says about a First Class hotel: "A dependable, comfortable hotel with standardized rooms, amenities and public areas—May have superior executive level or wing—May be safely recommended to average travelers not expecting Deluxe facilities or special services—Should also be satisfactory for better groups."

That definition probably about fits what you encountered in that First Class hotel—a far cry from the top. The real top is Superior Deluxe, which translates as: "An exclusive and expensive luxury hotel, often palatial, offering the highest standards of service, accommodations and facilities—Elegant and luxurious public rooms—A prestige address—Establishments in this category are among the world's top hotels."

4/23/2000

Figure 4-1. *Outrigger's site offers Internet-only discounts of 30 percent.*

Unfortunately, not all hotel chains are as diligent or open as Outrigger in posting their promotional rates. During most of 1999 and 2000, for example, the Thistle chain in the United Kingdom offered a "Pounds For Dollars" promotion for U.S. visitors: Pay the same number of dollars

The Art of the Deal

Not all your deals will be the result of your Internet expertise. Surprisingly, some of the easiest discounts to get are those that you simply ask for yourself. When you call for a reservation, check the price, but then—no matter what the response—ask if the hotel has a better deal available. While I was writing this chapter, I had to make a quick trip to Texas to appear on a program. I started by calling a big chain where I had often found outstanding senior deals. "Is the senior rate available?" I inquired. "No," said the agent, "the regular rate is $165." "That's too much," I responded, "I'll try somewhere else." But before I could hang up, the agent hastily interjected, "Oh, I can't give you a senior rate, but I can give you a corporate rate of $86." "Fine," I said, and I made the deal.

as the rack rate, expressed in pounds. Since a pound was about $1.60, that meant a rate reduction of some 40 percent. Thistle's Web site (*www.thistlehotels.com*) made no specific mention of that deal. The site did show a rate for "PFD promotion," but unless you knew that name, you'd never figure out the deal.

Another way that hotels cut prices is through packages—sometimes just for a room, but more often for a room plus one or more additional features: meals, entertainment, recreational activities, or sightseeing. Evaluating packages is tricky. Usually the reduction, if any, comes in the combined prices of all of the elements, and you can sometimes have trouble estimating the value of these elements.

Many hotel chains and individual hotels develop and sell their own packages. Typically, you find them on the regular hotel Web sites, often under a special heading such as "vacations" or "packages." Airlines and wholesale tour operators also sell hotel packages; see Chapter 6 for details.

Always take a quick look at packages when you're checking out hotel rates. In my experience, however, a package is seldom the cheapest option if all you want is a basic hotel accommodation. Take a careful look at what else is included, set a dollar value on it, and then compare the package price with what you can get by buying the room separately through any of the discount approaches mentioned. And beware: Many hotels quote package rates as per person rather than per room.

The Art of the Deal *(continued)*

That system works best when you call a hotel directly, but it can work through a national reservation office, too. However, you must talk directly to a reservationist: You can't dicker over the Internet.

How much can you save that way? In general, the percentage discount you get at a hotel varies inversely with your odds of getting it. Modest discounts of 10 percent or so are often available, even when the hotel is full, for AAA members, seniors, corporate travelers—and just about anyone else. But when a hotel is hungry, you can look for cuts as high as 50 percent. The amount of the discount—if any—is strictly up to local hotel management. Of course, you also have to be ready to back off and be really willing to try somewhere else. If you aren't flexible, you could wind up paying rack rate. Just remember, it's a bazaar—and act accordingly.

These same comments apply to self-contained resort vacations. You can look on them as the ultimate package: everything you need in a hotel or resort stay for a single price. Inclusive rates are great if you really take advantage of a good share of the recreational and social options that are available; not so great if you just want someplace to rest and relax. You often see peak and off-peak pricing and occasional sales at those resorts, as well. Again, you can find what's available on the individual chains' Web sites.

Big-City Discounters

Your toughest hotel challenges are in big cities and popular resort areas. That's where you find the highest list prices and the most buying options. Rack rates at the best-known upscale chains, such as Hilton, Hyatt, Inter-Continental, Marriott, Radisson, and Sheraton start at around $125 to $150 in dozens of large and midsize cities. Once you get down around $80 a night, you're likely to find the options either somewhat scruffy or at a fair distance from the city center—or both.

Rates in the world's top visitor cities are even higher. In London, New York, Paris, San Francisco, and a handful of other comparable cities, you're looking at $200 to $400 per night in one of the upscale chains, $100 to $150 a night in one of the midpriced spots. Even the fabled budget London B&Bs charge close to $100 a night these days.

Of course, these figures are rack rates. Generally, hotels establish their rack rates at the highest levels they might ever expect to charge—for example, when the Super Bowl or a major convention is in town.

Like the airlines, big-city hotels know that they can't often fill their hotels to capacity at rack rates, so they offer a variety of discounts. Knowing how they arrange these discounts sometimes helps you navigate the marketplace more smoothly.

Big-city hotels routinely cut rates using one of three different kinds of discount systems. Often, when you deal with an Internet (or any other) discount agency, you can't really tell which system is in use. But you probably don't care, either; what's important is the size of the deal, not how it was arranged.

Broker a Deal

Hotel brokers act for hotels in much the same way that consolidators act for airlines: They provide a low-profile channel through which hotels can unload rooms they don't expect to sell at full price. As is the case with airline consolidators, several discount brokers operate extensive Internet sites.

Most brokers handle a limited number of hotels, usually midpriced and high-priced. You'll find relatively few choices in airport locations and virtually none in small cities and along the highways.

Unless you find a really good hotel promotion, a broker is probably your best bet for finding a really good hotel deal in a big city. However, not even a broker can do much for you when hotel space in the city you're going to visit is tight. And, as with so many other travel buys, you're better off angling for the best deal in the city rather than first selecting a hotel and then trying to get a deal on a room.

However, broker deals aren't always the best you can find. You might do better with a half-price program (see the section "Half-Price Programs" later in this chapter). The only way you can be sure that a broker's rate (or any other discount) is a good deal is to compare it with the hotel's own best price for a room during the time you're considering visiting.

Discount Booking Agents

Some brokers operate as discount booking agencies: They arrange deals with hotels that need to fill rooms. Often, these deals are short-term and fluctuating: Reductions can be as high as 60 percent when a hotel is hungry, but they dry up when room availability is tight. Most big booking agencies sell through the Internet as well as by phone.

Brokers in the discount booking group act strictly as agents: They make reservations for you at the discount rates they've prearranged, but they can also negotiate individual rates (see "Negotiate a Rate," later in this chapter). In fact, when you're booking, you really can't tell the difference between a short-term rate the broker might have negotiated individually and a rate the broker obtains through one of the large negotiated-rate programs. But you really shouldn't care, as long as the deal is good.

Most brokers in this group handle hotels in only a limited number of cities. Among the largest of the discount booking agencies is Quikbook (*www.quikbook.com*), with hotel deals in 18 major U.S. business centers.

Figure 4-2 shows the map on Quikbook's home page, which indicates cities where deals are available. Earlier this year, the number of participating hotels in each city ranged from only 3 in Minneapolis to 47 in New York, but those numbers change from month to month.

4/23/2000

Figure 4-2. *Quikbook discounts hotel rooms in 18 major U.S. cities.*

Once you have selected a city, you can access Quikbook's deals in three ways:

- If you have a specific location preference, you can click a hotel's icon on the city map and view a detailed description of that hotel. From the hotel page, you can specify dates and number of occupants, submit your request, and determine availability and price—sometimes a single price, sometimes several prices depending on the type of room. If the hotel is unavailable (or at least unavailable at Quikbook's price), the page lists alternative hotels that are available.

- If you're looking for the best deal, regardless of location, you can start an "Express Search," entering dates, number of adults, and a general price range. The site displays a list of hotels that meet your needs. You can then select one of the options and make your reservations.

- A third option takes you to a combined list of "special" deals, usually short-term. Figure 4-3 shows a sample of Quikbook's special deals for Dallas and Denver.

4/23/2000

Figure 4-3. *Quikbook's site lists short-term "special" deals in major cities.*

Another large broker in the discount booking group is Central Reservation Service (*www.reservation-services.com*). It handles hotels in 10 major cities. As with Quikbook, most are midpriced or high-priced and are located in the central business districts, with a few airport locations as well. The Appendix lists other similar discount booking agencies. It also lists several brokers that specialize in only one or two cities.

Discount booking agencies also operate overseas; British Hotel Reservation Centre Online (*www.bhrc.co.uk*), a booking agency for London and the vicinity, is one such example. It operates in exactly the same way as its U.S. counterparts. You can access its database by name, quality rating, or location.

They Can Get It for You Wholesale

A different cluster of brokers acts as wholesalers: They contract to buy rooms at wholesale rates and resell them to travelers. You reserve through— and pay through—the broker. The broker sends you a voucher that you exchange for your accommodation when you arrive.

Wholesalers' price reductions are in the same ballpark as those of discount agencies—up to 65 percent off in a few cases, 20 percent or so at many locations. But you find one big difference between wholesalers and discount booking agents: Wholesalers require that you pay the entire amount, up front. You can cancel only through the wholesale broker (not directly with the hotel), and you usually face a cancellation fee of at least the first night's cost.

Other things being equal, you're better off with a discount booking agency or a negotiated rate than with a wholesaler. Having to pay your full bill up front limits your flexibility and seriously impedes cancellations and refunds.

However, other things aren't always equal. Frequently, a wholesaler's deal is the best you can find. So you either have to accept the risks of full prepayment or find a more flexible deal, even if it isn't quite as good.

The largest wholesale hotel broker, of any stripe, is Hotel Reservations Network, or HRN (*www.hoteldiscount.com*). In addition to its own sites, HRN has arranged to be linked by dozens of other travel sites. In fact, whenever you see a link to "hotel discounts" on an agency site, gateway site, or home page, chances are you'll reach HRN.

Figure 4-4 shows the primary HRN home page, which includes a listing of 50 major cities, worldwide, where the broker has its primary deals. If you don't see your destination city, clicking "More Cities" leads to a directory of many additional cities. Prices you see on that list are negotiated rates, obtained through one of the large programs mentioned in the next section. Other wholesale brokers, including some based overseas, are listed in the Appendix.

Figure 4-4. *HRN is the nation's largest hotel broker.*

Negotiate a Rate

Large travel agencies and consortiums of smaller travel agencies (that have banded together to increase their buying power) have negotiated reduced rates with thousands of hotels, worldwide. Reductions range anywhere from a few percentage points to as much as 40 percent to 50 percent off rack rates, depending on the hotel.

Negotiated rates are most common with city hotels in the midpriced range and higher, with the occasional budget hotel listed. You can also find negotiated rates for airport-area and suburban hotels, as well as for resort centers. The largest negotiated rate programs list thousands of hotels, worldwide, so you can find at least a few participating hotels in most medium-sized cities. However, you don't see many listings along the major highways and in rural areas.

As with discounts in general, you find far more hotels with small discounts than with big cuts. However, most negotiated rate programs usually include at least a few hotels in each city where the reduction is on the high end—these deals are sometimes called *preferred* rates. Obviously, for the best prices, you should head for the hotels that give these big discounts. On the other hand, if you insist on a specific hotel, you might or might not get any sort of price concession.

For the most part, negotiated rates are not highly restricted: As long as a hotel isn't sold out, you get the deal. However, some negotiated rates are seasonal, and many are blacked out during special events.

With negotiated rates, you arrange a reservation through just about any travel agency—online or storefront—including the agency Web sites listed in the Appendix and discussed in Chapter 3. The agency makes your reservation, probably asking for a charge card guarantee. When you arrive, you register in the normal way, and then pay by charge card, cash, or check when you leave the hotel. You usually face no cancellation penalty as long as you cancel before late afternoon on the day of arrival. However, during busy times, the cancellation period might be longer—as much as 24 hours in advance.

Name Your Price

Reverse auctions such as Priceline.com (introduced in Chapter 3) also handle hotel accommodations. The system works much as it does with airlines: You specify a city (and for big cities, a location within the metro area); you provide the dates of your visit, a general price category, and the amount you're willing to pay; and you give a charge card number. The system checks your bid against the available inventory and price guidelines of participating hotels. If your bid is accepted, you automatically buy the hotel room. If not, you can try again after you make a few adjustments.

Priceline.com gives you a choice of four classes: 1-Star Economy, 2-Star Moderate, 3-Star Upscale, and 4-Star Deluxe, and it provides an explanation of that rating scale, as defined by rack rates in the particular city you're checking. Overall, it's a pretty good approach to the problem of price and quality.

In one important way, a reverse auction works better for purchase of hotel rooms than for air tickets. With an air ticket, you can't specify flight times and you might have to accept connections; in effect, you risk considerable inconvenience to get your price. There are no equivalent limitations and risks to a hotel bid. You get the city, area, quality level, and price you want, with no real risks or inconveniences. Frequent travelers I know have been far more pleased with Priceline.com's performance on hotel accommodations than on air tickets.

As with purchasing airline tickets, if you use Priceline.com or a competitor, it should be your last stop: You really can't lose if you bid a bit under the best discount price you were able to find elsewhere.

Half-Price Programs

Half-price programs have been helping travelers cut their hotel bills for decades. While they don't always provide a big discount, they're still usually a good deal: The discounts are big enough, and you get them often enough, to justify spending the $40 to $60 you pay to buy into the program. Unfortunately, as of early 2000, none of the big programs was yet taking full advantage of the Internet.

Participating hotels range from lower midpriced to luxury. And they're available just about anywhere you might want to stay, including small cities and towns along major highways—places where you won't find any negotiated rates or broker deals.

The nation's biggest half-price program is run by Entertainment Publications (*www.entertainment.com*). You buy a directory of participating hotels, which includes an ID card valid for at least a year. Once you decide where you want to stay, you look up the hotels in that area on the Web site or in the directory, select a hotel, and call or fax the hotel directly to ask for the "Entertainment rate." You show your Entertainment ID card when you check in to secure this rate.

When a hotel signs up to participate, it agrees to provide the Entertainment discount any time it projects an occupancy rate of 80 percent or less. Some hotels offer smaller Entertainment discounts when they expect to be filled above that point. And some hotels impose blackouts at peak time periods.

Entertainment sells hundreds of national and local directories, but the best one for travelers is the *Hotel and Travel Ultimate Savings Directory* ($59.95). It lists more than 5600 hotels worldwide. Unfortunately, as of early 2000, although you could locate participating hotels on Entertainment's Web site, you could neither buy the *Ultimate* directory nor book half-priced rooms. Strange.

HEADS UP

Entertainment and its clones promise 50 percent off the regular room rate. However, that often works out to less than half off the price other travelers pay. The half-price rate is almost always calculated from the highest posted rack rate—a rate that few travelers actually pay. Still, using a half-price program usually gets you as good a rate—and often the best rate—as you're likely to get at a participating hotel.

Several competitors sell half-price programs similar to Entertainment's. Travel clubs often include half-price hotels as one of their features, and you might get a half-price deal as an employee benefit or through a charity sale. But if you don't have some other source, Entertainment is probably your best bet.

The Internet is weak in half-price programs. Entertainment's site is barely adequate, and its largest competitors—Encore, ITC50, and Quest—don't have Web sites at all. Other half-price programs with Web sites are listed in the Appendix.

Airline Tie-Ins

Several big hotel chains have joint marketing arrangements with airlines to provide reduced weekend hotel rates in the cities to which the airlines offer low-cost, last-minute weekend Internet airfares. Figure 4-5 shows a typical listing, from a weekly United e-mail bulletin (which anyone can subscribe to on United's Web site) for Hilton hotel deals associated with United's last-minute airfare promotions.

4/23/2000

Figure 4-5. *Hilton's weekend rates complement United's weekend airfares.*

You can book these hotel deals through either airline sites or hotel sites. Either way, you get the same rates and face the same restrictions.

HEADS UP

Several dozen big hotel chains operate frequent stay programs, modeled on the airline frequent flyer model. And like the airlines, big hotel-chain sites allow you to track your points, check current bonus-point promotions, and exchange points for various awards.

Out of Season

Rather than finagle discount prices—or in addition to finagling—many hotels, motels, and resorts establish a variety of peak and off-peak prices. You'll find these prices on their Web sites. Some variations are seasonal: You pay much less to stay in Aspen or the Caribbean in the summer than in the winter and much less in Bar Harbor, Maine in the fall or the spring than in the summer. Big-city hotels that cater to business travelers cut rates on weekends, resorts cut rates midweek, and motels along highways often cut rates in the winter. Rates are also higher when a local festival or program is going on than when stages are dark.

Some hotels don't offer much in the way of promotions other than off-peak deals. Hotels in Las Vegas and Reno seldom offer senior and similar discounts, for example, but they're big on attracting seniors with low advertised rates at off-peak times. The widest peak/off-peak swings are at expensive hotels and resorts, where there's a lot of padding in the peak prices. But even midpriced and budget hotels often vary their prices seasonally by at least a little bit.

Hotels and resorts sometimes label their off-peak rates as "discounted," but that's not quite accurate. Accommodations are really a different product off-peak than at peak times. A room in a resort on Jamaica in September, when it's hurricane season in the Caribbean and the weather is nice in New York, is different than that same room in February, when the Jamaican temperatures are mild and New Yorkers are shoveling snow. If you are willing to accept significant product differences, off-season rates that are often less than half of the peak-season rates might be a good deal for you.

Budget Motels:
When List Price Is a Good Deal

The American budget motel is arguably the world's best accommodation value. For under $50 a night, you get a good-sized room, usually with two queen beds, a desk, a dresser, and a modern bath with a shower; the room almost always includes at least one phone line (newer motels have two, to accommodate laptop computers with modems) and a large screen color TV, usually with cable. The motel typically has, at a minimum, ample parking and a swimming pool; many include a full or continental breakfast buffet at no extra charge, and a wide range of other features.

Given the low list prices, it's no surprise that you don't often find much of a discount at a budget motel. At best, AAA members, seniors, and corporate travelers might get a modest reduction of 10 percent or so.

All of the big chains have Web sites through which you can locate and book motels. In most cases, you can also find a detailed description of each property and can access a map for highway directions. Figure 4-6 shows part of the Motel 6 locator page (*www.motel6.com*) for Wisconsin, listing the options in that state. Other chains' sites operate in much the same way. Sites for all major U.S. motel chains are listed in the Appendix.

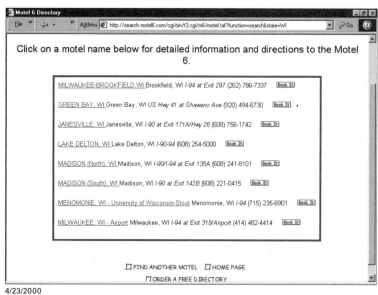

4/23/2000

Figure 4-6. *Motel 6 lists eight locations in Wisconsin.*

Although the budget motel idea originated in the United States, it has recently spread to Europe. The French chains are especially active: The giant Accor chain (*www.accorhotel.com*) includes budget brands Formule 1 and Etap, plus an economy brand Ibis. And the other big French chain, Groupe Envergure (*www.groupe-envergure.fr*), includes budget brands Nuit d'Hotel and Premiere Classe, plus economy brands Balladins and

Climat de France. The majority of both chains' locations are still in France, but both are expanding into Benelux, Germany, and the United Kingdom.

In the summer of 2000, prices at the bottom-end budget chains (Formule 1, Nuit d'Hotel, and Premiere Classe) started at under $20 a night for up to two adults and one child. The United States really has no equivalents of these super-budget motels. However, the rooms are barely 100 square feet, and, at the cheapest prices, toilets and showers are shared facilities, outside the rooms. Accommodations remind you more of college dormitories or military quarters than motels as we know them. However, if you go up to about $30 to $40 a night, brands such as Climat de France, Ibis, and Citadines provide accommodations quite similar to those you get for the same price in the United States.

You can locate and book all Groupe Envergure hotels through their Web site. As of the summer of 2000, most Envergure sites were available only in French, but the entries were fairly self-explanatory. You couldn't yet book Accor's budget brands through the Internet, but you could locate and book Ibis and Accor's more expensive brands.

The British, too, have their budget chains. The largest are Travelodge (*www.travelodge.co.uk*) and Travel Inns (*www.travelinn.co.uk*). Rooms in either are similar to what you'd find in a typical U.S. roadside motel; prices start at around $65 a night for up to three people. You can locate hotels and reserve rooms from the sites, which also provide locator maps and details on each property. Holiday Inn Express is also building budget sites in the United Kingdom.

Bed & Breakfasts

Bed & breakfasts remain a prime resource for budget travelers in Europe—especially in the United Kingdom. They've also become popular in the United States, but more because they're considered chic and quaint than for budget reasons. Either way, you can find lots of B&B Web sites for both sides of the Atlantic.

As of early 2000, BedandBreakfast.com (*www.bedandbreakfast.com*) appeared to have the most comprehensive set of worldwide listings. In all, the site claims more than 24,000 total listings, throughout much of the world. Figure 4-7 shows part of the primary directory page for Ashland, Oregon, listing eight B&Bs, with access to detailed backup information on each. That's several times more data than what's available for Ashland on any other B&B directory site.

However, that example also illustrates a common problem with the Web: Even the best gateway sites often don't have all the details. The top B&B site listed only eight bed & breakfasts in Ashland, while there are actually some 40 in the area. Where can you find them all? As far as I can determine, only the Oregon Shakespeare Festival's Visitor's Guide (*www.orshakes.org/Visitors/*—note that this URL is case sensitive), not a place many travelers would immediately think to look, lists all of Ashland's bed & breakfasts.

4/23/2000

Figure 4-7. *BedandBreakfast.com lists eight B&Bs in Ashland, Oregon.*

Discounts, however, are limited to last-minute availabilities and are offered through only a few sites. B&B Getaways (*www.bbgetaways.com*) and BedandBreakfast.com offer last-minute price cuts for B&Bs, nationwide. The concept is patterned after the last-minute deals offered by airlines and participating hotels. However, it's too early to tell if enough B&Bs will participate to make the programs worthwhile. And no matter how you book, if you want to confirm space more than a few days in advance, you're likely to pay list price. The online resources are therefore useful as guides and locators but not for cutting prices. Other sites are listed in the Appendix.

Several sites feature B&Bs in individual European cities. However, they don't all provide online rates or booking capability. Overseas sites are listed in the Appendix.

Overall, the various sites provide a wide choice of B&Bs. However, as the Ashland, Oregon example taught us, you should also check any destination sites for the area you plan to visit: A destination site might well have more local listings than the national or worldwide sites. It wouldn't hurt to check the generic travel sites, as well.

Vacation Rentals

The hottest accommodation market these days is for vacation rentals—apartments, houses, and cottages that you rent by the week or more. The people who arrange such rentals are fond of calling them "villas," but that's often a stretch. (I describe a villa as "a cottage with attitude.") Still, no matter what the name, vacation rentals provide several key advantages over hotel and motel accommodations, depending on where and how you rent. And you'll find a wealth of Internet booking resources.

Typically, in any given area, the cost of a two-room or three-room vacation rental is about the same as the cost of a standard room in a First Class hotel. You can use the extra space to spread out and avoid the claustrophobia of a hotel or to cut the per-person cost. Groups of four or more can spread out among several rooms for about the same cost as stacking themselves like cordwood in hotel rooms.

Vacation rentals are especially attractive overseas. Staying in a vacation rental allows you to get much closer to locals and to experience life as they know it.

But rentals aren't for everyone; they entail some disadvantages and risks that you don't face with hotel accommodations. The biggest disadvantages stem from the fact that you have to prepay the entire rental cost in advance—typically, months before you arrive. And once you have paid, you're locked in to the rental regardless of any adverse—and unadvertised—conditions that might be present when you arrive.

You can cancel your reservation with some vacation rental properties, but cancellation fees are usually stiff. Or, you might get no refund at all. In that case, you can protect yourself by buying trip-cancellation insurance. However, although insurance covers cancellation, it doesn't cover disappointment.

Financial risks aside, the last thing some travelers want to do on vacation is prepare meals and make beds. If you want to be pampered, either opt for a rental with full housekeeping services or stick with a resort hotel.

If you don't like to buy into a week's accommodation sight unseen, you can wait until after you arrive at your destination to arrange a rental. Book a hotel for one night or so, and immediately check local publications, real estate offices, or the tourist office for short-term rentals. This works off-season, but don't plan on it when rental space is tight.

Exchanging: Cheaper than Renting

The absolutely least expensive way to arrange a vacation house or apartment is to exchange homes with a family in an area you want to visit. Several Internet sites match travelers interested in home exchange; one of the largest of these is HomeExchange.com (*www.homeexchange.com*). You pay a fee of $30 a year to join, list your property, and search for other properties. During the initial search process, HomeExchange keeps your name and the names of possible exchange partners confidential to make sure you aren't inadvertently advertising your absence. Since you're potentially exchanging with strangers, HomeExchange encourages you to get acquainted over a period of months beforehand by e-mail, phone, photographs, and postal mail.

Given that so many vacation rentals are independently owned, or at least part of small complexes, the Internet is an ideal way to match individual renters with a diverse group of owners. It's no surprise that the Appendix lists close to 50 separate vacation rental sites. Some are worldwide, some deal in only a few countries, and many are limited to individual cities or resort areas. Some owners operate sites to rent just one unit (although I didn't list any of these).

Large or small, sites typically feature detailed information on accommodation size, number of rooms, equipment, and furnishings; location, within the building or complex and within the community; and rates. Most sites include either plans or photographs, or both.

CyberRentals (*www.cyberrentals.com*) is a typical worldwide site that claims to offer more than 4500 individual rentals. The home page alone links you to all 50 states, plus dozens of foreign countries.

Figure 4-8, on the next page, illustrates the kind of detail you can obtain about an individual rental. For the most part, the rental sites give you enough information to make an informed purchase decision—a degree of detail you don't always find in other Internet marketplaces.

Exchanging: Cheaper than Renting *(continued)*

Exchanges can go beyond just houses. If you and your exchange partners agree, the exchange can extend to automobiles and such. Even so, you'll probably want to lock up one room as "owner's storage," where you can stash anything you don't want other occupants to use and possibly damage.

Yet another possible approach to take is available through Servas (*www.servas.org/us*), an organization through which you can arrange reciprocal visits with residents of other countries. Unlike a home exchange, you stay with a foreign family while they are at home (and host a foreign family while you are at home). During these visits, the host family generally shows the visitors around, including at least some sightseeing and cultural activities, while also leaving time for independent exploration.

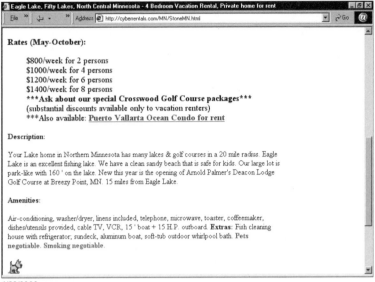

Rates (May-October):

$800/week for 2 persons
$1000/week for 4 persons
$1200/week for 6 persons
$1400/week for 8 persons
Ask about our special Crosswood Golf Course packages
(substantial discounts available only to vacation renters)
***Also available: Puerto Vallarta Ocean Condo for rent

Description:

Your Lake home in Northern Minnesota has many lakes & golf courses in a 20 mile radius. Eagle Lake is an excellent fishing lake. We have a clean sandy beach that is safe for kids. Our large lot is park-like with 160 ' on the lake. New this year is the opening of Arnold Palmer's Deacon Lodge Golf Course at Breezy Point, MN. 15 miles from Eagle Lake.

Amenities:

Air-conditioning, washer/dryer, linens included, telephone, microwave, toaster, coffeemaker, dishes/utensils provided, cable TV, VCR, 15 ' boat + 15 H.P. outboard. Extras: Fish cleaning house with refrigerator, sundeck, aluminum boat, soft-tub outdoor whirlpool bath. Pets negotiable. Smoking negotiable.

4/23/2000

Figure 4-8. *Web listings include extensive detail on individual properties.*

In general, if you know where (state or country) you want to rent, you're better off with a local site rather than a worldwide one. With all its global coverage, for example, CyberRentals lists just three rentals in London. By contrast, the Short Let Company (*www.short-term-lets.co.uk*), a London-based site, lists dozens. If you're heading for an area popular for vacation rentals—Florida, California, Colorado, the Caribbean, London, Paris, Provence, or Italy—you should always first try the specialized sites for these areas.

Vacation rental rates are almost always seasonal—high in summer, low the rest of the year in Europe and Northern North America; high in winter, low the rest of the year at tropical beach and ski resorts and warm climate areas. Seasonal rates are almost always reflected in Web listings.

Other Accommodations

If a type of accommodation is offered to travelers, you can probably find at least some sources for that accommodation type on the Internet. In virtually all cases, the Internet sites provide directories along with price and location information. Few if any, however, offer any special Internet discounts or reductions:

- **Hostels:** The American Youth Hostel (AYH) affiliate of Hostelling International maintains a site at *www.hiayh.org*, through which you can locate and book hostels throughout the world. Also check *www.hostels.com* and *www.hostelseurope.com*.

- **Campgrounds:** Kampgrounds of America, the largest commercial campground operator, maintains a site at *www.koa.com*, through which you can locate and book campgrounds. You can rent an RV through *www.cruiseamerica.com*.

- **National parks, national forests, state parks:** You can locate (and often book) in-park hotel and lodge accommodations and campgrounds through the sites maintained by the individual resource organizations (see Chapter 2).

- **University accommodations:** Many universities rent out their dormitory rooms when school isn't in session. The best way to find them is to use a search engine to check individual university or college sites.

- **Castles:** If you've ever wanted to stay in a castle or palace, you can find some of them on the Internet. Check *www.castlesontheweb.com* and *www.european-castle-tours.com*.

- **Dude ranches:** Several sites have compiled listings for individual dude ranches. These sites include *www.duderanches.com* and *www.gorp.com /oldwest/*.

- **Pet-friendly spots:** Several sites catalog hotels and motels that accept pets, including *www.dogfriendly.com*, *www.petswelcome.com*, *www.travelpets.com*, and *www.traveldog.com*.

A few specialized accommodations were not yet on the Internet as of early 2000. Among them are directories of monasteries that accept transient visitors, and retreat houses. For information on these and other obscure categories, you must still refer to guidebooks.

Beware: Hotel Price-Shopping Pitfalls

Price-shopping for hotels can sometimes be tricky. You're likely to encounter three major problem areas, on or off the Internet:

- Most hotels quote prices per room, even in promotions. However, you sometimes encounter prices featured as "per-person, double occupancy" at half the real price. Although it's deceptive, per-person pricing is deeply ingrained in cruise and package-tour promotions, and no amount of railing on my part is going to change that. However, per-person pricing for just a hotel room is inexcusable. Watch out for it in some of the promotions you see on the Internet (or anywhere else).

- When they advertise in Europe, European hotels are required to include value-added tax (VAT) in their featured prices. Unfortunately, some European hotels quote a pretax price in their U.S. ads. Read the fine print of these ads carefully to see which prices include VAT and which don't.

- Hotels often promote their ratings—a certain number of stars, for example—that might or might not mean anything. Some countries, including Austria, Belgium, Brazil, France, Greece, Hungary, Ireland, Italy, the Netherlands, Spain, Switzerland, Turkey, the United Kingdom (recently), and Yugoslavia, have government-run or industry-run hotel-rating systems. Presumably, they're policed and reliable, provided you know the system. But other important countries—including the United States—have no official standards and no standards at all other than proprietary (and often inconsistent) guidebook ratings. The net result is that any hotel here can declare itself to be "Five Star," with nobody to argue.

Floating a Deal

Quick Trip Through Chapter 5

At today's prices, taking a cruise is a good deal if you follow these rules:

- First decide where you want to cruise. You'll improve your odds of getting a good price if you are flexible about your sailing dates. Look for basic destination information on the Internet.

- Use the Internet to zero in on one or more preferred cruise lines. You might even want to settle on a specific ship—although if you do, you're sharply limiting your ability to get a good deal. If you need help, consult a travel agency for face-to-face counseling.

- Before you fire up your browser, settle on a general category of cabin you want: minimum price, least expensive outside, least expensive with a window, and so on. You can probably get a better price if you're willing to accept what comes your way on a "best available" deal.

- Next, search the Internet for the best prices that meet your requirements. Visit the Web sites of as many cruise discounters as you can, checking each for the best deals.

- Finally, check to see if a local full-service or cruise-only travel agency can match or improve the best Internet deal you found.

You can also use the Internet to locate cruise variants: barge tours, barge or boat rentals, and freighter trips.

The most important fact you need to know about taking a cruise is that it's a buyers' market—it has been for the last several years and will remain so for the foreseeable future. Although the cruise industry has been booming, the number of new ships and cabins has been growing even faster. The result: If you buy carefully, and if you have some flexibility, you can find some great cruise deals.

During the last year or so, discounted prices have started at about $200 a day per couple, though occasionally less. The base price of a cruise includes accommodations, most meals, entertainment, and local transportation. That's certainly competitive with the costs of a land vacation at even a midpriced resort.

The cruise marketplace is vastly simpler than the airline and hotel markets. You find comparatively few pricing gimmicks. What you pay depends almost entirely on what ship you choose, the type of cabin you choose, and when you buy your cabin. Cruising has none of those purchase and trip-related restrictions that complicate airline pricing—just the good old law of supply and demand. And since most cruise lines don't sell directly to the public, they're not competing—and fighting—with their travel-agent distributors.

HEADS UP

Taking a cruise is a great way to relax, enjoy a wide array of shipboard activities, watch the passing scenery, and make a fast pass at a handful of ports. But while a cruise gives you a quick look at different ports or countries, it doesn't allow you to "visit" them. You're in each port for no more than 12 hours, and often much less, giving you time only to sightsee the local blockbuster attractions from the window of a tour bus or taxi.

Although price is important in selecting a cruise, it isn't all-important. Undoubtedly the two most important decisions are where to take your cruise and which cruise line and ship to choose. You can find answers for both questions on the Internet. And, of course, once those are decided, you can shop for the best prices there, too.

Most cruises are stand-alone vacation purchases. Airfare from your home city to the port of embarkation—along with transfers between airport and port—might be included, but little else is. And the absolutely lowest prices are usually for the cruise alone.

Some cruises, however, are bought as part of larger package tours. Probably the most outstanding example is a Nile cruise, which is typically bundled with a more extended tour of Egypt or the Middle East. Greek Island cruises are often combined with stays in Athens, Istanbul, or other Eastern Mediterranean cities. And Rhine and Danube trips are sometimes included in extended European tours.

Where to Cruise

The most popular areas for cruising are the Caribbean and Mexico (year-round) and Alaska's Inside Passage (summer). The reasons for their popularity are simple:

- The Caribbean and Mexico provide a warm-to-hot year-round climate, with plenty of beaches and tropical scenery. Most cruises provide a port of call almost every day, with touring opportunities at each. The Caribbean islands, with their mix of African, British, Dutch, French, and Spanish heritage, offer a chance to observe some varied culture. And Mexican cruises provide opportunities to visit that country's outstanding pre-Columbian ruins.

- Alaska's Inside Passage is a protected waterway with perfectly calm sailing for all but a few hours of open sea. Moreover, for most of the trip, you're no more than a few hundred feet from land, which means you have continuous vistas of forests, mountains, streams, and wildlife. Ports are funky, with plenty of local color.

- Cruises for all three areas depart from ports in the continental United States (California, Florida) or Canada (Vancouver), minimizing the time and cost of getting from your home city to the ports of departure.

However, you'll also find plenty of cruising opportunities elsewhere. Among the areas with extensive cruise itineraries are the northeastern United States, eastern Canada, and the St. Lawrence; Alaska beyond the Inside Passage; the Hawaiian Islands; the Mediterranean and the Greek Islands; the Norwegian Coast; the Baltic Sea; southern South America and Antarctica; and Southeast Asia.

Positioning cruises, when ships move between their summer bases in Alaska and the Mediterranean and their winter bases in the Caribbean, take you through the Panama Canal or across the Atlantic Ocean. Travelers with a lot of time can take more extended cruises, including the ultimate round-the-world trips that operate several times a year.

River cruises provide still another alternative. As with Alaska's Inside Passage, waters are always calm, and you're never far from land. Among the most popular venues for river cruises are the Mississippi-Missouri-Ohio system, the Columbia, the Rhine, the Danube, the Nile, the Amazon, and the Moscow-St. Petersburg river and canal system.

ED'S NOTEBOOK

They've Come a Long Way

Today's luxury cruise ships are a far cry from the old transatlantic liners. My first trip to Europe was aboard one of those ships (at that time, transatlantic air travel was prohibitively expensive). Class distinctions were enormous. In the lowest class, I was assigned a dormitory cabin with a group of other men and boys. The cabin was little more than a bunk area; the shower and toilet were down the corridor.

Travelers in that class were strictly segregated by sex. One of the men in our cabin was traveling with his family: He and his teenage son were in our cabin; his wife and daughter were in a different cabin, on a different deck. Couples could travel together only if they paid the much higher fares for Cabin Class or First Class. Access to dining rooms and other public areas was strictly class-segregated, as well, with separate and distinctly unequal facilities.

Today, cabin sizes don't vary much until you get to the super-luxury and suite range. Price depends mainly on location, the number and type of windows, and whether the cabin has a balcony or veranda. And the numerous public areas are open to all travelers, regardless of how much they pay.

You'll find a good deal of information about the major cruise destinations on the Internet. I have found the following sites particularly helpful:

- A few Web-only sites include destination-planning materials. One such site is CruiseMates (*www.cruisemates.com*), which bills itself as an "Internet Cruise Magazine and Community." Note the other information also available on this site: ship reviews; information for singles, children, and gay and lesbian travelers; and lots more.

- Cruise Calendar (*www.cruisecalendar.com*) provides an extensive database of worldwide cruises, which you can search by date, ship, or itinerary. It's a subscription service: $5 for one day, $25 for a full year.

- The major guidebook sites mentioned in Chapter 2 have pages devoted to the main cruising areas.

The big cruise lines' sites (see the Appendix) also contain some destination information. However, these pages are generally filled with puffery rather than hard facts.

> **HEADS UP**
>
> Even the best Web sites cover only the high points of cruise ships and destinations. If you really want to research the differences among the major and not-so-major cruising areas, you'll want to buy a few printed cruise guidebooks. Among the better ones are Fodors' *Alaska Ports of Call, Europe Ports of Call,* and its annual *Best Cruises*; Frommer's *Cruises and Ports of Call* titles for Alaska and the Caribbean; the *Berlitz 2000 Complete Guide to Cruising & Cruise Ships*; and Ethel Blum's *The Total Traveler Guide to Worldwide Cruising*.

Which Ship?

With cruise ships, size matters. Major-line ships range from around 200 passengers to well over 3000. You'll find both advantages and disadvantages with different sized ships.

The new megaships are truly floating resorts, with lots of big public areas and plenty of specialized activities; some are akin to a seagoing Las Vegas casino hotel. Since they're new, most have a high percentage of outside cabins, and the cabins tend to be relatively large. But the ships are so big that some travelers feel lost in the shuffle. And when one or two (or even worse, three or four) dock in a port at the same time, the local facilities and shops can be overwhelmed.

The smaller ships are more like floating boutique hotels. Because they're small, they can negotiate some waterways and get into some ports that can't handle the megaships. And when they dock, they don't overcrowd local facilities. However, they provide far fewer activities and entertainment options than the giant ships do.

Beyond sheer size differences, cruise lines and ships have their own individual "personalities." Some attract a partying crowd, some attract families, and some attract an older crowd that wants a more sedate experience. On some cruise lines, you might still have to dress for dinner—at least in the formal dining room. On others, dress code has gone the way of Silicon Valley executive offices. There are even theme cruises, where entertainment and programs, such as performances, lectures, lessons and activities, are focused on some specific interest. Cuisines and service levels also vary.

The Internet can help you select a cruise line and a ship to suit your requirements. The big cruise lines all have their own Web sites, which typically provide extensive detail on individual ships. The site for Holland America (*www.hollandamerica.com*), for example, provides a detailed plan for each deck (see Figure 5-1). Other cruise line sites are listed in the Appendix.

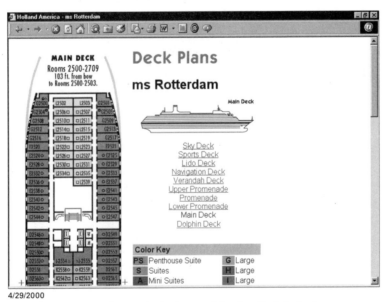

4/29/2000

Figure 5-1. *Holland America's site provides detailed deck plans.*

However, you get more realistic evaluations from one of the several independent sites that maintain extensive cruise ship reviews (most of them sell cruises, as well):

- CruiseMates, mentioned earlier, provides extensive reviews of both cruise lines and individual vessels, prepared by professional travel writers. Figure 5-2 shows the beginning of one such review, for the Carnival Destiny cruise.

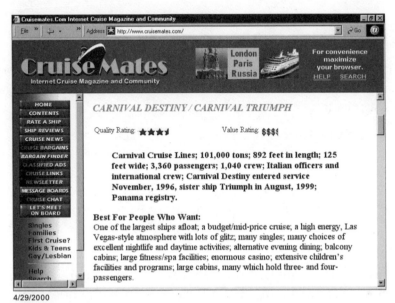

4/29/2000

Figure 5-2. *Professional reviews at CruiseMates.com are detailed but usually positive.*

- Cruise Critic (*www.cruisecritic.com*) also provides reviews by professional travel writers.

- CruiseReviews (*www.cruisereviews.com*) provides reviews written by individual cruisers—mostly ordinary consumers—rather than professional writers. These reviews have the advantage of being a great deal less gushy than the professional reviews usually are.

- The Cruise Professionals (*www.cruiseprofessionals.com*) provides extensive reviews of the more upscale ships and includes links to deck plans.

- Ship Stats (*www.shipstats.com*) provides a statistical database of cruise ships: sizes, capacities, and such.

These reviews discuss general ambience, public facilities, entertainment, and cuisine, and they also provide the basic nuts-and-bolts data you're likely to want: cabin size, numbers of passengers, and such. Overall, the reviews give you a pretty good idea of the experience you're likely to find on any of the big cruise lines and their individual ships. Of course, the professional reviews all tend to be positive (as are many of the amateur ones). But if you read the reports critically, you can readily discern the negative aspects among the many positives.

Getting the Best Price

Like so many hotels, cruise lines typically set high list prices (*brochure prices* in trade lingo) and then offer heavy—but selective—discounts on these nominal list prices:

- Many published brochure prices include generous early-booking reductions—price cuts that can reach 30 to 40 percent. *Early*, in this context, means six months or more before a sailing date. Whenever they get together at industry conventions, cruise executives vow to set attractive brochure price schedules for early booking, to keep to those published prices, and to "clean up" last-minute discounting. And each year they fail to keep that vow.

- Last-minute deals are still the best—at least, if you are prepared to accept what's available at the time you buy. No matter how strong the policy reasons against distress sales are, cruise lines would rather sell a cabin for even a minimum price than have it sail empty. Last-minute discounting—and, in the cruising industry, *last minute* means less than a month before departure—has been widespread for several years, and there's no reason to believe it won't continue in the future. However, last-minute cruise line bookings entail one risk: You might find airline seats to the main ports scarce.

In the spring of 1999, last-minute prices for cruises on the big cruise lines, in the most popular cruise areas, were under $200 per couple per day—sometimes well under $200 per couple. I saw one seven-night Mediterranean cruise quoted at $388 per person—just over $100 per couple per night. And prices around $700 per person ($200 per couple per night) were common.

Those featured "from" cruise prices apply to the lowest category of inside cabin. Most cruise lines have a dozen or more price categories, and the top cabins are priced at three to four times the "from" price. The one or two "captain's suites" or equivalent accommodations often run more than $1,000 a day.

You needn't reject the lowest-priced inside cabins out of hand. Although they have no windows, they're decorated to avoid a feeling of claustrophobia. And on the newer ships, even the lowest-priced cabins are about the same size as the midpriced ones. However, if you really want an outside cabin, you can usually upgrade to one for an extra $50 a day or so, space permitting.

HEADS UP

Some last-minute deals promise the "best available" cabin. If you're lucky, that means you could be upgraded several levels above the minimum category. Of course, what you get is the luck of the draw: The best available cabin might well be a minimum-priced inside one.

Cruising for Singles

Like so much else in travel, cruising is set up largely for couples. Most prices are per-person, double occupancy, and single travelers often have to pay a stiff "single supplement." When booking a cruise, single travelers have two options:

- Many big cruise ships have at least a few single cabins. Prices start at no more than 10 percent over the per-person, double-occupancy rates, although they're often higher. You can search for relatively good single deals on the Internet.

- Some cruise lines sell single passage at the per-person double rate. They'll try to find a roommate to share your cabin, but if they can't find one, you still get the per-person price. Alternatively, you can find your own roommate before you buy.

Cruise Discounters

Dozens of agencies claim to be cruise discounters. Most big general agency sites (mentioned in Chapter 3), such as Expedia and Travelocity, sell cruises as well as air tickets and hotel rooms. Some of these maintain their own cruise agencies; others link to a cruise specialist. When you begin shopping for cruise deals, you should certainly check one or more of the big agency sites. Figure 5-3 shows Expedia's Cruise home page, which indicates links to several cruise sellers.

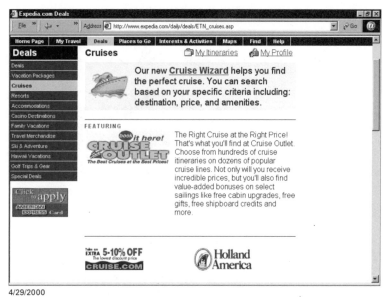

4/29/2000

Figure 5-3. *Expedia contains links to many cruise sellers.*

Other agencies specialize in cruises. For example, the home page for icruise (*www.i-cruise.com*) lists the various cruise categories on sale and highlights a few of the best current deals. Other discount cruise agencies are listed in the Appendix.

Never assume that Internet deals are the best you can find. Before you buy, check with one or more local travel agencies—either full service or cruise-only specialists. The big multi-office chains, such as AAA and Carlson, can often negotiate excellent cruise prices, as can the consortiums of independent agencies. And face-to-face contact with an agent can give you more help in selecting a cruise ship than you can get on the Web.

Cruise Lines

Most of the big cruise lines maintain their own sites. Several sites list individual itineraries and brochure prices, but most encourage you to book through a travel agency. The Appendix lists cruise line Web sites.

Renaissance Cruises (*www.renaissancecruises.com*) is the only big cruise line to claim better prices if you buy direct from its Web site. However, its Web site did not list any cruise-only prices as of early 2000; all cruises were bundled with round-trip airfare from New York and hotel stays before and after the cruise. You really couldn't negotiate a deal without calling the cruise line's reservation office.

Auctions

The big auction sites that sell travel usually include cruises as a product category. Figure 5-4 shows a page on the MSN auction site (*auctions.msn.com*) that lists several six-day to nine-day cruises. Other auction sites are listed in the Appendix. Although the page appearances vary, several individual auction sites apparently post identical listings.

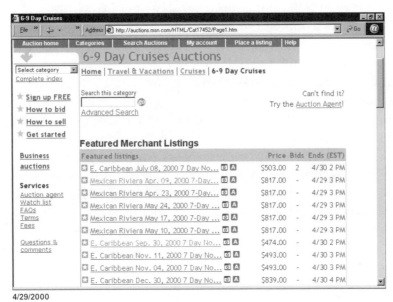

4/29/2000

Figure 5-4. *The MSN eShop Auctions site shows lots of cruise auctions.*

You can also post your desire for a cruise on an *I want* site—a site where you specify what you want to buy, and participating suppliers submit offers to you. It's too early to determine if travelers are successful with this gambit.

Hop a Freighter

Many modern freighter ships have accommodations for leisure travelers—some for a handful of people, others for as many as 100. The best freighter cabins are larger than conventional cruise cabins, with a private bath. Others are described as "dormitory," with shared facilities. As a freighter passenger, you typically enjoy the use of a public lounge and a library, often with a self-serve bar. You eat with the ship's officers. The ship might have a crew's fitness center or swimming pool, too.

You might call a freighter trip an *un-cruise*. You're on the open sea for days at a time; when you dock, you might stay in port several days. The only entertainment is videos or books from the library; there are no onboard shows or bands, stand-up comics, seminars, gambling, or shops. Prices run an average of $200 per couple per day—about the price of a minimum cabin on a discounted cruise.

Although complete round-trip freighter itineraries can last several months, you can usually book shorter one-way segments. Even so, you won't find many trips less than 12 days. From the East Coast of the United States, you can take freighters to England, France, the Netherlands, the Mediterranean, through the Suez Canal, and on to East Asia; you can also sail to the Caribbean and Latin America. Other trips run from the West Coast across the Pacific, and some originate at Great Lakes ports.

You don't buy freighter cruises directly from freighter lines. Instead, you go through one of the few agencies that specialize in freighter travel. Figure 5-5 shows a portion of the "transatlantic" pricing page from the site of Freighter World Cruises (*www.freighterworld.com*), one of the country's largest freighter brokers. Other major agencies are Maris Freighter Cruises (*www.freighter-cruises.com*) and the Cruise & Freighter Travel Association (*www.travltips.com*).

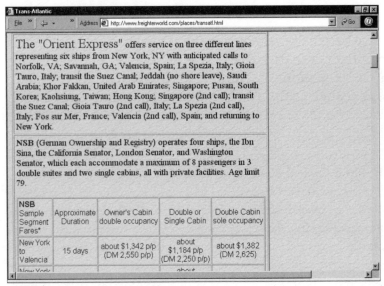

The "Orient Express" offers service on three different lines representing six ships from New York, NY with anticipated calls to Norfolk, VA; Savannah, GA; Valencia, Spain; La Spezia, Italy; Gioia Tauro, Italy; transit the Suez Canal; Jeddah (no shore leave), Saudi Arabia; Khor Fakkan, United Arab Emirates; Singapore; Pusan, South Korea; Kaohsiung, Taiwan; Hong Kong; Singapore (2nd call); transit the Suez Canal; Gioia Tauro (2nd call), Italy; La Spezia (2nd call), Italy; Fos sur Mer, France; Valencia (2nd call), Spain; and returning to New York.

NSB (German Ownership and Registry) operates four ships, the Ibn Sina, the California Senator, London Senator, and Washington Senator, which each accommodate a maximum of 8 passengers in 3 double suites and two single cabins, all with private facilities. Age limit 79.

NSB Sample Segment Fares*	Approximate Duration	Owner's Cabin double occupancy	Double or Single Cabin	Double Cabin sole occupancy
New York to Valencia	15 days	about $1,342 p/p (DM 2,550 p/p)	about $1,184 p/p (DM 2,250 p/p)	about $1,382 (DM 2,625)
New York			about	

4/29/2000

Figure 5-5. *The Freighter World Cruises agency specializes in freighter travel.*

HEADS UP

Health concerns might be your biggest barrier to a freighter trip. Most freighters carry no doctor, so if you suffer a health crisis, you'll have to make do with whatever the ship's officers can handle until you get to port. Because of the potential danger this creates for passengers, most freighter lines enforce a maximum age limit policy.

You almost never find any price discounting for freighter trips, on the Web or otherwise. Rather, the most desirable freighter trips sell out far in advance. If you like the idea, start checking options as soon as possible—and be prepared to travel when you find a good cabin.

Barges and Boats

Waterborne trips aren't confined to giant ships—or even modest-sized river cruisers. Some of the most popular trips are on vessels that hold only a dozen or so passengers; some are even just for you and a companion.

Barge Cruises

Barge cruises have become quite popular along smaller rivers and canals. As with ocean-going cruises, a barge cruise bundles an entire vacation experience—accommodations, food, and local transportation—into a single package at a single price. The best-known trips operate in France, from the rivers and canals of northern and central France and Burgundy to the Canal du Midi at the foot of the Pyrenees. You also find barge trips on the extensive canal and river systems of southern Britain, in several parts of Germany, in Benelux, and in the United States along the Erie Canal.

Barge cruises are great for exploration of a small area at a leisurely pace. Barges necessarily travel only a few miles per hour, to avoid disturbing other boaters and eroding the shorelines with excessive wakes. Many barges carry bicycles, which you can use to visit attractions not directly on the waterway and still easily get back to (or catch up with) the barge in time for the next meal. Trips in France, especially, feature outstanding onboard cuisine.

Barge-tour operators are well represented on the Internet. Figure 5-6 shows one listing from The Barge Connection (*www.bargeconnection.com*). Other barge agencies are listed in the Appendix.

4/29/2000

Figure 5-6. *The Barge Connection is one site for barge cruises on the Internet.*

Rates on barges are generally high, in the neighborhood of $400 to $500 per couple per night. And you seldom find really big discounts: Even last minute bookings generally cut no more than 10 to 15 percent off brochure rates.

Be Your Own Captain, Cook

One easy way to cut the cost of a barge tour in Europe is to do the barging yourself. You can find rentals ranging from small boats for just one or two couples to larger barges that are as big as those used for full-service cruises.

A typical page of rentals from H$_2$O (*www.barginginfrance.com*) is shown in Figure 5-7, displaying weekly rental rates in the South of France. Although prices change with currency fluctuations, you can see that barge rentals are competitive with vacation rentals. Other rental agencies are listed in the Appendix.

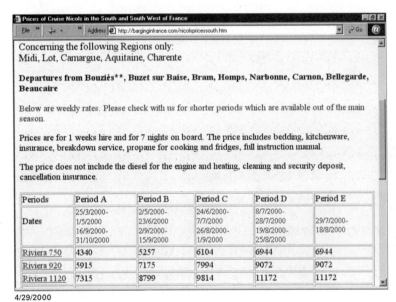

4/29/2000

Figure 5-7. *H$_2$O has rent-your-own barge rates that are far lower than cruise costs.*

Of course, you find plenty of boat rental opportunities in the United States, from cabin cruisers on the eastern lakes and rivers to houseboats on the big western lakes. Interested in renting a houseboat in the Florida

Keys, on the Mississippi, or on Lake Mead? Check The Houseboating Page (*www.houseboat.net*), a gateway site for links to rental agencies throughout the United States and Canada. And the Boating Yellow Pages section of the Yachtworld site (*www.yachtworld.com*) has links to more than 500 individual boat-rental agencies in the United States (and other countries).

Beware: Cruise-Buying Pitfalls

Price comparisons among travel services are always tricky; they're especially so when you're checking out a cruise. And both before and after you buy your tickets, you must beware of certain practices that can run your costs well above what you'd been led to expect:

- Cruise lines almost invariably quote prices as "per person, double occupancy." These figures obviously don't pass a buyability test; instead, two travelers pay double the highlighted price. Per-person cruise (and tour) pricing has become so ingrained that railing against it is pointless. Nevertheless, it is potentially misleading.

- Cruise lines and agencies almost always quote *per-person* prices, but they also almost always claim promotional "savings" on a *per-cabin* basis. Thus, when you see a price reduction from, say, $1,499 to $1,199 per person, the ad will most likely claim a saving of $600, not $300 per person.

- Some agencies slice out an arbitrary portion of the price, label it "port charges," and exclude it from the featured price. Of course, they add it back in when you pay. Unlike the case of immigration fees and airport charges, these "port charges" aren't a pass-through of per-passenger fees collected by the cruise lines on behalf of taxing authorities. Instead, they're simply part of the full price that has been deducted to make the price featured in big type look lower. In 1999, the Florida Attorney General's office reached agreements with the major cruise lines to stop using that particular deception, but the agreements apply only to the cruise lines. Agencies are still free to mislead—and some of them do.

- Cruise lines and agencies often advertise their lowest cabin prices, but their very lowest featured prices might be per-person rates for a *quad* cabin accommodating four people. Granted, prices are low, but four people in a tiny cruise cabin is more togetherness than most travelers want.

- Cruise lines sell shore excursions for most, if not all, ports of call. Some are simple sightseeing tours, others involve activities ranging from golf to ballooning, snorkeling, and helicopter rides. The one thing you know about any shore excursion is that it's profitable—to the cruise line that sells it, the local tour operator that runs it, and the souvenir store that pays off the tour operator to bring tourists into the store. Some shore excursions might well be a good buy (the guidebook and destination sites rate them). But you can often do better by arranging your own tour: Negotiate with a local sightseeing company or taxi driver, or rent a car.

- Cruise lines also invite "port lecturers" on board to brief you on what to expect when you get off the ship. Certainly, they can impart some local knowledge. But make no mistake: Their primary function is to shill for local merchants. Their suggestions about the "best" places to shop aren't personal recommendations, they're paid commercials. Act accordingly.

- Cruise lines are fond of touting their "one price covers everything" pricing. But that claim is not quite true. You usually pay extra for bar drinks (these days, often at inflated prices), and you might have to pay for wine with dinner. You must tip—generously. Shore excursions are almost always extra. What you spend in shipboard shops and what you lose in the casino are never covered (unless you receive a "shipboard credit" as a promotion). Lately, some cruise lines have even taken to charging extra for some "gourmet" meals and some of the more elaborate shipboard entertainment and recreational facilities.

For the most part, however, pitfalls are easy to spot and to avoid. If you're careful, you can have a great time on a cruise.

Vacation Packages

Quick Trip Through Chapter 6

If you're looking for a good deal on a package tour, you'll find the Internet a decidedly imperfect source; however, you will be able to find the following:

- Operators of narrowly focused, special-interest tours. You'll also find exactly what those operators offer in the way of destinations and experiences.

- Background information on group tours. You can find details on itineraries, hotels, and prices—sometimes close to what you'd find in a brochure, sometimes less, but almost never more.

- Some good last-minute tour prices—but read the fine print carefully.

In any case, you usually won't find prices any lower than you could get through a travel agency—and many top operators don't sell online at all.

Although airline and agency sites provide search engines that are supposed to locate the "best" deals on simple air-hotel packages, they're often more cumbersome and frustrating to use than they are when you use them to search for airfares or cruises. Yes, you can buy online, but you won't always feel confident that you've really found the best deal.

The Internet offers you fewer advantages in buying a vacation package than it does when you buy any other important travel service. This is the result of three main factors:

- Nobody—not even an Internet vendor—can give much of a discount on a package tour. Typical tour packagers in the United States (*tour operators* or *wholesalers* in industry terms) have very little wiggle room in their pricing. For every dollar they take in, they pay out at least 80 cents to suppliers and subcontractors. They almost always outsource air travel, bus travel, hotel accommodations, local sightseeing, and even some meals to independent businesses. As a result, even if a tour operator wanted to cut its own margin by a steep 25 percent, the effect on the retail price would be no more than four percent—hardly enough to generate a consumer buying frenzy.

- Many tour operators sell only through retail travel agencies and not directly to the public at all. And, among those that do sell direct, most charge the same retail price as agents charge. At least so far, tour operators have not heavily gone the route of "Internet specials" the way many other suppliers have.

- Selecting the right tour often requires the assistance of an experienced professional agent. Tour operators make such exaggerated claims about their tours that you have a tough time comparing them solely on the basis of the puffery they put on their Web sites, in ads, or in brochures.

That's not to say that the Internet can't help you select and buy a vacation package. But you use the Web mainly for tour information, not to find a huge price cut. And you might well decide that the hassle of Internet booking doesn't warrant the effort. Except perhaps for tracking down a few last-minute deals, you might prefer to forget the Internet and instead see a good travel agent.

Presumably, by the time you get to this chapter, you've decided where to go and what sort of vacation you want to have. Here, let's examine how you can use the Internet to zero in on the trip that best meets your needs.

I've separated tours into three different categories: simple air-hotel packages, group tours, and special-interest tours. For the most part, different groups of operators run each of these tours and sell them in different ways. Clearly, you'll find some overlap, but the separation is helpful in looking at the marketplace.

ED'S NOTEBOOK

The Good and Bad of Packages

Two visits to Hawaii, a few years back, illustrate the ups and downs of packages. In one case, someone in my family decided to go to Hawaii on short notice (three weeks), and quickly found that the only available airline seats were full-fare Coach. "Try a packager," I advised, "One of them might still have cheap seats." Sure enough, a local operator could still handle the trip. The cost was a bit higher than separate airfare and hotels, if cheap airfares had been available. But it was much less than the cost of the best airline tickets available at the time.

On a second trip, I found a package price that beat anything I could arrange separately, so I bought the package. The air trips and hotels were fine, but the transfers were a disaster. One difficulty with group travel is that everyone is held captive by the slowest member. The receiving agent took almost an hour to corral us and our baggage for the by-the-numbers lei greeting, and we didn't get away from the airport for almost two hours. We added another two hours when our bus stopped at seven or eight different hotels, on the same package program, before reaching ours. For the return flight, rather than assemble for the airport bus four hours before flight time, we took a cab.

Transportation and Rooms Only

The simplest vacation packages consist of airfare plus hotel, and include airport-to-hotel transportation (*transfers*, in travel-ese). Often, the basic package includes a rental car rather than transfers. Many operators also sell hotel-car packages without the air travel, for travelers who want to find their own best airfare or use frequent flyer mileage.

Basic packages often include a brief sightseeing tour (with the mandatory souvenir-store stops). In Hawaii, they almost always include a hokey flower lei greeting at the airport; you often find similar trifles at other destinations. And they often include a "free" tote bag and a handful of coupons you can use at local merchants and visitor attractions.

Why buy a basic air-hotel package rather than separate air travel and hotel accommodations? I know four possible reasons:

- Sometimes, the package price beats the best you could do on your own buying separately. Packagers typically get good bulk rates on hotel accommodations, and *tour-basing* airfares (wholesale fares the airlines sell only to packagers) are sometimes lower than the cheapest regular published excursion fares.

- Big packagers lock in a certain amount of air and hotel inventory on annual contracts. These operators might still have access to cheap seats, cheap rooms, or both, after the airlines and hotels have already sold out their own low-priced inventory.

- Tour-basing airfares typically are not subject to the same advance-purchase requirements as cheap Coach/Economy tickets purchased separately. Thus, you can sometimes find and buy a low-fare seat as part of a tour package, as late as a day or two before departure. However, that doesn't work if the tour operator uses published rather than tour-basing airfares.

- Even the most bare-bones tour packages provide some assistance when you arrive and depart. You might like the idea of prearranged (and prepaid) airport-to-hotel transfers—with someone from the tour company to make sure the baggage gets collected and delivered properly. And, at popular destination areas, the big tour operators maintain some on-site staff to answer questions and help solve problems that might arise.

On the other hand, packages have some disadvantages. Chief among them is the fact that you have to prepay your entire tour—air, hotel, rental car, sightseeing, and whatever else is bundled into the package price—before you start your trip. Cancellation penalties can be much higher than the $75 you risk if you cancel an air ticket. Also, you have less flexibility with travel dates and schedule choices than you do with independently purchased tickets. Some tour-basing fares don't earn frequent flyer mileage. And the transfers are usually handled in busload-sized groups rather than by taxi or shuttle—which means waiting for stragglers and perhaps stopping at many hotels.

HEADS UP

Always compare the best package price you can find with the best deal you can get buying separately. Beyond the transfers (which I figure are worth no more than $20 per person, round-trip), the package gains you very little other than price. If the package is significantly cheaper, by all means buy it. But if costs are comparable, skip the package.

Airline Sites

Virtually all the giant airlines and quite a few small ones sell basic air-hotel tours—on the Internet as well as through storefront travel agencies. Let's use United as an example. Its vacation package site (*www.unitedvacations.com*) is separate from the main airline site, but the two are (inconspicuously) linked. Here's how it worked in early 2000.

If you weren't sure of a destination, clicking a Destinations button on the home page brought up a page with headings for Asia, Europe, Latin America, and the South Pacific. United covered the United States with headings such as *America's Cities, Florida, Hawaiian Islands, Nevada,* and *Ski & Mountain Summer*—a reasonable reflection of the vacation preferences of most Americans. Each heading listed from 3 to 12 specific destination cities or regions.

For a test, I entered a request for a trip from Seattle to Las Vegas, departing July 17. On the next screen, I was given a choice of air-hotel-car, air-car, and hotel-car options. I chose air-hotel-car for this test, and then specified my length of stay as four nights and my class of service as Economy. Next I selected a flight from a list of optional schedules. From there, I scrolled down to a list of hotels (more than three dozen options in Las Vegas; I chose the Luxor), ranked by price, with a sample price shown. If you wanted to know more about each hotel, you could take a detour to a separate page full of hotel details, with photographs.

Before finalizing the package, the United Vacation site provided a chance to accept or reject a number of add-on features, including a rental car (if not already included) and sightseeing tours. It selected "yes" to travel insurance as a default; if I didn't want it, I had to specify "no" myself. After I made all those choices, the site gave a final itinerary and price (except for airport charges), followed by the usual entry boxes for a charge-card buy. For the most part, this screen sequence was a model of clarity and full disclosure, right down to the on-time rating of each flight and what kind of room I would get.

HEADS UP

The United site, and many others, use the term *run of house* to describe some hotel choices. This simply means the hotel could assign you to whatever room was available rather than to a specific floor level, view outlook, or room class.

Figure 6-1 shows the final package price for the sample trip I checked. I was especially pleased to see that the final price was really for two people, not per-person as it is with so many travel services. (Most other airline sites were similarly honest about the price basis.)

Overall, United's process was quite smooth—provided you knew enough about the destination to make an informed choice of hotel location and specific hotel. The biggest problem was that it was impossible to know if you could have found a cheaper price by selecting different flights. United told you "We suggest checking alternative flights as promotional or sale fares may be available." My question was "Why should I have to reiterate that tedious entry process eight or nine times? Why can't the computer check that for me, instantly?" I still wonder.

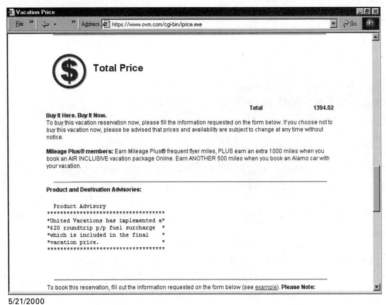

Figure 6-1. *The United Vacations site computes a final trip price for two people.*

Other airline vacation sites (listed in the Appendix) are functionally similar. However, during my tests, I found some interesting variations:

- Several of the airline sites featured "deals" that they claimed represented "savings" from regular prices.

- The package pages for Continental (*www.continental.com/vs/*) and Northwest (*www.nwaworldvacations.com*) located each hotel on a map, at least in some destinations. That's a useful addition if you want to be sure you're near the beach, ski base, city center, or whatever. However, Northwest noted it couldn't sell some of its vacation packages on the Web: no Europe, no ski trips, and no Asian or Hawaiian trips that involved stays at more than one city.

- American (*www.aavacations.com*) offered a free CD-ROM version of all its printed vacation brochures. And American designated those flights on its flight list that qualified for a "special discounted fare."

- Delta's vacation site (*www.deltavacations.com*) sold packages online but requested that you call for some package locations.

Agency Sites

Travel agencies of all stripes sell package tours on their Web sites. The big online agency sites offer much the same sort of system as the airlines, although they can obviously offer a greater selection of suppliers. The two largest such sites, Expedia and Travelocity, have pages for vacation packages, with two key features:

- A box where you enter departure dates, destinations, and activity preferences into a search engine that locates packages, from all participating suppliers, that meet your criteria.

- Links to other tour operator sites, including several of the airline sites mentioned earlier.

Several of the smaller online agencies claim they specialize in searching for vacation packages (although they might offer some separate air tickets and hotel accommodations, as well). Among these smaller online agencies are Travelscape (*www.travelscape.com*), EUROPEonsale.com (*www.europeonsale.com*), Go-Today (*www.go-today.com*), and Online Vacation Mall (*www.onlinevacationmall.com*). Others are listed in the Appendix.

Big multioffice retail chains also sell vacation packages on their affiliated Web sites. Liberty Travel (*www.libertytravel.com*) provides a full-service site, with plenty of package-tour options. So do three of the largest nationwide chains. Carlson Wagonlit Travel (*www.carlsontravel.com*) permits online booking, but encourages you to contact a local Carlson Wagonlit agent. Uniglobe (*www.uniglobe.com*) has a user-friendly interface, but when you inquire about a package tour, you're seamlessly shifted to Online Vacation Mall. American Express (*www.americanexpress.com*) displayed only around 100 packages in early summer 2000—a very small fraction of the total products available.

You'll also find several sort-of-gateway sites for tour packages. Last Minute Travel (*www.lastminutetravel.com*) lists what are promoted as last-minute deals on a variety of travel services, including vacations. You enter your origin city, your destination, and a time frame (for example, next 7 days, next 14 days); the site provides a list of current packages from a variety of suppliers. If you're interested, the Last Minute Travel site links you directly to the supplier's site—where you might or might not find the featured deal. (I couldn't locate one of Last Minute's trips from Los Angeles to Hawaii on the supplier's site, but I found others.)

Travel Hub (*www.travelhub.com*) is also something of a gateway site, with travel listings that include vacation packages. Prices and availability are posted for some vacation packages; for others, you are invited to post your trip details and ask for an e-mail response.

Many of the agency sites promise reduced prices on last-minute tour packages, and that's one area where the Internet seems to work reasonably well. Take EUROPEonsale.com as an example. Figure 6-2 shows part of a page listing "Tag Sale" tour prices, as of early summer 2000. This is one of the clearest presentations you'll see of last-minute tour pricing. Unfortunately, it also presents two problems you'll often encounter on the Web: Most of the prices shown are only from New York; travelers from other cities (and that's most of you) have to call for your real cost. Even worse, at the time I wrote this, the site was still displaying a few deals that had already expired.

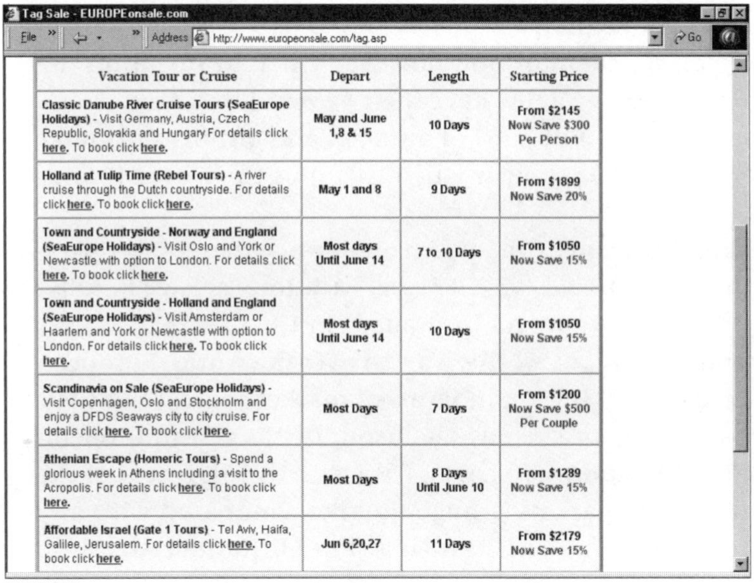

Vacation Tour or Cruise	Depart	Length	Starting Price
Classic Danube River Cruise Tours (SeaEurope Holidays) - Visit Germany, Austria, Czech Republic, Slovakia and Hungary For details click here. To book click here.	May and June 1,8 & 15	10 Days	From $2145 Now Save $300 Per Person
Holland at Tulip Time (Rebel Tours) - A river cruise through the Dutch countryside. For details click here. To book click here.	May 1 and 8	9 Days	From $1899 Now Save 20%
Town and Countryside - Norway and England (SeaEurope Holidays) - Visit Oslo and York or Newcastle with option to London. For details click here. To book click here.	Most days Until June 14	7 to 10 Days	From $1050 Now Save 15%
Town and Countryside - Holland and England (SeaEurope Holidays) - Visit Amsterdam or Haarlem and York or Newcastle with option to London. For details click here. To book click here.	Most days Until June 14	10 Days	From $1050 Now Save 15%
Scandinavia on Sale (SeaEurope Holidays) - Visit Copenhagen, Oslo and Stockholm and enjoy a DFDS Seaways city to city cruise. For details click here. To book click here.	Most Days	7 Days	From $1200 Now Save $500 Per Couple
Athenian Escape (Homeric Tours) - Spend a glorious week in Athens including a visit to the Acropolis. For details click here. To book click here.	Most Days	8 Days Until June 10	From $1289 Now Save 15%
Affordable Israel (Gate 1 Tours) - Tel Aviv, Haifa, Galilee, Jerusalem. For details click here. To book click here.	Jun 6,20,27	11 Days	From $2179 Now Save 15%

5/21/2000

Figure 6-2. *The EUROPEonsale.com "Tag Sale" features reduced prices for immediate departures.*

Tour Operator Sites

Many tour operators, large and small, have Web sites. Often, however, the Web is simply a way to provide background information: If you want to check prices or buy, the site suggests you call or visit a retail travel agency.

Inside the System: Those Invisible Tour Operators

Tour operators that sell mainly air-hotel-car packages are largely in the invisible part of the travel spectrum. They assemble the components of a vacation, mainly from outside suppliers, and then bundle and sell them at a package price. But you see very little of these tour operators in the marketplace. In a recent Sunday travel section of *The New York Times*, for instance, I saw only two ads placed by companies I knew to be tour operators, and both were small. Instead, the big tour ads were from retail travel agencies (American Express, Liberty, and such) and giant airlines.

Whether you see them or not, however, the tour operators are there. Some retail agency chains have their own in-house tour operators, as do some airlines. But most of agencies and airlines outsource the tour operator function, even when they put their own brands on the tours.

In fact, about the only time you really notice these tour operators is when one of them fails (see "Beware: Vacation Package Pitfalls" later in the chapter, and "Travel Insurance" in Chapter 8).

Tour operators don't work this way all over the world. European tour operators are much bigger, in terms of market share, than their U.S. counterparts. A giant such as Thomson, the largest tour operator in the United Kingdom, can control as much as 10 percent of the total British vacation market—a huge number, compared with any U.S. firm. Thomson even owns its own airline (Britannia Airways); other giant European operators own airlines and hotels, as well. As a result, they can cut last-minute prices by percentages the U.S. operators can't touch.

In a few years, U.S. tour operators might consolidate into a small number of giant firms, as the European operators have. Now, however, you're looking at a fragmented marketplace where even the biggest players can't do much with their prices.

Still, a few big operators that specialize in air-hotel packages do provide for online purchase. For example, Funjet Vacations Pleasure Break (*www.pleasurebreak.com*) provides the same sort of sequence as some of the agency sites. Once you enter your origin, destination, and dates, you proceed to select airlines, type of package (air-hotel, air only, or hotel only), and length of stay, with airfare differences not shown. You move next to choose a preferred hotel from a long list, with prices shown; and then you select the extras you want from a laundry list of excursions, admissions, and such. Finally you receive a complete price for the packages, including fees and charges.

Pleasant Holidays (*www.pleasantholidays.com*) illustrates a different tack for its packages to Hawaii, Mexico, and Tahiti. You can get to the usual entry box (dates, destinations, and such), but the end result is an e-mail message to the agency's office. The site has plenty of interesting destination background, but you can't really buy over the Web.

Even when you can buy a package directly from a tour operator, you don't pay any less than if you bought through an agency site—or, for that matter, a storefront travel agency.

Don't Miss the Bus

Pick up the travel section of your weekend hometown newspaper, and chances are you'll see plenty of ads for airfares, cruises, air-hotel packages or escorted package tours, hotels, and resorts. What you might not see many of are ads for bus-hotel tours. Nevertheless, they're big-time, hauling thousands of busloads of travelers to some of America's most popular visitor meccas.

Bus-hotel tours are conceptually similar to air-hotel tours. The big difference is that, for the most part, bus tours serve more limited regional markets—usually destinations that are within a day's drive of the origin city. Thus you find lots of bus-hotel tour packages from Boston, New York, Philadelphia, and Baltimore to Atlantic City; from Des Moines, Kansas City, Memphis, Omaha, and St Louis to Branson, Missouri; and from Los Angeles and San Francisco to Yosemite.

Although a few large tour operators run big programs, the bus-hotel tour business is largely a cottage industry, with individual tour companies working out of their home areas. Many such tours are organized by small retail travel agencies.

I didn't find any good gateway sites for bus-hotel tours on the Internet, and the trade association with the most bus tour operators, the National Tour Association, doesn't provide an online directory of members. But you can find sites for a few dozen companies through most search engines. The Appendix lists some representative operators of bus-hotel tours. Some of the bus-tour sites permit online booking; others are merely informational.

Let's take California Parlor Car Tours (one of the nation's larger operators) as an example. Figure 6-3 shows the company's home page (*www.calpartours.com*), listing summaries of its three main touring programs. You can click each tour name and get to subsequent pages with extensive detail: tour highlights, a description of the hotel, and a detailed schedule of travel and local sightseeing. Finally, another click takes you to a familiar entry box for your name, travel dates, and tour selections. However, you don't actually buy online; instead, your entry is an e-mail "request," and you buy the tour only after you hear back from the operator. Web prices are the same as you'd pay through a travel agency or at a hotel desk.

In providing specific price information and at least the initiation of an online booking, California Parlor Car is the exception rather than the rule. Most of the sites I checked provided, at best, pricing for destination packages. You had to call the bus operators for specific tour prices including long-haul transport. Those sites that didn't list prices were merely informational, again suggesting that you call for specific itineraries and prices.

All in all, you'll probably have a tough time finding a bus-hotel tour on the Internet. You'll save time by checking whatever section of your local newspaper the bus tours use for advertising, or checking with a local travel agency.

Riding the Rails

Amtrak sells tour packages that involve train travel. Although its site (*www.amtrak.com*) describes these tours and lists illustrative minimum prices, you can't buy on the Web. (See Chapter 7 for more about train travel.)

2000 - Page 1 of 4	Yosemite National Park 2 Days - One Night	California Coast 3 Days - 2 Nights	Coast & Monterey 2 Days - One Night
Departs From:	San Francisco Round Trip	San Francisco to Los Angeles One Way or Round Trip	Los Angeles One Way to San Francisco
What You See	Yosemite Valley, El Capitan, Bridaveil Fall, Yosemite Falls, Half Dome, Merced River. Glacier Point in Summer	Monterey, 17 Mile Drive Carmel, Big Sur, Highway 1 Hearst Castle, Solvang, & Santa Barbara	Solvang, Hearst Castle, Highway 1, Big Sur, Monterey, 17 Mile Drive, Carmel by the Sea
Where You Stay	Yosemite Lodge, Ahwahnee Hotel or Yosemite View Lodge	Hyatt Regency Monterey and Royal Scandinavian Solvang	Hyatt Regency Monterey
Meals Included	Lunch at The Ahwahnee	3 Lunches and 2 Dinners	2 Lunches
Cost Per Person based on two persons staying in one room	US $272 for Yosemite Lodge or View Lodge US $345 for Ahwahnee Hotel	US $548 - One Way Add Train Fare for Return	US $308 - One Way April to October
	Click Here for	Click Here for	Click Here for

5/21/2000

Figure 6-3. *The California Parlor Car Tours' home page includes summaries of its tours.*

HEADS UP

Want to organize a bus tour for your own group? You can do that online. Motorcoach.com (*www.motorcoach.com*) operates a clearinghouse for bus charters. Enter the key facts—origin, destination, number of passengers, travel dates, features you want—and the site passes your requirements along to participating bus operators. The site also includes a list of "tips" for first-time charterers. Many of the individual bus companies listed in the Appendix also solicit charters.

For Extended Hand-Holding

Buying an air-hotel package is really just another way to travel on your own. If you want someone else to take most of the work out of travel, you should look for a group tour. As the name implies, you travel a set itinerary with typically around 30 other travelers, the number that conveniently fills most tour buses. Although group tours usually involve a good bit of assistance, the amount varies depending on the tour.

The most basic group tours include round-trip airfare to and from a major gateway airport in your destination area, hotel accommodations, transfers, internal transportation (within your destination region), and some sightseeing. Others include some or all meals, admissions to local attractions, and scheduled entertainment.

Typically, group tours move around extensively within the main destination region. (That classic movie *If This Is Tuesday, It Must Be Belgium* was a send-up of a prototypical European group tour.) You might stay only one night at some hotel stops, several nights at others. Usually, internal transportation is by tour bus, which also doubles as local sightseeing. Occasionally you travel by train—especially in Europe and Japan, where train service is exceptionally good—or, less often, by plane or boat.

Representatives of the tour operator typically meet your plane; make sure everybody and their baggage get on the right bus to the right hotel; and show up during the tour, at least occasionally, to answer questions and solve problems. More comprehensive *escorted* tours provide someone who stays with the group, serving as a combination facilitator, guide, and gofer. Even with escorted tours, however, your escort in one city might remain behind when you leave and a new one might greet you at the next stop. If you want to have someone along the entire trip, look for a *fully escorted* tour.

Operators of group tours are better known than those largely anony-mous operators of simple air-hotel packages. They tend to specialize in terms of the clientele they serve, the destinations they feature, or both:

- Among the better-known upscale operators are Abercrombie & Kent (*www.abercrombiekent.com*), Tauck Tours (*www.tauck.com*), Maupintour (*www.maupintour.com*), Intrav (*www.intrav.com*), and Travcoa World Tours (*www.travcoa.com*). Figure 6-4 shows the top portion of A&K's list of added-value tours—including a round-the-world tour by Con-corde for $62,000 per person. None of these five operators encouraged online booking; none of their sites had the usual entry boxes. Al-though all listed a phone number for inquiries and reservations, the main thrust was to have you call a travel agency.

- The broad midpriced mass market is exemplified by such well-known names as Apple Vacations (*www.applevacations.com*), Collette Tours (*www.collettetours.com*), Globus & Cosmos (*www.globusandcosmos.com*),

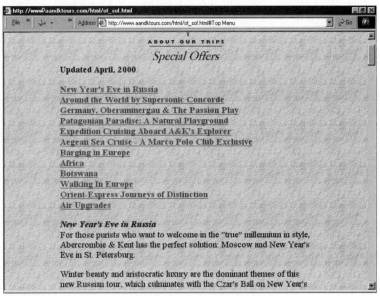

Figure 6-4. *Abercrombie & Kent features upscale group tours.*

GoGo Worldwide Vacations (*www.gogowwv.com*), and Funjet Vacations (*www.funjet.com*). Of this group, only Funjet lists "hot deals" and provides for online bookings (see Figure 6-5 for a typical last-minute listing). The others refer you to a travel agency; GoGo even restricts site entry to travel agents.

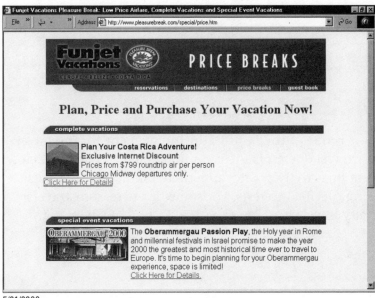

Figure 6-5. *Funjet lists last-minute "hot deals."*

- Well-known operators that focus on a limited number of destinations include Homeric Tours (*www.homerictours.com*), concentrating on Greece; Pleasant Holidays (mentioned earlier), with tours to Hawaii, Mexico, and Tahiti; and Perillo Tours (*www.perillotours.com*), concentrating on Italy (but also offering tours in Hawaii and Israel). They all provide for online reservations but not complete charge-card bookings. Contiki (*www.contiki.com*) focuses on young (age 18 to 35) travelers and provides for online booking; as shown in Figure 6-6, it also offers last-minute reductions.

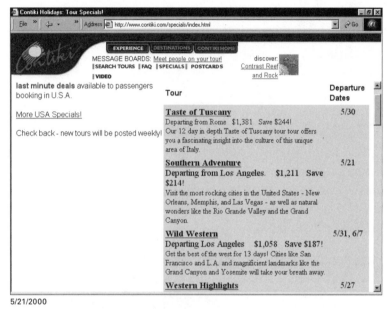

5/21/2000

Figure 6-6. *Contiki arranges tours for young travelers age 18 to 35.*

For Focused Tours

Specialty travel is one of the fastest growing segments of the travel industry. Specialty travel operators focus on individual activities, or closely related clusters of activities, and aim their marketing at travelers with corresponding specific interests. For some of the reasons travelers might enjoy specialty travel, see "Travel with a Focus," in Chapter 2.

For entry into the extended world of special interests, most trade experts would direct you to Specialty Travel Index (*www.spectrav.com*), the 800-pound gorilla of sites (note that you can also get the *Specialty Travel Index* in magazine form). Figure 6-7 shows just the first part of the site's listing of individual categories, which contains more than 300 individual line items.

5/21/2000

Figure 6-7. *The Specialty Travel Index site lists more than 300 activities.*

I recommend searching this site first by activity. Interested in bicycle touring? Click that subject, and you see a list of more than 100 destination areas. Pick a destination and the site returns a list of one or more tour operators that run bicycle tours there. Finally, choose an operator from the list, and then go directly to its Web site for details.

Or if you're interested in a safari, you select Safari/Game Viewing, which returns more than 50 individual entries—continents, countries, and states. If you select Kenya, you see a list of more than two dozen operators of safaris for that country. (In this and in most cases, search results for a selected country will include options in neighboring countries, as well.) Many of the listed operators include links to their own Web sites (but I was surprised to find that a few operators apparently aren't online).

Alternatively, you can narrow your search initially by destination and then see what activities are available there. Even an area as desolate as Antarctica yields a list of some 24 activities.

If you check the site, you quickly find that the individual listings are a bit of an apples-oranges mix. Some of the Antarctica listings are activity-centered, such as bird-watching, marine biology, and photography; others focus on participant groups, such as women or people over 50. However, these diverging paths often lead to the same endpoint. Nevertheless, the Specialty Travel Index is clearly the place to start for tours focused on diverse, specific subjects.

However, as I noted in Chapter 2, you can also find other gateway sites that are specific to individual activities: golf, tennis, opera, theme parks, and such. These sites are noted in the Appendix.

One of the huge benefits of the Web is its ability to level the competitive playing field. Small operators can set up Web sites and list themselves in the Specialty Travel Index (or other gateway sites) at a fraction of the cost of mounting any kind of ad or PR campaign in print, radio, or TV. Many of the most intriguing specialty operators are very small businesses—some literally one-man (or one-woman) operations. But on the Web they're right up there with the big boys. Thanks to the Internet, you can find these small gems in what would otherwise be a vast slag heap of giant suppliers.

Even so, the Internet doesn't catch everyone. By a combination of word-of-mouth and serendipity, I've found quite a few fascinating small operators that don't bother with Web sites at all. They're content to keep selling to their prior clients and to new clients referred by earlier customers. I frankly have no clue as to how you can locate these hidden treasures other than the way I did—a combination of determination and luck.

Beware: Vacation Package Pitfalls

The tour operator segment has always been one of the most trouble-prone elements of the travel industry. Despite a variety of safeguards, it seems that every year or so a tour operator fails, leaving hundreds of travelers with neither their trips nor their money—maybe even stranded in a foreign country. I know two main reasons:

- Tour operators operate on thin margins: Even a small budget miscalculation can throw them from a profitable situation into a loss.

- The standard requirement for full prepayment—often months in advance—gives tour operators control over a cushion of cash that really doesn't belong to them.

That combination has all too often been a recipe for the disaster you can easily foresee: A weak operator dips into new customers' prepayments to pay off obligations for prior customers. Obviously, that process can't last very long.

Travelers have at least three safety nets that are supposed to protect them against operator failure, but none of them applies across the board:

- On any tour that includes charter air travel, Federal law requires operators to deposit travelers' prepayments into escrow accounts that must be used to pay subcontractors in full before the operator can withdraw any profit. Although that system works reasonably well, every year or so a few operators figure out how to get their hands on the escrow accounts. And some travelers have unwittingly abetted the misuse by making their checks out to the tour operator rather than the escrow company.

- The US Tour Operators Association (USTOA), a trade association, operates a robust consumer protection plan: Each member must demonstrate financial resources of at least $1,000,000 to cover potential customer losses should the member go bankrupt or otherwise fail. The resources can be in the form of a bond, a letter of credit, or a certificate of deposit. It's a fine program; the main problem is that only some 126 tour operators, out of the thousands that sell tours, belong to USTOA. Members tend to be the larger, more stable operators. For a full membership list or more information about the consumer protection plan, check the USTOA Web site (*www.ustoa.com*).

- The National Tour Association (NTA) is an association of mainly smaller tour operators, including many bus-tour companies. Although NTA also promises a consumer protection plan, it's much weaker than USTOA's program. The financial requirement is just $250,000 per operator. An even greater problem is that the protection kicks in only if a member becomes bankrupt—and, unfortunately, many tour operators have gone broke without ever filing for bankruptcy. The NTA site (*www.ntaonline.com*) provides additional detail on the consumer plan. You can also check to see if a tour operator you're considering is a member, but you can't view a full membership list.

Individual states might provide additional protection. California is clearly ahead of the pack: It maintains a fund, supported by fees from travel agencies and tour operators, to reimburse travelers in case of failure of any "seller of travel." Unfortunately, it applies only to sellers registered with the state of California and to consumers who live in California. Other states offer a variety of weaker protection plans; ask a local travel agent for specifics about your state.

Internet Caveats

In early summer 2000, my tests of airline and agency sites produced somewhat disappointing results—especially when compared with the relative ease I found searching for just airfares, hotel rooms, and cruises. Among my gripes (at least one applies to each site I checked; some sites suffered from several) are the following:

- Sites widely varied in what each site claimed was the best deal on a given test trip.

- Some sites allowed you to enter a desired destination, but didn't ask for an origin city. Once you found a destination package you liked, you were supposed to call for airfares.

- Many sites displayed hotel-only or hotel-car packages without airfare, even when I asked for a complete vacation package on every test.

- On the agency sites, almost all hotel-only price quotations were on a per-person rather than a per-room basis. That's an inexcusable deception. To give credit where it's due, most airline sites quoted prices for two people.

- Some of the supposedly independent sites came up with (to put it kindly) idiosyncratic airline and flight choices. In one case, I asked for tours from Portland, Oregon to Honolulu, and the site routed me via San Francisco on United rather than nonstop from Portland on Hawaiian.

- All of the sites were lavish with their claims of "lowest prices," "discounts," and "savings," all of which would be very difficult to verify. Watch out for fluff like "fourth night free"; this is just a more compelling way for the operator to present the final price.

- The end result on quite a few sites was an inability to book a complete package. Quite often, the Internet gave a reasonable amount of information about hotel features, prices, and availabilities, but the final instructions were to call a toll-free number to finalize the details or determine the exact airfare.

In sum, none of the sites allowed me to feel confident I'd found a good deal for the test trips I selected, much less the best available deal. My advice? When you're shopping for a simple air-hotel package to a popular destination, use the Internet to research options and compare prices (if you can), but call a travel agent to make the final deal.

I felt more comfortable with the sites that offered last-minute specials. The information seemed to be more complete, and many of the prices really looked like good deals.

I also fared much better in tracking down special-interest tours. The Internet opened up avenues of communications with operators I would never have located any other way.

7

The Rest of It

Quick Trip Through Chapter 7

You can find extensive information on rail travel, rental cars, insurance, and communications on the Internet, though the services and cost-cutting opportunities are limited:

- You can easily locate railroad schedules and fares for just about anywhere in the world online. Amtrak offers a few Internet-only specials, but most other systems don't. You can buy tickets and passes for European trains online, but for many other countries, you can't.

- You can use the Internet to check availability and reserve rental cars for just about anywhere in the world. The rental-car companies are also offering a few Internet-only specials.

- You can use online ATM locators to guide you to sources of cash (and low-loss currency exchange) worldwide, and you can use Web data to compare the costs and benefits of various charge cards.

- You can compare rates of and buy trip-cancellation insurance. Seniors on Medicare who might need medical or hospital coverage outside the United States can also find coverage information online.

- You can use the Internet to help you find a good call-home long distance service and to rent a cellular phone, but you might need to call some phone companies directly to get the best deals.

You can get information about—and buy—just about any travel service you might want, on the Internet. As with airfares, hotels, cruises, and tours, the Web gains you access to a tremendous wealth of information and puts you in contact with just about all of the significant suppliers. However, online buying is somewhat more limited in certain market niches, where you find fewer Internet-only special deals than you find with airfares or hotels.

Riding the Rails

In North America, rail travel remains a significant means of intercity transportation in only a few heavily populated corridors. In other parts of the world, however, governments have pumped huge investments into rail in order to make it a legitimate alternative to flying or driving for trips under 300 miles or so. These systems set the world's standards.

You can use the Web to examine schedules and buy tickets on most of the world's important rail systems. Here, your primary reason for using the Web is as a convenient way of collecting information and making a purchase, although a few rail systems are starting to offer Internet specials.

Trains in the United States

Whether your interest in Amtrak is practical or romantic, you can check routes, schedules, and fares on the Internet, and you can make reservations and buy tickets. In fact, the Amtrak site (*www.amtrak.com*) is, in many ways, a parallel to airline sites. Figure 7-1, for example, shows a portion of the online timetable for the Metroliners, currently Amtrak's top trains (I've magnified the text to make it easier to read). You can also download and view these timetables using Adobe Acrobat Reader.

HEADS UP

Presumably, by the time you read this, Amtrak will have finally been able to get its new high-speed *Acela Express* trains running. They'll be close to a year late, but—travelers hope—worth the wait.

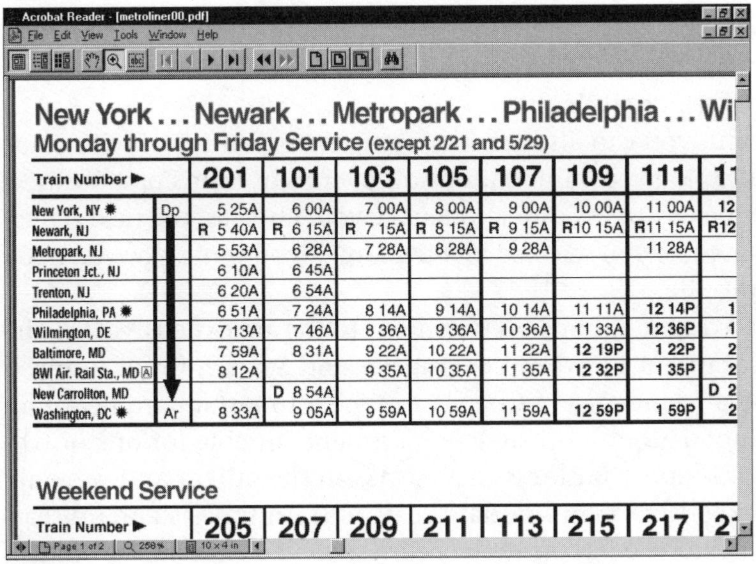

New York ... Newark ... Metropark ... Philadelphia ... Wil

Monday through Friday Service (except 2/21 and 5/29)

Train Number ▶		201	101	103	105	107	109	111	11
New York, NY ✻	Dp	5 25A	6 00A	7 00A	8 00A	9 00A	10 00A	11 00A	12
Newark, NJ		R 5 40A	R 6 15A	R 7 15A	R 8 15A	R 9 15A	R10 15A	R11 15A	R12
Metropark, NJ		5 53A	6 28A	7 28A	8 28A	9 28A		11 28A	
Princeton Jct., NJ		6 10A	6 45A						
Trenton, NJ		6 20A	6 54A						
Philadelphia, PA ✻		6 51A	7 24A	8 14A	9 14A	10 14A	11 11A	12 14P	1
Wilmington, DE		7 13A	7 46A	8 36A	9 36A	10 36A	11 33A	12 36P	1
Baltimore, MD		7 59A	8 31A	9 22A	10 22A	11 22A	12 19P	1 22P	2
BWI Air. Rail Sta., MD Ⓐ		8 12A		9 35A	10 35A	11 35A	12 32P	1 35P	2
New Carrollton, MD			D 8 54A						D 2
Washington, DC ✻	Ar	8 33A	9 05A	9 59A	10 59A	11 59A	12 59P	1 59P	2

Weekend Service

Train Number ▶	205	207	209	211	113	215	217	21

5/28/2000

Figure 7-1. *You can view all Amtrak timetables on the Internet.*

Booking a train trip online is much like booking a flight. You start by registering with the Web site (Amtrak adopted that annoying requirement from the airlines). You then ask to plan an itinerary, and enter your origin, destination, and date information in the ubiquitous itinerary box. Next, you see a display of trains that meet your requirements; if there is

Inside the System:
Amtrak's Split Personality

Amtrak, operator of the U.S. passenger rail system, is really two different railroads. In the Northeast Corridor (from Boston to Washington, D.C.) and in a few other short-haul corridors radiating from a few big cities, Amtrak seriously competes with airlines and cars to provide efficient point-to-point intercity transportation. The Boston-New York portion is also improving dramatically: Electrification of this line was completed in early 2000, and new high-speed trains were due to enter service sometime in the year.

Amtrak's long-haul system is completely different. These trains, with their roomy double-deck cars and average speeds of around 40 miles an hour, are "land cruisers" rather than practical transportation. They're both slower and more expensive than flying—or even taking Greyhound. People ride them because they like to ride trains, not to get from point A to point B.

more than one, you see them all and select the one you prefer. The next screen asks for the names of passengers traveling and which are adults, seniors (62 or over), or students.

At that point, you can also ask for "accommodations," which means some form of sleeping accommodations on overnight trains or a Business Class seat on some day trains. After you make your choices, the next screen gives you the schedule you selected and the fare. If you want, you can book directly from the site.

Sleeping accommodations on overnight trains are expensive. On the popular Coast Starlight between Los Angeles and Seattle, for example, a couple pays $404 round-trip in Coach, and $998 in a standard bedroom sleeping accommodation (a private compartment suitable for one or two passengers). Extra-roomy Business Class seats, on the other hand, are only slightly more expensive than standard seats. But Amtrak's standard seating is far better than Coach on most airlines, so you probably wouldn't need anything better for daytime travel.

Like the airlines, Amtrak now posts short-term Internet-only specials; they're mainly for short trips, both in distance traveled and in time allowed at your destination. Figure 7-2 shows a list of such specials.

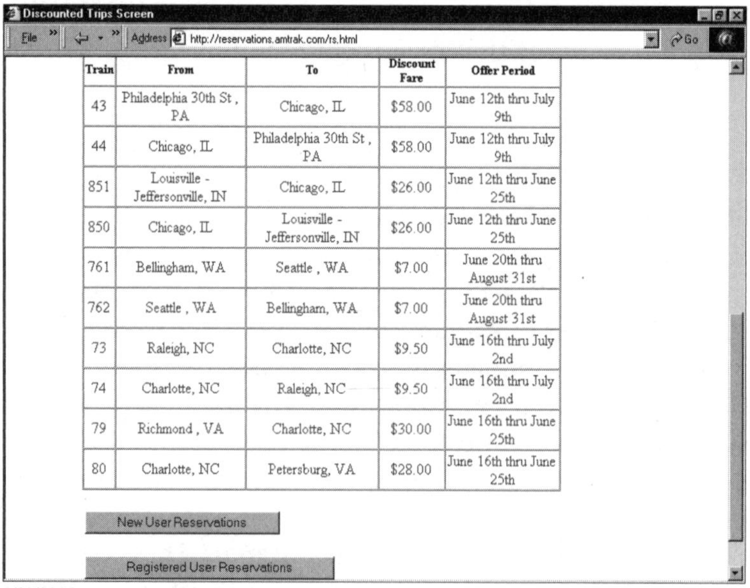

Train	From	To	Discount Fare	Offer Period
43	Philadelphia 30th St., PA	Chicago, IL	$58.00	June 12th thru July 9th
44	Chicago, IL	Philadelphia 30th St., PA	$58.00	June 12th thru July 9th
851	Louisville - Jeffersonville, IN	Chicago, IL	$26.00	June 12th thru June 25th
850	Chicago, IL	Louisville - Jeffersonville, IN	$26.00	June 12th thru June 25th
761	Bellingham, WA	Seattle, WA	$7.00	June 20th thru August 31st
762	Seattle, WA	Bellingham, WA	$7.00	June 20th thru August 31st
73	Raleigh, NC	Charlotte, NC	$9.50	June 16th thru July 2nd
74	Charlotte, NC	Raleigh, NC	$9.50	June 16th thru July 2nd
79	Richmond, VA	Charlotte, NC	$30.00	June 16th thru June 25th
80	Charlotte, NC	Petersburg, VA	$28.00	June 16th thru June 25th

6/23/2000

Figure 7-2. *Like the airlines, Amtrak offers frequent Internet-only specials.*

Amtrak's site also has information about other rail-based services. However, all you get is information; to reserve or book these services, you must call or go to a travel agency. Here is some of what you'll find out:

- Auto Train is a service that carries you and your car overnight between Alexandria, Virginia and Sanford, Florida.

- Amtrak offers occasional special promotions. Last spring, for example, three-person families could take advantage of a special deal: The first person paid full fare, the second paid half fare, and the third paid nothing.

- Amtrak, like airlines, organizes package tours.

- Amtrak and United Airlines team up for *Air-Rail* packages: Ride the train one way and fly the other, without having to pay an outrageously high one-way airfare.

- Amtrak teams with Via Rail Canada to sell a North American railpass that provides 30 days of unlimited rail travel in the United States and Canada. In previous years, Amtrak has also sold regional and national passes for just the United States; presumably, if it does so again, you'll see these advertised on the Web site.

Although the value of rail as a mode of transportation for longer trips generates a great deal of disagreement among transportation mavens, there's no question that rail, of various sorts, plays an increasing role in urban transportation. And most of the cities with rail transit have Web sites devoted to rail services. You can access these sites most easily through city sites (discussed in Chapter 2).

You can locate many of the country's small, scenic, and excursion railroads either through destination sites or gateway sites devoted to commercial tourist attractions. Among the best sites for rail trips is Web Union Station (*www.webunionstation.com*).

HEADS UP

Although it's not rail service, you sometimes find that Greyhound is the only available alternative to driving or flying. Its excellent site at *www.greyhound.com* follows the usual pattern: Enter an itinerary, select a schedule, and find the price. However, Greyhound doesn't take seat reservations, and you can't buy tickets online.

Canadian Rails

Canada's national passenger railway program closely parallels Amtrak, as does its Web site. Figure 7-3 shows the English version of the VIA Rail Canada home page (*www.viarail.ca*), with a number of options.

6/23/2000

Figure 7-3. *From VIA Rail's home page, you can access schedules, fares, specials, passes, and much more.*

VIA Rail has one heavy traffic corridor with fast, relatively frequent train service, incorporating Montreal, Ottawa, and Toronto. But its long-haul trains are land cruisers, just like their Amtrak counterparts.

Rail buffs consider the three-day trek from Toronto to Vancouver to be one of the world's great train rides, and the overnight trip from Montreal to the Maritimes is also popular. Other equally dedicated rail fans like the services to the far North—on some routes, to places you can't reach by highway at all. VIA Rail splits one of its most scenic trips—between Jasper, Alberta, and Prince Rupert, on the British Columbia coast—into two all-daylight segments, with an overnight stay halfway between, at Prince George. I've often wondered if that formula might work for some of Amtrak's scenic routes, too.

VIA Rail offers two types of railpasses. Canrailpass provides unlimited train travel on any 12 days out of a 30-day period (at a cost of US$410 from June 1 to October 15, US$260 at other times; sleeping accommodations are extra; discounts are available for children, students, and seniors). Corridorpass provides unlimited train travel for 10 days in the region between Quebec City and Windsor, Ontario (at a cost of US$190 in Coach, US$345 in First Class).

Although the Web site describes these and other specials in some detail, you can't book or buy on the VIA Rail site. You can enter information in a form, send it via e-mail, and then wait for a response, or you can reserve and buy at least some kinds of tickets through a link to the Travelocity (*www.travelocity.com*) agency site.

BC Rail, with a scenic route from Vancouver to Prince George, maintains a site at *www.bcrail.com* that provides information on routes and schedules but has no reservation or buying capability.

Great Trains in Europe

Europe's rail system is fantastic—mainline trains are fast, frequent, and comfortable. The high-speed *Premier* trains clip along at close to 200 miles per hour on dedicated high-speed tracks, and 120 to 150 miles per hour on conventional roadbeds. Express trains operate every hour or two on the main intercity routes, and the rail network reaches many of the continent's small cities, as well. Traveling in Second Class is perfectly acceptable—its cabins are much roomier and more comfortable than are Economy cabins on airlines.

Rail Europe (*www.raileurope.com*) is the leading multicountry rail agency operating in the United States. Although run by the French railroads, it represents most other European rail systems as well, including the United Kingdom, but not including Germany. It's largely a one-stop shopping center for just about any European rail ticket you might want: individual point-to-point tickets, national or international railpasses, and rail-based package tours. In fact, it's a comprehensive agency site that also arranges rental cars, hotel accommodations, and even transatlantic airline tickets.

Train or Car?

Most of the time, if you want to visit more than one city or country in Europe, your real choice is between taking trains and renting a car, with flying a distant (and expensive) third. Although this choice depends on your exact itinerary, I've found some general cost and convenience patterns.

Rail almost always beats renting a car:

- When you're traveling solo

- If you think you will be logging a lot of miles in a fairly short time

- In areas where car rentals are expensive, such as Italy and most of Scandinavia

- When you want to stay at downtown hotels in midsize to large cities

Renting a car is preferable:

- When three or four adults share one car

- When you want to tour the countryside at a leisurely and relaxed pace

- In regions where rentals are inexpensive, such as Germany, Benelux, and the United Kingdom

- When you rent a cottage in a small town or in the country, or when you plan to stay at country inns

One way to solve the train vs. car dilemma is to do some of each. Quite a few European railpasses are available in *Rail 'n Drive* versions: a certain number of rail-travel days plus a certain number of driving days. You can use trains for long intercity links and use cars for local exploration.

Figure 7-4 shows part of Rail Europe's site, emphasizing the breadth of services available. It's an easy site to use. If you want a railpass, for example, you can select either "single country passes," "multicountry passes," or "Rail 'n Drive passes" from the drop-down menu. If you opt for single country, you get a list of 16 countries, each of which has its own detail page. If you select Italy, for example, the page you call up lists two different kinds of Italy Rail Cards plus a Rail 'n Drive Card.

6/23/2000

Figure 7-4. *Rail Europe is the U.S. representative for most European railroads.*

HEADS UP

European railpasses come in two basic flavors. Standard, or *full-time*, passes allow you to ride trains, as much as you want, over the entire validity period of the pass, which can range from one week to several months. *Flexi* passes (just about all the countries use that term) allow unlimited train travel on only a limited number of days out of the total validity period—8 days out of 15, for example, or 4 days out of a month. For equivalent total periods of validity, the flexi passes are always less expensive, but for an equivalent number of train-travel days, the full-time passes cost less.

Also, several regions and countries now offer companion, or *saver*, passes. For couples who travel together, they cost less than individual one-person passes.

A click on the specific type of pass you want takes you to a price table; Figure 7-5 shows the one for Italy's flexi passes. After you check out prices, it's an easy scroll down to a box where you can add the pass to your shopping cart and buy it online.

6/23/2000

Figure 7-5. *Italy's Flexi Rail Card is available for three periods of train travel.*

DER Travel Services (*www.dertravel.com*) is currently the primary U.S. representative for the German rail system. Like Rail Europe, it's really an agency site: It handles rail tickets and passes for several other European countries, as well as rental cars, hotel accommodations, air tickets, and package tours.

Although it still sells through Rail Europe, BritRail now has its own site (*www.britrail.com*) where you can get information but (as of the summer of 2000) can buy tickets or passes only through links to other sites. Britain's several privatized railroads are a bit of a jumble: For schedule information, the best site is Railtrack (*www.railtrack.co.uk*) which also has links to individual private rail companies.

Another site, Rail Connection (*www.railconnection.com*), specializes in railpasses. Last year, it promoted express delivery of two or more passes at no extra charge—thus undercutting most rivals by at least a few dollars. Although affiliated with Student Advantage, the Rail Connection site is happy to sell to any traveler.

In much of Europe, bus systems are operated by the rail agencies. One special bus site you might want to look at is Busabout (*www.busabout.com*), a system that serves Europe's top tourist cities with daily trips (on most routes). You can buy a pass that permits unlimited stops and on-and-offs for however long the pass is valid. It targets mainly young travelers as a lower-cost alternative to Eurailpass, but travelers of any age are welcome.

Pass or Tickets?

The question of railpass vs. individual tickets, like the question of rail vs. driving, is complex, depending on your specific itinerary. If you want to be rigorous, the Rail Europe and DER sites both display prices for point-to-point tickets (in the summer of 2000, Rail Europe's site was the better). You can use that information to estimate what you'd pay for a trip if you bought separate tickets, and compare that total with the cost of the cheapest railpass that would cover your trip.

If you plan mainly short rail trips, individual tickets are often your best bet. But if your comparison shows that the cost of individual tickets adds up to anything close to the cost of a railpass, stick with the pass for its greater flexibility and ease of use.

Senior Travelers

In some European countries, senior travelers are entitled to big discounts on railpasses and individual rail tickets. Seniors age 60 or over can buy First Class BritRail passes for 15 percent below the regular First Class pass price (but regular Second Class passes cost even less). Scanrail Pass offers senior reductions in both classes of 11 to 12 percent for travelers 60 or over traveling in Denmark, Finland, Norway, and Sweden. Seniors 60 or over can also buy First Class tickets on Eurostar trains through the Chunnel at 27 percent below the regular First Class fare (but, again, regular Second Class tickets cost even less). You can buy all of these senior railpasses and tickets through links from the BritRail site.

If, however, you just plan no more than one longish one-way or round-trip train journey, buying individual tickets as you need them, with a senior discount, might cost less than any pass. (Discount-rate travel might be blacked out on peak days or at peak times.) Senior discounts of between 50 and 60 percent are available for individual tickets in Denmark, Finland, Luxembourg, Norway, and Portugal; all you need to qualify for your senior rail discount is your passport. You must first buy official senior ID, issued by the railroad, before you can buy discounted tickets in Austria, France, Germany, Greece, and Sweden. The maximum cost for ID is $66 (for Coach), but you'll get discounts of anywhere from 25 to 50 percent. You can have your ID issued on the spot at most main rail stations (have two passport-size pictures ready). Unfortunately, you can't buy these senior-discount tickets over the Internet (and U.S. travel agents generally don't sell them, either). You have to wait until you arrive in Europe to make reservations and buy tickets.

Other Countries

Japan opened its high-speed rail system even before Europe did, and it's one of the world's best. Several national and regional railpasses are available for extended touring. For Japan, a good place to start looking is a site operated by the San Francisco Office of the Japan National Tourist Organization (*www.sfjnto.org*), with information on individual tickets, routes and maps, railpasses, and airport train services. However, you can't buy through this site.

You might consider rail for local transportation in Korea and Taiwan (good service, but no passes). For train travel in Australia, check out the Australian site at *people.enternet.com.au/~cbrnbill/maps/austrail.htm*; it has basic route and ticketing information, plus links to the several independent rail operating companies, where you can reserve and buy some rail tickets online. You can also find at least some attractive train trips in many other parts of the world, but they're slow and infrequent—land cruises and sightseeing excursions rather than efficient transportation.

I wasn't able to locate any really good gateway sites to worldwide railway systems (the bulk of the rail sites seem to be designed for rail fans rather than travelers). The best place to start looking for rail information for your destination is at the country or region's general tourist site.

Wheels and Deals

For many travelers, driving a rented car is the only satisfactory way to explore a destination area. Fortunately, you'll find very few areas of the world where you can't rent cars for reasonable rates—and where you can't reserve online. However, except for a few very limited Internet specials, online booking won't cut your costs.

Driving the United States

You'll find it very easy to reserve a car over the Internet. As with airlines, you can search for the best rates among different suppliers, and some of them display Internet-only specials.

Hertz's site (*www.hertz.com*) is a good example of a convenient rental-car Web site. Once you're on the "Rates and Reservations" page, you start out with the usual dates and locations input boxes. Next, you have a lot of choices to make: the model of car you want to rent; the airline to which you want to apply the frequent flyer credit you earn on the rental; whether you're eligible for a discount or corporate rate; a promotion code (if you saw one in an ad or brochure); and whether you want such accessories as a ski rack, child's seat, cellular phone, hand controls (for some disabled drivers), or the Neverlost satellite navigation system. After you've entered all these specifics, Hertz responds with a detailed price estimate, including applicable local taxes and fees. After making your decisions and adjustments, if necessary, you can reserve and put down a deposit online. All in all, it's a very efficient site; other rental car sites, listed in the Appendix, are similar.

Although each rental is unique, I can pass along a few overall guidelines you might consider when you rent a car:

- No one company always has the best deals in every city, country, or region: To get the lowest rates, you must compare prices from as many different sources as you can find (or until you run out of patience). You can easily do these comparisons online (although you might get a still different quote over the phone).

- The cost per day of a rental is almost always lower when you rent by the week or weekend than when you pay by the day. All the sites I reviewed could easily handle weekly and weekend rates.

- Almost everybody qualifies for some sort of "discount." The amount of the discount can be substantial on expensive daily-rate rentals, but it's usually no higher than 5 to 10 percent on weekly and weekend rates. As one rental-car manager put it to me, "Just fan out all the charge cards, airline cards, car cards, and discount coupons you have, and the agent will select the best one."

- One-way rentals from one city to another are usually extremely expensive, except that you can sometimes pick up and return at different cities within the same state at no extra cost. Ditto for individual European countries.

Many of the big rental-car companies now list some Internet specials. Figure 7-6 shows the online special page from Avis (*www.avis.com*). You'll find similar deals—and similar pages—on the other companies' sites.

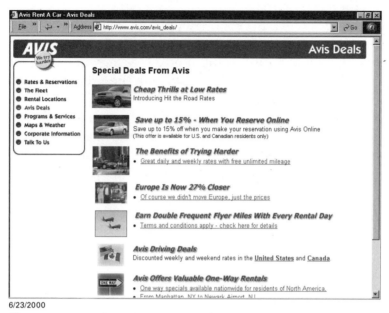

Figure 7-6. *Rental-car companies, like airlines, occasionally feature Internet-only specials.*

ED'S NOTEBOOK

Don't Go Too Small

In my experience, the most common rental-car mistake travelers make is trying to cut costs by renting a car that's too small. Any time your group includes three or more adults, or even two adults and a child or two, an economy or compact car is simply too small. The "guidelines" rental companies post aren't much help, either: They typically overstate the carrying capacity of various models. My take is that the minimum acceptable size for three or four people is "intermediate," and a notch up from that is even better.

Nobody wants to waste money on a rental. But moving up a class or two costs only $100 to $200 a week. That's far less than the cost of upgrading even one airline seat, and you'll probably spread it out over three or four people and over many hours of driving.

Rentals Outside the United States

Generally, when you rent a car in the United States, you can drive it into Canada with a minimum of additional paperwork, and vice versa. Let the rental company know, of course. You'll probably have to show proof of your right to have possession of the car and your liability insurance (and of course proof of U.S. residence for your re-entry). Your regular U.S. insurance probably covers you in Canada, but check to make sure. And renting a car in Canada is just like renting it in the United States.

Driving a U.S. rental car into Mexico can be a problem, especially if you want to drive beyond Baja California or a narrow border zone of a few miles into other Mexican areas. Some companies flat out prohibit you from taking cars into Mexico; others allow it, but with elaborate paperwork. Your U.S. insurance probably doesn't cover you in Mexico, so you'll have to buy extra insurance at the border. You can avoid the cross-border problems by renting on the Mexican side (such as in Tijuana rather than San Diego), but local rates are usually much higher than in the United States.

Many American tourists rent cars in Europe as casually as they rent in the United States. And most of the big rental-car companies handle car rentals in some European countries. A few independent rental agencies, such as Auto Europe (*www.autoeurope.com*) and Kemwel Holiday Autos (*www.kemwel.com*) specialize in European rentals. Figure 7-7 shows Auto Europe's rate page for France, with useful detail about individual models.

5/28/2000

Figure 7-7. *Auto Europe's Internet listings show car details and rates.*

HEADS UP

Rental-car offices in some European countries won't rent to travelers over 70 years of age. The policy varies by country and by company. If you're over 70, make sure the company you're considering will accept you in the country where you plan to rent. If you're facing a problem, you want to find out about it while you're making your reservation, not when you show up at the counter. Unfortunately, I've found no reference to upper age limits anywhere on the Internet.

Kemwel Holiday and Renault Eurodrive (*www.eurodrive.renault.com /anglais/*) also handle the *French lease* program. Basically, you buy a factory-new car, drive it, and resell it at a guaranteed price to the company at the end of your trip. All you have to pay is the difference between the buying and selling price; this system works for some arcane tax reasons. The minimum rental period is 17 days, and ordinary rentals can often beat lease rates for terms that short. But if you're touring for a month or more, the French lease is hard to beat. You can check options and reserve cars on the Internet.

Renting a car in Europe is no more complicated than renting in the United States. You can reserve and guarantee in advance on the Internet or through a travel agency. When you arrive, you'll find rental counters in the airport just like at home. All you need to rent is your U.S. driver's license and a credit card—even with MasterCard or Visa branding, a debit ATM card won't do.

HEADS UP

Although you don't need it at the rental counter, you might need an International Driving Permit if a police or traffic officer stops you. It's not really a separate license; it's an official translation of your regular license that, by U.N. rules, is acceptable in most countries of the world. You don't need it at all in an English-speaking country, and France and Switzerland generally don't insist. But other countries do, so get one at an AAA office for $10 (but not through the AAA Web site, where it isn't listed at all).

Like renting, driving in Europe is also easy. Almost all traffic signs are in graphic symbols rather than text, so you need the local language only to cope with street names and destination signs. Beware of one unexpected problem: Instead of collecting tolls, some European countries finance superhighways by selling special tax "stickers," which you must post on your windshield. If your rented car already has them for the areas you'll drive in, you don't need to buy new ones; but if the car doesn't have them, it's your responsibility. Check with the rental counter when you arrive. To familiarize yourself with European cars, check out the Moto Europa Web site (*www.ideamerge.com/motoeuropa/*), which provides lots of useful information about European car models; it also has information on buying new cars overseas, buying and selling used cars, and such.

Some Americans are a bit queasy about renting in the British Isles and driving on the "wrong" side of the road. My memory is that the first 15 minutes were sheer terror, after which it became routine. However, I do recommend an automatic transmission—with all the other differences, coping with a manual shift on the left side is disconcerting even for those of us who feel thoroughly comfortable with stick shifts elsewhere. The only places I hesitate to recommend driving are those where all traffic and street signs are in an alphabet you can't decipher.

Taxers Target Travelers

One of the more unwelcome developments in recent years is the targeting by taxing authorities of people who rent cars. The reason is obvious: For the most part, people who rent cars don't live in the jurisdictions that assess the taxes and therefore can't express their displeasure at the ballot box. It's today's ultimate taxation without representation. Nevertheless, today's compounding of multiple taxes and fees can add as much as 25 percent to the cost of a car rental in many parts of the world.

For the most part, avoiding these taxes is difficult, since many of them apply no matter where in a metro area you rent the car. However, you can sometimes avoid airport taxes and fees by renting from a downtown office (off-airport locations near the airport usually don't escape these taxes). The tradeoff is that the extra cost and hassle of taking a taxi or bus to a downtown rental office might be worse than the tax bite. However, some airport taxes are now in the 10 percent range. On an expensive rental, it might pay for you to go offsite for your rental.

Piling On the Extras

Rental-car companies have been notorious for keeping the featured prices low, and then piling on the extras when you arrive at the rental counter. Taxes and fees, of course, they're forced to collect. But they have their own extras, as well.

The worst offender over the years has been the collision-damage or loss-damage waiver (CDW or LDW). In exchange for a payment up to $20 a day (often more overseas), rental-car companies waive their right to charge you for any damage to the rented car while it's in your possession. Most of you can avoid this gross overcharge. There's a good chance that your regular auto insurance covers you in a rental car at no extra cost; check your policy for particulars. Also, most American Express cards, all Diners Club cards, and most Gold or Platinum MasterCard or Visa cards provide no-cost collision coverage when you use the card to rent a car. Buy the CDW/LDW only if you don't have either protection. Other forms of rental car insurance are also overpriced and, for the most part, they duplicate coverages you probably already have through umbrella, homeowners', or tenants' policies.

Another gouge is the charge some rental car companies assess for an extra driver—anyone other than the person who rents the car. Charges can run as high as $5 a day or $20 a rental. That charge is pure gouge: I can't see how trading off the driving with your sister-in-law increases the car rental company's costs by as much as a penny, let alone several dollars a day. Some companies exempt spouses and business colleagues from this charge; others don't. If you plan to share the driving chores on a trip, make sure you rent with a company that doesn't assess an extra-driver charge. Unfortunately, I didn't see any Web sites where you could check on that particular charge.

Insurance: Hate It but Need It

Whenever you take more than a short trip, you need to consider one or two types of travel insurance to fill any gaps your regular life and household or tenant policies don't cover. You can buy any needed travel insurance online, either from an agency site or directly from an insurance company or broker.

You must consider trip-cancellation or trip-interruption insurance (TCI) any time you put up a large deposit or prepayment for any form of travel. TCI makes up the difference between the amount you paid and what, if anything, you can collect in the way of refunds if you should unexpectedly need to cancel a trip between the time you pay and your departure date. It also covers any extra costs when you have to interrupt a trip you've already started. You need it whenever the up-front money you have at risk is more than you could afford to walk away from if you had to cancel.

HEADS UP

Do you need special medical or hospital insurance for travel? If you have health coverage at home, either fee-for-service or HMO, it probably covers you outside the country, as well; check your program to be sure. However, Medicare does not cover seniors outside the United States. If your Medicare supplement doesn't include such coverage (some programs do, others don't), you will need special coverage. Fortunately, the better TCI policies include as much medical coverage as you're likely to need as part of the base price.

You must usually prepay in full for a cruise, tour package, vacation rental, or other big-ticket travel product, often up to a year in advance. Some prepayments are totally nonrefundable; with others, cancellation penalties can be stiff, especially close to departure date. And after you begin your trip, changing your return plans can be very costly, especially if you need special emergency transportation.

TCI pays off in the event that you, a traveling companion, or a close family member at home falls sick or suffers a severe accident, either before or during a trip; if your tour operator or cruise line fails; if your destination area is suddenly hit with terrorism or a natural disaster; if your house is severely damaged; if you're called to jury duty; or if similar situations arise. TCI also pays the difference if you have to return home early and your travel companion has to continue the trip alone. And most pay for emergency medical evacuation, should you need it.

The cost of TCI is based on the amount of money you have at risk; prices on the best policies also vary with your age. Rates run from a little over $3 per $100 of coverage to as much as $9 per $100 of coverage. The least expensive TCI policies are available on the Internet from CSA Travel Protection (*www.csatravelprotection.com*), TravelGuard International (*www.travel-guard.com*), or a CNA policy from an independent agency such as Travel Protection Services (*www.travelprotect.com*). Figure 7-8 shows one of CSA's rate pages.

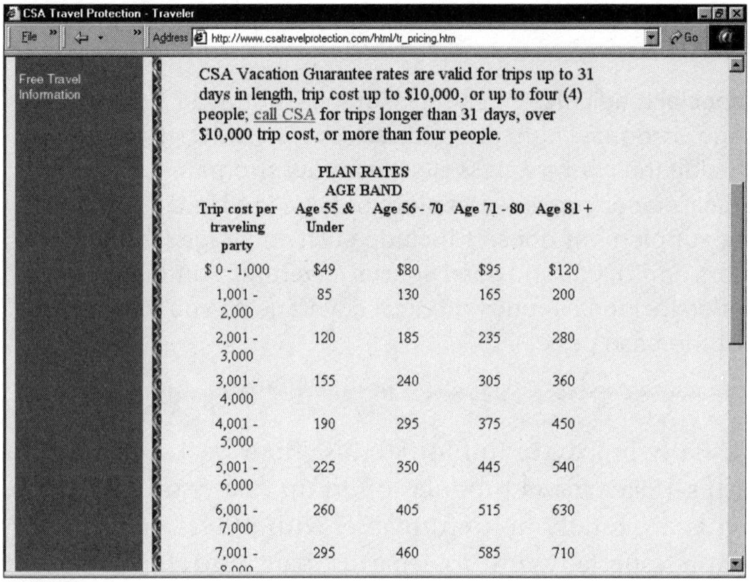

CSA Vacation Guarantee rates are valid for trips up to 31 days in length, trip cost up to $10,000, or up to four (4) people; call CSA for trips longer than 31 days, over $10,000 trip cost, or more than four people.

PLAN RATES
AGE BAND

Trip cost per traveling party	Age 55 & Under	Age 56 - 70	Age 71 - 80	Age 81 +
$ 0 - 1,000	$49	$80	$95	$120
1,001 - 2,000	85	130	165	200
2,001 - 3,000	120	185	235	280
3,001 - 4,000	155	240	305	360
4,001 - 5,000	190	295	375	450
5,001 - 6,000	225	350	445	540
6,001 - 7,000	260	405	515	630
7,001 - 8,000	295	460	585	710

5/28/2000

Figure 7-8. *Age-based insurance from CSA and competitors is the best TCI deal.*

Agency sites (and storefront travel agencies) sell TCI, and you can buy it when you buy your other travel services. In fact, many agencies now automatically bill you for TCI, with a disclaimer that you must sign if you want to decline it. That's OK, as far as it goes; unfortunately, some agencies sell insurance that costs more than you need to pay. Use the low-cost policy prices as a benchmark: If anyone tries to sell a more expensive policy, decline it and buy one of the low-cost policies instead. Or just buy one of the low-cost policies from the start.

Don't buy TCI from a tour operator: If the operator that sells you the insurance fails, the insurance won't cover the failure. Don't buy a cancellation waiver from your cruise line or tour operator, either; although it's sometimes cheaper than true TCI, its coverage is far too limited.

An important detail: If you pay for your TCI in full within 7 or 14 days (it varies among insurance companies) of your first prepayment or deposit, most insurance companies will waive any exclusions due to pre-existing medical conditions.

Using Plastic Money

Nothing frustrates travelers more than foreign exchange. When you buy something outside the United States, it seems as if everyone has a hand in your pocket: merchants, banks, and exchange offices. Actually, the facts are fairly straightforward: You always lose something when you exchange currencies, but judicious use of plastic can keep those losses to a minimum. Here's my advice:

- Put as many of your expenses as you can on a charge card. If you use one of the right cards, you'll lose no more than about 1 percent on each transaction. That's much better than the 5 to 10 percent you can lose if you exchange dollars or travelers checks for foreign currency at a bank or exchange office; you lose even more if you exchange at a hotel. By "right" card I mean a MasterCard or Visa that does not slap its own surcharge on top of the 1 percent that the banks pay the international MasterCard or Visa networks to do the actual exchange. Also relatively good: American Express and Diners Club, which add a total of 2 percent to foreign billings.

- Use an ATM debit card for the bulk of the local currency you need. The exchange fee is that same 1 percent for the international networks. Beyond that, you pay a transaction fee—up to $5, but usually closer to $3—each time you use a foreign ATM, regardless of the amount you withdraw. Obviously, if you take out at least $200 each time, the percentage loss is small. Worldwide ATM locators are at *www.mastercard.com/atm/* (shown in Figure 7-9 on the next page) for Cirrus/MasterCard, and *www.visa.com/pd/atm/* for Plus/Visa cards. Do not use a credit card to withdraw cash, if you can help it: You'll pay surcharges, extra fees, and increased percentages on your entire balance.

6/23/2000

Figure 7-9. *MasterCard (and Visa) both have comprehensive worldwide ATM locators online.*

ED'S NOTEBOOK

Which Card Is Best?

The question of what's the best charge card for travelers is complicated. I favor a MasterCard or Visa card that earns one mile of frequent flyer credit on the airline I fly most for every dollar I charge; and Diners Club, which also earns a mile of credit per dollar in any big airline's program, while offering the industry's best rental-car collision coverage.

But each traveler's decision depends on a large number of factors: annual fee, APR, airline mileage, and other benefits. If you're shopping around, useful sites include CardWeb (*www.cardweb.com*) and Bankrate (*www.bankrate.com*), both of which provide extensive comparison tables for dozens of cards. Unfortunately, as of the summer of 2000, neither site showed which cards applied surcharges to foreign transactions.

When you travel outside the United States, take $100 or so in U.S. $20 bills for times when you need to exchange for just a little extra foreign currency to get you out of the country. Given the worldwide distribution of ATMs, I see no further need for travelers checks.

You probably don't need those currency-in-advance packages that are promoted in the United States. The old scare pitch about "arriving in a foreign country with no local currency, at a time when banks are closed" is no longer valid. These days, you can find ATMs at every important international airport.

The Web is full of sites that quote current exchange rates and calculate foreign equivalents of whatever amount you enter. Most home pages of large gateway sites have links to at least one. Among them are Oanda (*www.oanda.com*) and Universal Currency Converter (*www.xe.net/ucc/*).

Making the Call

Keeping in touch by phone while traveling has always been a problem for some travelers. The needs are even greater now, with so many of us demanding frequent access to e-mail and the Internet.

Away-From-Home Long Distance

Finding the best way to make long-distance calls when you're traveling is one of those perennial small-dollar, big-annoyance hassles. As with charge cards, the question is complicated, but I can set down a few guidelines for making long distance calls at reasonable rates while traveling in the United States:

- Hotels and pay phones in tourist areas often route your calls through very high-priced long-distance services, which rebate part of the inflated revenue to the owner of the phone. You can usually avoid the gouge by using a calling card.

- Your regular long distance carrier, local service provider, or both probably have nationwide calling-card plans. You can check out options online with AT&T at *www.att.com*, MCI WorldCom at *www.wcom.com*, Sprint at *www.sprint.com*, or your local operating company at its site.

- Although sometimes cumbersome to use, many prepaid phone cards also provide low per-minute rates from any phones in the country.

Overseas hotels are much more likely to slap you with a really big surcharge than hotels in the United States or Canada. Finding some way around hotel switchboards is therefore more important when you're on a foreign trip.

Contrary to what you might expect, the international call-home services operated by AT&T, MCI, and Sprint aren't always the least expensive way to call home. If you read their promotions carefully, you'll see that they don't even make that claim. What they do claim, rightfully, is that they're usually less expensive than charging calls to your hotel room—which can be astronomical from overseas hotels. What they don't tell you is that you can often cut costs even more by buying a calling card from the local phone company and using public phones.

When you buy overseas call-home service as part of a combined U.S. calling-card plan, however, the international calling-card rates from AT&T, MCI, and Sprint can be quite low. Unfortunately, you might not find their best deals on the Internet. The last time I did some digging into rates from these three companies, some of the better options weren't listed on the Web pages; instead, I had to call the phone companies.

Independent telephone companies often have lower-cost international calling programs than major U.S. or foreign phone companies. Probably the least expensive is the call-back system: You sign up with a service, which assigns you a dedicated number in the United States. When you want to make a call, you call that number from overseas and hang up after the first ring; the U.S. call-back switchboard then immediately calls you back, at very low U.S. rates rather than higher foreign rates, and provides you with a U.S. dial tone you can use to call out to any desired number—in the United States or even in another foreign country. Some callback systems even have voice prompting to ask for your room at a hotel switchboard; how well that works depends on how each hotel reacts to automated incoming calls.

Several Web sites provide extensive information and comparisons of overseas phoning options. Among these overseas phoning options are CallNOW.com (*www.callnow.com*), EZTEL Long Distance & Callback Services (*www.eztel.com*), and WorldWide Plus Telecom Services (*wwplus.net/longdist /#callback*).

As to Internet access, more and more hotels are equipping rooms with two telephone lines—one for voice, the other for hooking up your laptop computer or portable e-mail reader. Check with your Internet service provider (ISP) for away-from-home access numbers and procedures. If you travel overseas a lot, you're probably better off signing up with an ISP with worldwide local access numbers, such as MSN. Or, for casual use, drop in on one of the many Internet cafes that are sprouting up all around the world.

One warning: Apparently, these days, some hotel guests check in and immediately go online for hours at a time. Because that practice ties up hotel telephone lines, hotels have been retaliating by surcharging even local and toll-free calls after a certain period of time—20 minutes, for example.

Schlep a Phone

One way to avoid the hassles of both hotel switchboards and foreign pay phones is to bypass both of them: Rent a cellular phone, and keep it with you throughout your trip.

Your own cellular phone probably does not work outside North America (only a very few do), but you can easily rent a cellular phone from online vendors for extended trips in most developed parts of the world. Among these online vendors are Cellhire (*www.cellhire.com*), InTouch USA (*www.intouchusa.com*), and Planetfone (*www.planetfone.com*).

You can also rent cellular phones in the arrivals areas of some major world airports. Unfortunately, most airport Web sites don't tell you whether this particular service is available.

Beware...

In a chapter of grab-bag topics, here are a few possible pitfalls you might encounter on your journey:

- U.S. marketing agencies find it easier to sell railpasses than individual train tickets, so they push passes. But passes aren't always your best deal. Decide what you want first, and then buy what you want to buy, not what someone wants to sell you.

- U.S. rental-car offices are pretty much used to having savvy travelers decline CDW/LDW and rely on their charge cards for collision coverage. Overseas, however, you still find offices that try very hard to sell you CDW/LDW—even to the point of bending the truth about what is covered and what isn't—even though you have a card that covers you. True, charge-card coverage is invalid in a handful of countries (check with your card issuer); in those places you can't avoid the rental company's bad deal. Elsewhere, however, stick to your guns and refuse to pay the gouge prices.

- Some insurance or travel agencies will try to sell you much more expensive policies than the minimum TCI-medical plans I've noted, and they'll try to add additional coverages. Forget them: They either duplicate coverages you already have, are grossly overpriced, or both.

- A few hotels and pay phones block access to the more popular toll-free calling-card services, such as 800-CALLATT (for AT&T). If your call is blocked, you'll have to find a phone that isn't blocked, or just pay the higher calling rates. Alternatively, call the number you want to reach, stay on the line only long enough to pass along (or record) your current hotel number and room number, and have your party call you back at cheap direct-dial rates.

8 Troubles, Scams, and Deceptions

Quick Trip Through Chapter 8

Travel provides fertile soil for misdirection, deception, and scam, and you can encounter troublesome traps online and offline. Common ones are:

- Hidden extra charges on Internet auction and sale prices.

- Tie-in deals that pad the price of one tour component to claim that something else is "free."

- Vacation certificates that, at best, require you to pay far more than the promotion would lead you to believe or that demand your presence at a high-pressure timeshare sale; at worst, they're outright frauds.

- Card mills that promise you'll make a lot of money selling travel or that you'll "travel like a travel agent." Both claims are, at best, questionable; at worst, they're lies.

I'm not talking about just scamsters here; the travel industry's big-name suppliers—airlines, hotel chains, cruise lines, and tour operators—make many wild promotional claims. And because consumers tend to trust big-name companies, people are willing to swallow just about any claim about travel. In effect, the industry has erected an umbrella of deception under which scamsters can flourish.

Protecting yourself is fairly easy, however. The worst of the problems are easily recognizable; you can just reject them.

Arguably, promotional standards in the travel industry are lower than in any other large consumer marketplace. I see two main reasons:

- Travel has a powerful allure—people want to believe that the exaggerated claims they see are real.

- It's easier to get people excited about a trip to Hawaii than about a refrigerator.

Greedy promoters have been quick to take advantage of the umbrella of deception that the travel industry has created. They continually bombard you with offers and claims that range from slightly overstated to out-and-out fraud, with just about every conceivable intermediate variation.

You can spot—and avoid—most of the deceptions and scams by applying a simple rule: "If it looks too good to be true, it probably is too good to be true." Granted, that rule might exclude a few genuine offers. But, in general, nobody ever lost anything by following it.

Although the fine print and communications media change, the basic deceptions and scams are fairly simple. Here's my list of the major ones you can currently expect to find online.

Hidden Extras

Beyond being outright fraud, hidden extras are perhaps your greatest risk of deception when you buy on the Internet. They're especially prevalent in online auctions, although you see them in other promotions, as well. They generally take one of two forms: phony fees and charges, and tie-ins.

Phony Fees and Charges

Suppliers often tack what they call "fees" or "service charges" onto the highlighted prices. In cruise promotions, the extras are often labeled "port charges and taxes." No matter what the promoters call them, such add-ons are phony. They're really nothing but a portion of the full price, broken out and given a plausible label for the sole purpose of making the featured price look lower than it really is.

Add-on fees are legitimate when travel suppliers collect them on behalf of governments, port authorities, or airports and pass them through directly to the taxing agency. Legitimate fees like these are pretty much confined to air tickets, where you can pay up to $90 round-trip in a combination of airport fees and charges for customs and immigration agencies.

Cruise lines, too, collect legitimate customs and immigration charges. However, as noted in Chapter 5, some online cruise agencies split out an arbitrary portion of the true price, call it "port charges and taxes," and deduct that amount from the true price to highlight a phony lower price.

Of much smaller dollar value, but still confusing, are fees and charges for "handling" and "delivery" of travel documents. Some agency sites charge up to $20 per ticket; others don't. Ditto the $20 "fuel surcharge" you see on some tour packages that include airfare. Although $20 might not break your budget, the tail-end addition of an extra $20 to your bill can seriously distort a price comparison, especially when some suppliers include the extras in their advertised prices while others don't.

If Others Advertised Like the Travel Industry

"Brand-new 2000 Cadillac, only $6,999!*" at a car dealership.

"Free Breakfast Bacon!*" at a restaurant.

"32-inch TV Set just $199!*" at an electronics store.

These are the sorts of ad headlines you'd see if sellers in other markets advertised the way the travel industry does. How would the ads work? The reality would all be in the fine print. The car footnote would say "*per person, based on a six-passenger sedan." The restaurant fine print would say "*with the purchase of eggs and toast at $5.99." And the TV footnote would say "*plus $199 service and handling fee."

Mislead the consumer in big type; correct the distortion in fine print: This practice pervades travel advertising. Unfortunately, even governmental agencies—supposedly those charged with consumer protections—are willing to buy off on these tactics. *Caveat emptor* was never more relevant than in travel.

Tie-Ins

You often see "free" or very low-cost airfares in online promotions or auctions, with fine print indicating that you must buy at least a week's hotel accommodations from the same promoter to qualify for the low fare.

ED'S NOTEBOOK

Sloppy Words, Sloppy Thinking

The travel industry encourages sloppy thinking by its sloppy or misleading use of certain "hot button" words. For example:

"Discount" (as I noted in Chapter 3) is one of the most abused words in the travel lexicon. You get a true discount only when you buy something for less than the supplier's regular price for the exact same thing. A Geo Metro isn't a "discount" car because it's cheaper than a full-size Chevrolet, and a restricted excursion isn't a "discount" air ticket because it's cheaper than an unrestricted Coach ticket. Lower fare, yes; discount, no.

"Free" is another grossly abused term. Something is truly free only if you can get it without buying anything else, or if a supplier receives it at no cost from some other source and passes it along to you. Airfare to a cruise port, a companion air ticket, or a sightseeing excursion might be "included in the price" or "at no extra cost," but if you have to buy something else to get it, or if the supplier paid for it, it's not really free.

"Save" and "saving" are also badly mangled. The only way you can truly save money on travel is to stay home. When a hotel claims a reduced room rate "saves" you money, you could make a case for "saving" only if you're fully prepared to pay rack rate and unexpectedly get a lower price. But if, in the absence of a sale price, you'd actually shop around for a deal at some other hotel, you might not save anything. A supplier can specify the dollar amount of a price reduction, but only an individual consumer can determine how much of that reduction, if any, is really a saving.

I sometimes think that travel-ad copywriters' word processors are programmed to insert either "only" or "just" before every price figure. Yes, that's petty, but it's annoying to see these words used so often.

Other industries play these word games, too. But none play more assiduously than travel. Take care not to be subtly influenced.

Alternatively, you might find free or low-cost hotel rooms if you buy airfare from the same supplier.

You don't have to be an intellectual giant to figure out what's behind either of these promotions: The cost of what you do buy is padded enough to cover the cost of what you supposedly get free or at a give-away price. Yes, I know that the fine print says you pay the hotel's or airline's "regular" price, but you and I know that said regular price is, in fact, padded one way or another.

Often, the final price of a tie-in deal is not appreciably lower than the price of a comparable air-hotel tour package conventionally advertised. One promoter of tie-in schemes told me something to the effect that "we supply a good product; that's just the way we choose to promote it." Maybe so, but my take is that anyone who tries to fool you into thinking you're getting something free isn't above trying to fool you in other, less obvious ways, as well. Accordingly, I can only recommend you stay away from any supplier using this sort of promotional tactic.

"Pack Your Bags" Certificates

If you've never received a letter, fax, or e-mail message promising a Florida, Bahamas, or Mexican vacation or cruise for under $200, you've led a sheltered life. A few years ago, most so-called "vacation certificates" arrived by mail, looking like stock certificates, with a salutation such as "Pack your bags, Ed, you will receive a fabulous vacation." These days, you see them as e-mail messages and faxes. To avoid running afoul of fraud laws, promoters are careful not to promise you've "won" something free, but the sellers don't mind if you get that impression.

No matter what the medium, the end result is the same: an offer that looks like a fantastic buy. What's really happening is a different story. In general, you're looking at one of three scenarios:

- Some offers are bona fide—if misleading—promotions, in that if you pay the money, you eventually get the promised service. The catches are that everything is hyped (the "Bahamas cruise" is really a day-trip sightseeing excursion); you're usually required to pay a hefty service fee or equivalent in addition to the featured price; you're charged extra for practically everything (including a deck chair on the "cruise"); and the hotels at the promotional price are such fleabags that you're almost forced to upgrade—at extra cost, of course. The upshot is that, by the time you're through with fees and upgrades, you pay as much as if you'd bought a conventional tour package from a conventional supplier.

- Some offers are out-and-out frauds, where the promoter never intends to give you anything. You pay the featured price, perhaps pay an additional fee, and you're told to call for reservations a month or more in the future. When you first call, you're told that the program is so popular that your preferred dates are already sold out, and to try again in a month for different dates. About the third or fourth call, instead of a reservation agent, you hear "We're sorry, you have reached a number that has been disconnected or is no longer in service." Frauds of this type actually provide one or two travelers with a trip at a great price, so promoters can post rave testimonials.

- Other offers are promotions for timeshares. Yes, you actually get your cheap resort weekend at the promised price. But you get it only after you sit through a half day or full day of very high-pressure sales pitching for a timeshare (see "Timeshare Tribulations" later in this chapter). No matter how much sales resistance you think you have, beware: Those sales pitches are carefully scripted and very good. That free or low-cost weekend trip could wind up costing you $10,000.

HEADS UP

Vacation certificates often include the logos of well-known and respected suppliers, such as major hotel chains, cruise lines, and rental-car companies. But that's no guarantee that the promotion is sanctioned by the owner of the logo. I've found that most big travel companies give blanket permission to franchisees and independent agents to use their logos in promotional materials, and they make no effort to police misuse of those logos.

"Travel Like a Travel Agent"

Some agencies, including a few on the Internet, offer to sign you up as one of their outside travel agents. The industry calls these agencies *card mills* because they're so profligate in issuing travel-agent ID. "You can make money selling travel," goes the pitch; even if you don't, the travel agent

ID you get with the program allows you to claim big discounts on your own travel. You usually pay $495 to enroll in a program, although a few charge far more. Some of them are near-pyramid schemes (*multi-level marketing* is the euphemism of choice), where you're told you can make big bucks selling additional memberships rather than selling just travel.

What are the catches? First is the "make-money" claim. Yes, you do receive about half the commission on the sales you make, and yes, if you're diligent, you can make money selling travel that way. Home-based or "outside" agents are an important and recognized part of the travel distribution system, and some of them—and the agencies they work with—make good money. But selling enough travel to make a living, let alone a killing, is hard work—just ask any full-time travel agent. To do it right, you need to know a great deal about airlines, cruise lines, tour operators, destinations, and such. According to trade data, only a tiny percentage of cardmill agents actually make a significant amount of money.

As to the "travel like a travel agent" claim, the reality is that airlines, hotels, cruise lines, and such are well aware of the card mills and can easily distinguish between real and fake travel agents. Most suppliers give good deals only to agents who actually sell significant amounts of travel. Those that do give big discounts to fake agents usually give similar deals to any individual who wants to buy.

In early 2000, *Consumer Reports Travel Letter* had a staffer enroll in several of the programs to test the "discount travel" claims. The result? In most of the tests, the staffer actually paid more than the going price in discount markets open to anybody. Even in the few cases where the "agency" price was lower, differences were small, and nowhere near enough to offset the $495 fee.

Timeshare Tribulations

Some of the most troublesome travel promotions involve timeshare sales—where you buy the ongoing use, over a period of many years, of a week or a series of weeks (*intervals*, in timeshare-ese) in a resort development. Once the almost exclusive province of shady operators, the timeshare business has matured and now boasts such big names in the accommodations business as Marriott and Hilton. But just because they're honest doesn't mean these are good deals.

The biggest problem with timeshares is that, although they share many of the characteristics of conventional real estate, they lack one essential ingredient: resale value. If you buy a condo or cottage in a resort area—and buy it carefully—you can legitimately expect to retain the capital value, and perhaps even enjoy some appreciation. If you ever want to sell a timeshare, on the other hand, you'll be lucky to get back 10 cents on the dollar. Although the industry is striving to develop a viable resale market, it hasn't happened yet.

A second problem is that the timeshare developers' markups are in the range of 40 percent, rather than the 6 percent or so that you pay in real estate commissions. That's why timeshare promoters will go to such lengths to get their hands on you: They're so sure of the power of their sales pitches that they're willing to spend $200 or more for a "free" or subsidized vacation just to get you into the showroom.

Given these market realities, I've developed two rules about possible timeshare purchases:

- View the price of a timeshare as a cost, not as an investment. If the idea appeals to you, figure the buy-in as the price you pay for access. Of course, you still have to pay yearly maintenance and other fees.

- If you like the idea—and millions of satisfied owners do—buy from someone who wants to sell, not from a developer. Even with resale agency markups, you'll pay far less than the developer's asking price.

The Internet is an ideal medium for timeshare resale, and several resale sites are now in operation. One such is Timeshare Resales Worldwide (*www.vacation-realty.com*), which lists timeshares at no cost to owners; other sites are listed in the Appendix.

Choose a resale agency carefully, however; one of the more pernicious current scams is run by people who promise to resell a timeshare you no longer want. Often, the promotion will claim "People in Timbuktu are eager to buy unwanted American timeshares," or similar nonsense. Forget those promotions. All the scamsters really want is the fee of $500 or so they charge to "register" or list your timeshare: Once you pay, you'll never hear from them again.

Maybe I'm being a bit unfair by including timeshares in the misdirections and deceptions category rather than treating them as a subset of vacation rentals; many developers will surely accuse me of anti-timeshare bias. Moreover, quite a few of my friends are happy and satisfied timeshare owners. But I've seen so many deceptive timeshare promotions that, at least for now, I believe a warning is in order. Perhaps in the future industry practices will change and timeshare resale values will increase, and I will feel better about including timeshares in a discussion about vacation rentals.

Building Your Scam Firewall

Protecting yourself against Internet deceptions is straightforward. First and foremost, just being aware of them—knowing what to look for in the fine print—is enough to keep you out of lots of bad deals. Ditto keeping in mind the "if it looks too good..." rule.

Be wary about giving your charge card information to an online supplier you don't know or recognize as a legitimate player. Be especially careful about responding to e-mail spam from unknown promoters. Never give checking account numbers to any online source but an online bank.

Here are a few other scam warning signals—online or offline:

- Be careful with any promotion that tells you that you've been "specially selected" or singled out for a deal—a deal that isn't being offered to just anybody. Sure, if you're a prior customer, a supplier might give you early notice of a sale or even a good-customer discount. But when someone you've never heard of says you've been targeted for special treatment, chances are you won't like the "treatment" the promoter has in mind.

- Be wary of any offer with a really tight purchase deadline of a day or two: If you don't act immediately, you'll lose out on this opportunity. In reality, the opportunity you're likely to miss is the chance to be scammed.

- Watch out for promotions that ask you to make a telephone call where you pay a fee (beyond just the telephone charge). You know that 900 numbers are fee calls, but other promotions come with offshore fee-call numbers that you don't immediately recognize. In fact, be wary of any promotions from offshore outfits—the reason they're offshore might well be to elude the long arm of U.S. law.

- Be very cautious about any offer that requires you to "invest" up front in a long-term program. Yes, some programs are legitimate. But the potential for abuse is very high.

- Be suspicious when a promoter refuses to send written materials and give you enough time to review them; flat out forget the offer.

If you suspect outright fraud, check with the Federal Trade Commission (FTC) and file a formal complaint at *www.ftc.gov/ftc/consumer.htm*. You can also file at the National Consumer League's National Fraud Information Center & Internet Fraud Watch (*www.fraud.org*).

Safety and Security, Too

Not all travel troubles are the result of deceptions or scams. You must still watch out for possible safety and security problems. Several Internet sites provide information you might find useful:

- The U.S. State Department keeps tabs on foreign developments that might impact your travel plans. In particular problem areas, it issues travel warnings that, in effect, tell you to stay away from certain countries or regions that pose a serious security threat. You can access these warnings, along with a lot of other background information, at *travel.state.gov/travel_warnings.html*. Although these warnings are widely touted by various travel writers, I've found them to be only marginally useful. For the most part, the trouble areas listed are the ones you see in your daily headlines and on CNN. After all, do we really need the State Department to wave us away from visiting Eritrea or Bosnia?

- The U.S. Centers for Disease Control and Prevention routinely runs sanitation inspections on all cruise ships that call at U.S. ports. The results of those inspections are available online at *www.cdc.gov/nceh/vsp/vsp.htm*. The inspection scores are useful for identifying ships in real trouble—those with below-passing grades. However, differences of five or ten points within the passing-grade range don't seem to be significant enough to warrant influencing your choice of ship.

- The U.S. Federal Aviation Administration regularly grades the aviation safety practices of foreign countries. You can download these ratings (in Microsoft Excel or Adobe Acrobat format) from *www.faa.gov/avr/iasa/index.htm*. For the most part, the ratings don't contain many surprises: The economically advanced nations all earn good marks.

As an Internet shopper, you automatically enjoy one scam barrier: the chargeback provisions on charge-card sales. If you don't receive something you paid for with a charge card, you have the legal right to demand that your card issuer remove the charge from your bill or, if you've already paid, give you a refund. As far as I can tell, that provision is somewhat ambiguous, in that at least one of the applicable laws specifies that the provision applies only to dealings with suppliers in or near your home. There's also a 60-day limit, which can be inadequate for travel services you buy far in advance. However, I also understand that the charge-card companies are relatively liberal in the way they interpret the chargeback limitations.

Still, chargeback isn't a cure-all. It applies only if you fail to get a service entirely (as would be the case in an outright fraud), not if you got the service but didn't like it (as in a fleabag hotel accommodation). Avoiding a scam in the first place is far better protection than trying to get a refund after the fact.

When Things Go Bad

Quick Trip Through Chapter 9

The best way to avoid complaint hassles is to prevent problems from arising. This means examine the fine print before you buy any travel service, check and verify suppliers' claims, and avoid prepayments whenever possible—all of which you can do when you buy online.

If you do face a problem, either get it fixed quickly or bail out and make alternative arrangements. Enjoy your vacation time; argue about the money later.

You can initiate formal complaints against most travel suppliers online. But don't start a complaint process unless you're willing to follow it through to some resolution. Always ask for some specific compensation. And use whatever resources are available to you, online and off, to press your claim.

Over the course of a year, the travel industry satisfies the traveling needs and expectations of millions of people. During that same year, however, it also disappoints many thousands—some over relative trifles, others over serious failures to deliver. The Internet provides resources both for avoiding problems and for taking action when they occur.

An Ounce of Forethought...

"...is worth a pound of complaint," to reshape the old cliché. Clearly, the best solution to travel problems is to avoid them in the first place—and that's often easier than you'd think. Here are some suggestions:

- Examine the fine print before you buy anything—especially over the Internet, where you aren't working with a knowledgeable travel agent. A basic rule about travel packages is "If it isn't specifically promised, you won't get it." Disappointment often arises out of an assumption about what is actually included or a failure to understand some limitation or exclusion.

- Don't rely on the suppliers' blurbs for basic information about destinations, hotels, cruise ships, and such: A good copywriter and a photographer with a wide-angle lens can make a tiny ship cabin seem luxurious and a fleabag hotel look comfortable. Check out as much as possible in an independent online guidebook, as discussed in Chapter 2.

- Don't prepay unless you can't avoid it. Many of the most serious travel complaints center around refunds for unsatisfactory travel services. Paying as you go, as you do with hotels you book independently, solves this problem completely: If you're dissatisfied, pay for one night, move out, and find something better. When you're searching for deals on the Internet, seek out those that don't require prepayment.

Fix It or Leave It

A few years ago, my wife, Eleanore, and I prepaid for a four-night stay in Taipei at what looked in the tour operator's brochure like a perfectly adequate hotel. But when we arrived, we found a dump: shabby furnishings, uncomfortable beds, and an unsavory neighborhood. It wasn't just a single problem that could be solved; the entire operation was sloppy. Rather than put up with ongoing frustrations, we immediately repacked and headed for the Sheraton. Clearly, even with a discount, we paid a lot more. But we thoroughly enjoyed our stay in Taipei. And we negotiated a satisfactory (although only partial) refund of the original hotel payment from the tour operator when we returned.

We had one other alternative: Stay at the dump and agree not to let it get to us. Had we been on a tight budget, that would have been our reluctant choice—but only after promising ourselves that we wouldn't obsess about a "ruined" vacation.

That experience in Taipei illustrates a very important rule: The worst way to deal with a serious problem on a trip is to endure it and figure you'll make a complaint later. Instead, take quick and decisive action right away. As soon as you encounter the problem, decide on the minimum fix that will solve the problem, and request an immediate correction—a mechanical fix to an air conditioner that isn't working properly, a move to a different hotel room or cruise cabin, or whatever—from whomever is responsible. Set a realistic time limit for the fix and stick to it.

If the supplier can't or won't fix the problem by your deadline, bail out and find something else, even if you have to pay extra. That way you avoid wasting your irreplaceable vacation time and you strengthen your basis for a refund. All too often, suppliers refuse a refund on the basis that "the problem couldn't have been as bad as you say since you stayed the full week."

- Avoid "from" priced accommodations. Tour operators often include at least one really cheap hotel so they can feature a low price in big type (as in those "a week's stay *from* only $499" promotions) in a brochure or online. In my experience, all too many minimum-priced hotels are shabby. Going up one or two levels is usually a good investment in trip enjoyment.

- Keep detailed records of the purchase process—receipts, dates, places, and contact names—in case you later need to bolster a complaint and justify your request for refund. Where feasible, take photos and download or print screens; if other travelers are affected, try to record their names and addresses.

Inside the System: The Rights Stuff

Though people might have their own opinion about what might be the world's shortest book, my candidate is *Air Passengers' Rights*. As an air traveler, though, you should consider yourself lucky to have even this small amount of protection; for other travelers, there aren't any such books.

Air travelers have only one specific right, established by law: compensation when they're bumped due to overbooking. If an airline overbooks a flight and then bumps you, Federal law requires that it get you to your destination as quickly as possible; in addition, the airline is required to pay you up to $400, depending on how late you are, the price of your ticket, and where you're flying.

Lots of travelers know about that rule—if anything, it's overpublicized by the travel press. What many travelers don't realize is that it applies only in the narrow instance of bumping because of overbooking. It does not apply if you're bumped for any other reason, or if your flight is cancelled or seriously delayed.

The only other legal requirement that applies strictly to air travelers is one mandating that each U.S. airline develop policies about how they handle various consumer problems, and that they make these policies available to travelers. There are no specific policy conditions—just that the policies be there. For the most part, these policies are pretty vague: "We will do what is appropriate to the circumstances."

Make Your Complaint Work

Except in the most egregious cases, getting a refund from a travel supplier is a challenge. You could be involved for months and months, with extensive paperwork, phone calls, or e-mail messages.

If all you want to do is to get your dissatisfaction on the record, one letter should do the job. No matter how much an airline stiffs you, your complaint will at least count on the consumer complaint reports. And even if it does nothing, a complaint against some other supplier will at least be counted in a consumer database such as that maintained by the Better Business Bureau.

But if your complaint is significant, and if you're seeking real compensation, don't start unless you intend to finish—and unless you're

**Inside the System:
The Rights Stuff** (continued)

Last year, the airlines—acting under the threat of genuine passenger-rights legislation in Congress—agreed to develop "Customer Service" plans. The only significant improvements were promises to publish seat dimensions and the number of seats allocated to frequent flyer awards—promises that the giant airlines have, by and large, implemented. The rest of the plans, for the most part, are vaporware—simply repeating promises the airlines had already been making (and not keeping) in one form or another, for years. Moreover, the plans provide no accountability: lots of promises, but nothing about what happens when the airlines fail to keep even their modest promises.

One other legal protection is afforded, but just to travelers who buy package tours using charter air travel: mandatory escrow accounts that protect prepayments against misuse by tour operators (discussed in Chapter 6). In addition, several states have traveler-protection laws.

Despite the absence of other specific travel laws, however, ordinary contract law does apply to travel transactions. Most successful suits by consumers against travel suppliers are based on contract law rather than any specific rights provisions.

The Department of Transportation's (DOT) "Fly rights" pamphlet is some 58 pages long (the online file at *www.dot.gov/airconsumer /flyrights.htm* is 81 KB). But more than 90 percent of the text is just a laundry list of familiar travel "tips," having nothing to do with real rights. The true rights stuff is limited to a few short paragraphs—mainly about overbooking.

willing to endure the inevitable anger and frustration you'll feel during the process.

If you decide to press a complaint, here is my nine-step formula. It won't work with a supplier that intends to stiff you, no matter what, but it will give you your best shot with a supplier that at least tries to be responsive to customers:

1. Gather all the evidence and paperwork and file it where it's safe but accessible. Specifically, make sure you have backup materials (brochures, contracts, and such) that describe what you were promised and what you actually received, if different. Download or print screens from the company's Web site, as appropriate.

2. Total up your losses—especially any out-of-pocket expenses or the costs of substitute arrangements. Where appropriate, add a reasonable figure for loss of vacation time, discomfort, and other intangibles.

3. Know your rights. If your problem is with an airline, check out the DOT's consumer protection site at *www.dot.gov/airconsumer/* (see Figure 9-1). Non-airline travelers have no comparable rights specified by law. Regardless of fine print and disclaimers, however, a reservation or a ticket is a binding contract, and your rights under contract law are substantial.

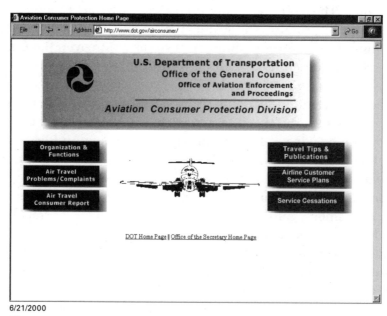

6/21/2000

Figure 9-1. *The DOT's site lists travelers' rights and accepts airline complaints.*

Online Travel

4. Decide what you want as a settlement: cash, a voucher for future service, frequent flyer or frequent stay points, or some other tangible compensation. In submitting a complaint, the biggest mistake travelers make is failure to ask for some specific compensation. If you're willing to use the supplier again, suppliers are usually far more willing to part with future credit than cash.

HEADS UP

Think carefully and check the conditions thoroughly before you accept a supplier's voucher as compensation. If you're mad enough, you might never want to use that supplier again. Vouchers often have a relatively short validity period—and a voucher that expires before you're prepared to use it is totally worthless. Also worthless: a voucher for a few dollars off or a small percentage discount, if you can apply it only to the list price of a service (such as a cruise) that is widely discounted.

5. Write or e-mail the first letter. Many supplier Web sites (see the Appendix) provide e-mail addresses or postal mail addresses for consumer complaints. Or find the supplier's contact information through a gateway site such as PassengerRights at *www.passengerrights.com*. State exactly why you're complaining; include dates, times, ticket/flight /room/cabin numbers, and the names of personnel you dealt with; and include photos and statements from other travelers, when available. Document your losses and extra payments, with *copies* of receipts (be sure to keep copies for yourself). Say exactly what you want; don't rely on the supplier to volunteer an offer. Keep your letter concise and focused on the key problem. If you feel compelled to recite a laundry list of mistakes and miseries, send it as an appendix. State your case in a positive way; you want to gain sympathy, not anger the person who reads your letter.

6. Give the supplier a chance to respond to your first letter before you escalate the confrontation. If the initial response includes any sort of compensation, treat it as an admission that your case has merit. If it's at all reasonable, accept it; otherwise, prepare a counteroffer.

7. Send your second letter. Only rarely does your first letter elicit more than a form response: "We're sorry for the problem; we value your opinion; we strive to please all our customers; we hope to see you again soon; have a nice day." The success of your complaint really hinges on your second letter. You restate your complaint, showing point-by-point how the supplier failed to address it or respond to your suggested settlement. Emphasize that you're really serious about compensation and expect a genuine response to your specific problem, and set a date for a response. If the supplier gave you an inadequate original offer, counter it.

8. If the second letter doesn't elicit some reasonable settlement, it's time to call for the cavalry of outside assistance, for which you have several options:

- You can submit your complaint through an online complaint agency such as PassengerRights.

- With an airline, you can register your complaint through the DOT site.

- If your argument is with a travel agency that belongs to the American Society of Travel Agents (ASTA), you can ask the Association to mediate your dispute—its site at *www.astanet.com* explains the process, but didn't accept online requests as of the summer of 2000.

- With a tour operator that belongs to USTOA or NTA, you can ask for the association's consumer aid, but only if a member operator fails (see Chapter 6).

- Better Business Bureaus (*www.bbb.org* and *www.bbbonline.org*) can provide mediation or arbitration services (see Figure 9-2), but only if suppliers agree. If nothing else, you can register your complaint in the BBB database.

- Travel and consumer media might help, but only if your complaint has news value.

Unfortunately, you'll find no specialized government or industry agencies to deal with consumer complaints against cruise lines, hotels, or car-rental companies, online or offline. If you want to let off a little steam, log on to one of the consumer complaint sites or newsgroups.

Unless you suspect fraud, don't bother a district attorney or an attorney general.

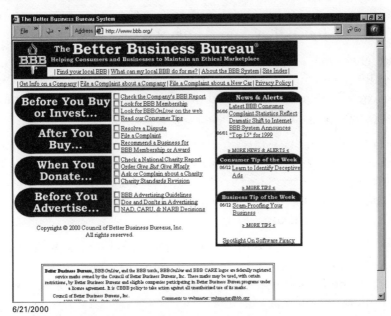

Figure 9-2. *Better Business Bureaus can provide mediation, but only if the supplier agrees.*

9. If a supplier stonewalls you—and your complaint has real substance—haul the supplier into court. You can handle a small-claims court action yourself. A lawyer is justified only if the complaint involves some big money.

If all these steps seem to entail a lot of potential aggravation, it's because they do. But in my experience, if you're not willing to follow through as far as court, you might as well not begin the process at all.

Heading for Court

Fortunately, I've never had a complaint with a travel supplier so severe that I even considered legal action. But when I was editor of *Consumer Reports Travel Letter*, I heard from many readers who had been mistreated badly enough that they went for legal action. Here are some of the conclusions I drew from those experiences:

- Travelers with realistic complaints tend to do reasonably well in small claims court, provided their claims are documented. In the decisions I've read, judges had little patience with big corporate suppliers' bluster and evasion.

- Small consumer lawsuits are feasible only against suppliers that have some sort of office or official presence in or near a consumer's home city. "Long arm" doctrines make it possible to sue an airline, for example, if the airline has nothing more than a sales office in the area.

- On the other hand, small lawsuits against remote suppliers are almost impossible to pursue. That's one of several reasons why I recommend that consumers deal with hometown or national suppliers as much as possible.

Endnote:
Using a Travel Agent

As I noted in Chapter 1, you don't have to choose between using the Internet and a travel agent. Many of the online agencies discussed in the various chapters and listed in the Appendix are travel agencies that provide help with travel services, and many personal-service travel agencies maintain Web sites, as well. Ideally, you can combine the best features of both.

Internet for Data

You can't beat the Internet for amassing a lot of information, quickly, about almost any travel subject. That characteristic has both an upside and a downside. The upside is how much and how varied the information is that you can get without ever leaving your desk. The downside is that you might have to filter through thousands of hits to get the information you need. Also, you often find that none of those thousands of hits exactly answers your question.

The Internet is at its best when you are searching for airfares and hotel rates. Provided you get off to a reasonable start (which, I hope, this book helps you do), you definitely can find the lowest airfare for any given trip. You also stand a good (but not perfect) chance of finding out how to get an even lower airfare by tweaking your itinerary. Similarly, you can probably find the best available hotel deal anywhere you're likely to head. Given enough online time, in fact, you can do as well as a travel agent at those tasks—maybe better, in the case of Internet-only deals.

The Internet can also do a good job of locating last-minute tour and cruise deals, although probably no better a job than a travel agent could do. And it's a great resource if you're looking for operators of unusual special-interest tours.

So far, Internet-only travel agencies have not bridged the personal-service gap. They can't offer counsel based on personal experience and knowledge. However, given the rapid pace of online change, I wouldn't be surprised to see one or more of the online agencies provide some sort of personal-service mode in the near future.

Travel Agents for Savvy, for Speed

You can't beat a good travel agent for knowledge and background in travel details, for exercising judgment about the bewildering variety of options in the travel marketplace, and for having ready answers to many of your likely questions. A good travel agent, for example, should know whenever the giant airlines mount a sale and how long the purchase window will remain open; which low-fare airlines serve your home city and where they go; which nearby airports might offer lower fares than your regular home airport (and which other destinations, close to your target travel area, might be cheaper to fly into); and which hotel and rental-car chains are offering promotions. The agent should be able to tell you, immediately, what it might take you hours to find on your own.

A travel agent is at his or her best when matching you to the right package tour, cruise, or resort vacation. The agent should know, without having to check each time, which tour operators have the best deals from your home city to popular destinations ranging from Las Vegas to London. The agent should have a good feel for the personalities of individual resorts and cruise lines and be able to recommend ones that best fit your particular requirements. The agency should have reliable, prescreened sources for discounts: consolidator air tickets, hotel broker rates, and cruise deals. And the agent can provide these features to you without you having to spend hours searching the Internet.

As mentioned in Chapter 1, a good travel agent should be able to come up with "Plan B" when your first plan turns out to be impractical, for one reason or another. An agent can also help with problems that arise during a trip. If you miss a connecting flight, for example, or suddenly need to change your plans, you can usually solve your problem more quickly by calling a travel agency back home than by standing in line at a mobbed hub airport or trying to reorchestrate your trip from a pay phone.

There's also a question of cost, at least in some cases. These days, most travel agents charge a small fee—in the neighborhood of $20—to issue an airline ticket. But the fee question has been somewhat overblown: With most other travel services—package tours, cruises, hotel and resort accommodations, and rental cars—agents continue to receive their compensation from suppliers, not clients. And very few other suppliers have tried to squeeze travel agents out of the picture, as the airlines have. Even then, that squeeze isn't total: While airlines' policies force most agencies to charge for issuing ordinary tickets, they still compensate agents the traditional way for selling their tour packages.

Many personal-service agencies encourage clients to use the Internet for exploration and for gathering information. They can also handle some client inquiries online through their sites and by e-mail. They can even obtain Internet-only deals, although they might have to charge you a fee.

Which Way?

In many ways, your buying strategy boils down to a matter of your buying preference. If you enjoy doing your own digging, the Internet gives you essentially as much information as professional agents get from their computer reservation systems. But by choosing to do all your own digging, you are, in effect, betting your personal skills against those of a trained professional. Some of us do that routinely in certain situations: when we invest on our own, when we do fix-it chores around the house, or when we install our own sound systems. We're less likely to do it when confronted with a legal or medical problem. So where does travel fit in the spectrum between do-it-yourself work and work that requires professional assistance? That's your call. Either way, the Internet can be a valuable tool: as the avenue through which you do your own planning and buying, or as a channel to a professional if you think you need help.

Appendix: Travel URLs

The Appendix is organized in alphabetical order by broad topic; you'll find that each broad topic is broken down into several smaller subtopics, which are also organized alphabetically for quick access. To cut down on the total length of the Appendix, each URL is listed only once—I hope in the category where it fits best. A few of these sites require that you enroll and pay a fee or dues in order to have access to all of the site content, but I've tried to avoid those when possible.

Accommodations

You'll find a wide range of information about accommodations on the Internet. I've listed several types of accommodations, although you might be able to find even more through a gateway site. I've listed only sites that cover multiple hotels, resorts, B&Bs, rentals, and such—that means agencies and large chains. Many individual accommodations also have Web sites, which you can find via the gateways or through a search engine.

Agencies

Many online agencies sell a broad range of travel services: air tickets, hotel accommodations, cruises, tours, and other services. Most agencies claim to offer "discounts" of one sort or another. The decision to list any given site here rather than as an airline, hotel, cruise, or tour agency is a judgment call, because most of the airline agencies also sell other travel services. My decision was based on relative emphasis; feel free to disagree. The list also includes the 10 largest full-service travel agencies in the United States, all of which have Web sites. Certainly, if you're looking for all possible information, check out the airline agencies as well as these general agencies.

11th Hour Vacations: *www.11thhourvacations.com*

1travel.com: *www.1travel.com*

4Airlines: *www.4airlines.com*

4GOING.TO: *www.4going.to*

AltaVista Travel with TRIP.com: *thetrip.onlinevacationmall.com*

American Express: *travel.americanexpress.com*

American Travel Abroad: *www.amta.com*

Best Fares: *www.bestfares.com*

ByeByeNOW.com: *www.byebyenow.com*

Carlson Wagonlit Travel: *www.carlsonwagonlit.com*

CheapAirlines: *www.cheapairlines.com*

Club Tripmakers: *www.clubtripmakers.com*

Concierge.com: *www.concierge.com*

The Connected Traveler: *www.connectedtraveler.com*

DER Travel Services: *www.dertravel.com*

EconomyTravel.com: *www.economytravel.com*

ETN: *www.etn.nl*

Expedia.com: *www.expedia.com*

The Experienced Traveler: *www.x-trav.com*

Getaway.com: *www.getaway.com*

Global Online Travel: *www.got.com*

Interworld Travel: *www.interworldtravel.com*

Jalpak America: *www.jalpak.com/English/*

LastMinuteTravel.com: *www.lastminutetravel.com*

Lastminute.com (London): *www.lastminute.com*

Leisureplanet: *new.leisureplanet.com*

Liberty Travel: *www.libertytravel.com*

Lowestfare.com: *www.lowestfare.com*

MaritzTravel Company: *www.maritztravel.com*

mytravelco.com (cruises and airfares): *www.mytravelco.com*

Navigant International: *www.navigant.com*

Rosenbluth International: *www.rosenbluth.com*

Sato Travel: *www.satotravel.com*

Site59.com: *www.site59.com*

Smarter Living: *www.smarterliving.com*

TTRIP.com: *www.thetrip.com*

TicketPlanet.com: *www.ticketplanet.com*

TravelHUB: *www.travelhub.com*

Travelbreak: *www.travelbreak.com*

Travelocity.com: *www.travelocity.com*

Travelconsolidators: *www.travelconsolidators.com*

Travelscape.com: *www.travelscape.com*

Travelsites.com: *www.travelsites.com*

TravelSmarter: *www.travelsmarter.com*

Travelzoo: *www.travelzoo.com*

Uniglobe.com: *www.uniglobe.com*

Web Travel Secrets: *www.web-travel-secrets.com*

Worldtravel Partners: *www.worldtravel.com*

Auctions

The auctions on most of these auction sites are traditional: You, the customer, bid on a service. A few sites have reverse auctions: You offer a price and suppliers react.

Bidtripper.com: *www.bidtripper.com*

Boston.com Auctions: *www.auctions.boston.com*

CityAuction: *www.cityauction.com*

TheDailyAuction.com: *www.thedailyauction.com*

Egghead.com: *www.egghead.com*

Excite Auctions: *auctions.excite.com*

Inntopia.com: *www.inntopia.com*

iWant.com: *www.iwant.com*

MSN eShop Auctions: *www.auctions.msn.com*

Priceline.com: *www.priceline.com*

Respond.com: *www.respond.com*

SkyAuction: *www.skyauction.com*

eWanted.com: *www.ewanted.com*

Bed & Breakfast Agencies

The following online agencies locate and arrange bed & breakfast accommodations. Discounts are rare. Quite a few specialize in limited areas.

1-888-Inn-Seek: *www.1-888-inn-seek.com*

B&B Getaways: *www.bbgetaways.com*

B&B My Guest (United Kingdom): *www.beduk.com*

Bed & Breakfast Inns ONLINE: *www.bbonline.com*

Bed and Breakfast Inns of North America: *www.cimarron.net*

Bed And Breakfast Network: *www.bedandbreakfastnetwork.com*

BedandBreakfast.com: *www.bedandbreakfast.com*

Beds, Breakfasts & Inns: *www.bedsbreakfastsandinns.com*

InnCrawler: *www.inncrawler.com*

INNRoads: *www.inns.com*

InnSite: *www.innsite.com*

The Internet Guide to Bed & Breakfast Inns: *www.traveldata.com*

Lodging On The Web: *www.lodgingontheweb.com*

London Bed & Breakfast: *www.londonbandb.com*

North American Bed and Breakfast Directory: *www.bbdirectory.com*

Paris B and B: *www.parisbandb.com*

Rome Bed & Breakfast: *www.romebandb.com*

Home Exchange Agencies

The following sites facilitate no-rental exchanges of homes.

American-International Homestays, Inc.: *www.spectravel.com/homes/*

Gateway Home Exchange: *www.gatewayexchange.com*

European Holiday Home Exchange Club: *www.prodat.no/ehhec/*

Apollo Home Exchange (Denmark): *www.sima.dk/haneys/*

Home Base Holidays: *www.homebase-hols.com*

HomeLink International: *www.homelink.org*

International Home Exchange Network: *www.homexchange.com*

Ridéf: *www.exchange-of-homes.com*

Seniors Vacation and Home Exchange: *www.seniorshomeexchange.com*

SERVAS International: *www.servas.org*

Trading Homes International: *www.trading-homes.com*

Timeshare Agencies

The Internet might become an effective resale market for timeshares. Here are a few agencies that buy and sell *intervals,* or timeshares.

All Islands Timeshare Resales (Hawaii): *www.timeshare-hawaii.com*

Preferred Timeshare Resales of Lake Tahoe: *www.preferredtimeshare.com*

Resort Condominiums International: *www.rci.com*

Timeshare Resales Worldwide: *www.vacation-realty.com*

Timeshare Travel: *www.timesharetravel.com*

Vacation Rental Agencies

The Internet is an ideal source of information and a great booking channel for vacation rentals. In the following list, I did not include any sites that cover just one property.

1001 Villa Holiday Lets: *www.1001-villa-holidaylets.com*

1st Choice Vacation Properties: *www.choice1.com*

A1Vacations: *www.a1vacations.com*

About London: *www.aboutlondon.com*

Accessible Vacation Home Exchange (for disabled travelers): *www.independentliving.org/VacationHomeSwap.html/*

At Home in France: *www.athomeinfrance.com*

Barclay International Group (Europe; the Caribbean; the United States): *www.barclayweb.com*

Caribbean Villas on the Web: *www.cvillas.com*

Condominium Travel Associates: *www.condotravel.com*

CyberRentals.com: *www.cyberrentals.com*

Doorways (Europe): *www.villavacations.com*

Dordogne Rental: *www.dordognerental.com*

Drawbridge To Europe: *www.drawbridgetoeurope.com*

EProperties: *www.eproperties.com*

Farm Holiday Bureau (UK): *www.farm-holidays.co.uk*

France For Rent: *www.franceforrent.com*

French Connections: *www.frenchconnections.co.uk*

GetAwayRentals.com (California, Oregon, Washington): *www.getawayrentals.com*

Guest in Italy: *www.guestinitaly.com*

Hideaways International: *www.hideaways.com*

Holiday Zone (United Kingdom): *www.holidayzone.co.uk*

Homebase Abroad (Italy, Paris): *www.homebase-abroad.com*

HomeExchange.com: *www.homeexchange.com*

HomeRentalGuide.com: *www.homerentalguide.com*

Insightful Travelers (Paris): *www.latoile.com*

Intervac International Home Exchange: *www.intervac.com*

Italian Vacation Villas: *www.villasitalia.com*

ItalianVillas.com: *www.italianvillas.com*

Just France: *www.justfrance.com*

Leisure Link International (condo rentals): *www.leisurelinkintl.com*

Locaflat (Paris): *www.locaflat.com*

Lodging On The Web: *www.lodgingontheweb.com*

OneWorld Travel (France, Scotland): *www.oneworld-travel.com*

Panache (Paris): *www.panacherental.com*

Personal Touch Relocation: *www.luxuryhousing.com*

Paris Short-Term Rentals: *www.qconline.com/parispsr/*

Quartier Montorgueil Properties, Inc.: *www.forparis.com*

Rentvillas.com (Europe): *www.rentvillas.com*

ResortQuest International: *www.resortquest.com*

ResortSource: *www.resortsource.com*

Rome Sweet Home: *www.romesweethome.com*

Sandcastle Realty (Martha's Vineyard): *www.sandcastlemv.com*

The Short Let Company (London): *www.short-term-lets.co.uk*

Toscana International: *www.toscanainternational.com*

Unusual Villas & Island Rentals: *www.unusualvillarentals.com*

Vacanza Bella (Italy): *www.vbella.com*

Vacation Homes Abroad (Europe): *www.vacationhomesabroad.com*

Vacation Direct (owner rentals): *www.vacationdirect.com*

Vacation Rentals by Owner: *www.vrbo.com*

VacationSpot.com: *www.vacationspot.com*

Villas and Voyages/The Savour of France: *www.villasandvoyages.com*

Villas by Linda Smith, Inc. (Jamaica): *www.jamaicavillas.com*

Ville et Village (France, Italy, Spain, Portugal): *www.villeetvillage.com*

World Wide Nest: *www.wwnest.com*

Camping

The following sites can help you make camping arrangements. You can also get camping information from some of the major park sites.

Camping-USA: *www.camping-usa.com*

Go Camping America (directory): *www.gocampingamerica.com*

Kampgrounds of America (KOA): *www.koakampgrounds.com*

Trek America: *www.trekamerica.com*

Dude Ranches

In addition to the following site, you might also find dude ranch information on some states' destination sites.

DudeRanches.com: *www.duderanches.com*

Hostels

For budget travelers, the following sites can help with hostel accommodations.

Hostelling International - American Youth Hostels: *www.hiayh.org*

Hawaiian Hostels: *www.hawaiian-hostels.com*

The Hostel Handbook: *www.hostelhandbook.com*

Hostels.com: *www.hostels.com*

Hostels of Europe: *www.hostelseurope.com*

Hotels and Resorts

You'll find a wealth of hotel and resort information on the Internet, whether by accessing a specific hotel chain, checking out an agency site, or using links from destination sites.

Agencies

The following agencies arrange hotel and resort accommodations. Most of them claim to provide discounts, but a few are simply list-price room locators. A few agencies specialize in just one or two areas or cities (as noted).

1 800 USA Hotels: *www.1800usahotels.com*

Accommodations Express: *www.accommodationsexpress.com*

All-Hotels: *www.all-hotels.com*

Amisto.com: *www.amisto.com*

Asia-hotels.com: *www.asia-hotels.com*

Association of Business Travellers (United Kingdom): *www.abt-travel.com*

British Hotel Reservation Centre: *www.bhrc.co.uk*

Budgethotels.com: *www.budgethotels.com*

Capitol Reservations (Washington DC): *www.hotelsdc.com*

Central Reservations Services, Inc.: *www.reservation-services.com*

Citywide Reservation Services, Inc.: *www.cityres.com*

Discount Asia Hotels: *www.discountasiahotels.com*

EURHOTELS: *www.eurhotels.com*

Eurotrip Accommodation Links: *www.eurotrip.com/link/Accommodation/*

Traveller Services (HK) Ltd.: *www.traveller.com.hk/*

Hostels.com: *www.hostels.com*

Hotel-Assist.com (London): *www.hotel-assist.com*

HotelBook.com: *www.hotelbook.com*

HotelBoulevard.com (France): *www.hotelboulevard.com*

Hoteldiscount.com: *www.hoteldiscount.com*

Hotel!Hotel! (London Paris): *www.dialspace.dial.pipex.com/hotel.hotel/*

HotelsOnline: *www.hotelsonline.com*

Hotel-UK: *www.demon.co.uk/hotel-uk/*

HotelWorld: *www.hotelworld.com*

Hot Rooms (Chicago): *www.hotrooms.com*

Impulse Preferred Travel: *www.impulsepreferred.com*

Las Vegas Hotels and Casinos: *www.las-vegas-travel.com*

Lodging.com: *www.lodging.com*

Motels.com: *www.motels.com*

PlacestoStay.com: *www.placestostay.com*

Quikbook: *www.quikbook.com*

ReservHOTEL: *www.reservhotel.com*

ResortLocator.com: *www.resortlocator.com*

Resorts International: *www.resorts-international.com*

Resorts OnLine: *www.resortsonline.com*

ResortSource: *www.resortsource.com*

SDHR, Inc. (Palm Springs, Phoenix, San Diego): *www.savecash.com*

Topaz Hotel Services, LLC (San Francisco, San Jose): *www.hotelres.com*

Travelnet: *www.orientaltravel.com*

TravelNow: *www.travelnow.com*

Travel Pick: *www.travelpick.com*

Travelscape.com: *www.travelscape.com*

USAHotelGuide.com: *www.usahotelguide.com*

Vacationland: *www.vacation-land.com*

WorldHotel: *www.worldhotel.com*

WorldRes.com: *www.worldres.com*

World Reservations Center (Mexico): *www.mexicohotels.com*

All-Inclusive Resorts

The following are representative all-inclusive resort chains that bundle room, meals, and most recreation activities into a single price.

Allegro Resorts: *www.allegroresorts.com*

Almond Resorts: *www.almondresorts.com*

Club Med: *www.clubmed.com*

Palace Resorts: *www.palaceresorts.com*

Sandals Resorts: *www.sandals.com*

SuperClubs Resorts: *www.breezes.com*

Chains

Most of the major hotel chains—and many smaller ones, too—maintain active Web sites. I've tried to list the more important ones here. A few of the foreign sites are in the local language only, but most of them have an English option.

Accor (France): *www.accor.com*

Adam's Mark Hotels & Resorts: *www.adamsmark.com*

AmeriSuites: *www.amerisuites.com*

Aston Hotels & Resorts: *www.aston-hotels.com*

Baymont Inns & Suites: *www.baymontinns.com*

Best Inns & Suites: *www.bestinn.com*

Best Western International, Inc.: *www.bestwestern.com*

Budget Host International: *www.budgethost.com*

Campanile (France): *www.campanile.fr*

Choice Hotels International (Clarion, Comfort Inn, Comfort Suites, Econo Lodge, MainStay, Rodeway, Quality, Sleep): *www.hotelchoice.com*

Coast Casinos: *www.coastcasinos.com*

Courtyard by Marriott: *www.courtyard.com*

Days Inn: *www.daysinn.com*

Doubletree: *www.doubletree.com*

Embassy Suites Hotels: *www.embassy-suites.com*

Fairfield Inn: *www.fairfieldinn.com*

Fiestamericana Hotels & Resorts (Mexico): *www.fiestamericana.com*

Forte: *www.forte-hotels.com*

Groupe Envergure: *www.groupe-envergure.fr/marque/marques.htm/*

Hampton Inn: *www.hampton-inn.com*

Hawaiian Hotels & Resorts: *www.hawaiihotels.com*

Hawthorn Suites: *www.hawthorn.com*

Hilton Hotels: *www.hilton.com*

Holiday Inn: *www.holiday-inn.com*

Howard Johnson: *www.hojo.com*

Hyatt Hotels & Resorts: *www.hyatt.com*

Inter-Continental Hotels and Resorts (includes Forum): *www.interconti.com*

Kempinski Hotels & Resorts: *www.kempinski.com*

Knights Inn: *www.knightsinn.com*

LaQuinta Inns & Suites: *www.laquinta.com*

The Leading Hotels of the World: *www.lhw.com*

Marriott International: *www.marriott.com*

Microtel Inns & Suites: *www.microtelinn.com*

Millennium Hotels and Resorts (includes Regal Hotels): *www.millennium-hotels.com*

Motel 6: *www.motel6.com*

Mövenpick Hotels & Resorts: *www.moevenpick-hotels.ch*

Outrigger Hotels & Resorts: *www.outrigger.com*

Posthouse (United Kingdom): *www.forte-hotels.com/hotel/posthouse /posthouse_f.html*

Première Classe (France): *www.premiereclasse.fr*

Radisson Hotels: *www.radisson.com*

Ramada: *www.ramada.com*

Red Roof Inns: *www.redroof.com*

Ritz-Carlton Hotels: *www.ritzcarlton.com*

Sheraton Hotels & Resorts: *www.sheraton.com*

Sofitel Hotels & Resorts: *www.sofitel.com*

Sol Meliá: *www.solmelia.es*

Sonesta Hotels, Resorts & Nile Cruises: *www.sonesta.com*

Super 8 Motels, Inc.: *www.super8.com*

Swissôtel Hotels & Resorts: *www.swissotel.com*

Thistle Hotels: *www.thistlehotels.com*

Top Resa (France): *www.topresa.com/liens.htm#hotels*

Travel Inn (United Kingdom): *www.travelinn.co.uk*

Travelodge (United Kingdom): *www.travelodge.co.uk*

Travelodge (United States; includes Thriftlodge): *www.travelodge.com*

Trump Hotels & Casino Resorts: *www.trump.com*

W Hotels: *www.whotels.com*

Westin Hotels & Resorts: *www.westin.com*

Wyndham: *www.wyndham.com*

General Information and Gateway Sites

Several of the following sites provide links to many individual hotel systems. Others provide a search capability.

All Hotels on the Web: *www.all-hotels.com*

Boutique Lodging International: *www.boutiquelodging.com*

Florida Hotels & Discount Guide: *www.flhotels.com*

Hotelamerica.com: *www.hotelamerica.com*

Hotelguide.com: *www.hotelguide.com*

HotelsTravel.com (contains links to dozens of hotel chains): *www.hotelstravel.com*

HotelView: *www.hotelview.com*

Official Hotel Guide Reviews: *www.traveler.net/ohgreviews/*

ResortQuest International: *www.resortquest.com*

ResortsandLodges.com: *www.resortsandlodges.com*

Resorts OnLine: *www.resortsonline.com*

Spafinder.com: *www.spafinders.com*

Pet-Friendly Accommodations

The following sites list accommodations that cater to travelers who are traveling with pets.

DogFriendly.com: *www.dogfriendly.com*

Dogpark.com: *www.dogpark.com*

Pet Vacations: *www.petvacations.com*

petswelcome.com: *www.petswelcome.com*

Takeyourpet.com: *www.takeyourpet.com*

TravelDog.com: *www.traveldog.com*

Privilege Card Accommodations

I found only one site focused on accommodations for half-price program members.

Privilege Card International (membership): *www.privilegecard.com*

Air Travel

The following sections provide listings of airline sites as well as sites that address other air travel–related issues.

Baggage Delivery

Using the following sites, you can arrange to have your baggage shipped ahead of you.

Excess Baggage: *www.excess-baggage.com/index.stm/*

Virtual Bellhop: *www.virtualbellhop.com*

Domestic Airlines

These are the giant U.S. airlines and the smaller airlines that generally offer the same levels of service and prices. I did not include any of the commuter airlines, because they operate almost all their flights under the banner of a major airline with which they are affiliated.

Giant Airlines

American Airlines: *www.aa.com*

Continental Airlines: *www.continental.com*

Delta Air Lines: *www.delta-air.com*

Northwest Airlines: *www.nwa.com*

Trans World Airlines (TWA): *www.twa.com*

United Airlines: *www.ual.com*

US Airways: *www.usairways.com*

Low-fare Airlines

The low-fare airlines listed here were those actually up and running as of mid-2000.

AirTran Airways: *www.airtran.com*

American Trans Air (ATA): *www.ata.com*

Frontier Airlines: *www.frontierairlines.com*

JetBlue: *www.jetblue.com*

National Airlines: *www.nationalairlines.com*

North American Airlines: *www.northamair.com*

Pan American Airways: *www.flypanam.com*

Pro Air: *www.proair.com*

Shuttle America: *www.shuttleamerica.com*

Southwest Airlines: *www.southwest.com*

Sun Country Airlines: *www.suncountry.com*

Vanguard Airlines: *www.flyvanguard.com*

Smaller Airlines that Follow Giant Airline Pricing

Alaska Airlines: *www.alaskaair.com*

Aloha Airlines: *www.alohaair.com*

America West Airlines: *www.americawest.com*

Hawaiian Airlines: *www.hawaiianair.com*

Horizon Air: *www.horizonair.com*

Legend Airlines: *www.legendairlines.com*

Midway Airlines: *www.midwayair.com*

Midwest Express Airlines: *www.midwestexpress.com*

Frequent Flyer Sites

The following several sites are not affiliated with any airline compile frequent flyer information; some also sell various travel services.

FrequentFlier.Com: *www.frequentflier.com*

MaxMiles: *www.maxmiles.com*

milesource.com: *www.milesource.com*

WebFlyer: *www.webflyer.com*

Wise Flyer: *www.wiseflyer.com*

Gateway Sites

This handful of sites provide links to a long list of individual airline, airport, and ticket-agency sites.

Air and Space Links: *www.abanet.org/forums/airspace/aslinks.html/*

Airline Directory: *www.airlines.com*

Airlines of the Web: *www.flyaow.com*

The Aviation Home Page: *www.avhome.com*

Air Nemo: *www.geocities.com/CapeCanaveral/4285/*

Everybody's Airline-Hotel Directory: *www.everybody.co.uk*

www.infoairports.com: *www.infoairports.com*

PlaneBusiness: *www.planebusiness.com*

Wheels Up (airlines and airports): *www.pathcom.com/~fshska/*

International Airlines

The following are some of the most important airlines based outside the United States.

Conventional Airlines

These are the counterparts of the major U.S. airlines. In quite a few cases, the airlines' home pages indicate several language options, one of which is almost always English.

Air Canada: *www.aircanada.ca*

Air France: *www.airfrance.com*

Air Jamaica: *www.airjamaica.com*

Alitalia Airlines: *www.alitaliausa.com*

All Nippon Airways (ANA): *svc.ana.co.jp/eng/*

British Airways: *www.british-airways.com*

British Midland: *www.iflybritishmidland.com*

Cathay Pacific Airways: *www.cathay-usa.com*

EVA Air: *www.evaair.com.tw/*

Finnair: *www.finnair.com*

First Air: *www.firstair.ca*

Iberia Airlines of Spain: *www.iberia.com*

Icelandair: *www.icelandair.com*

Japan Airlines: *www.jal.co.jp*

KLM Royal Dutch Airlines: *www.klm.com*

Korean Air: *www.koreanair.com*

LanChile Airlines: *www.lanchile.cl*

Lufthansa German Airlines: *www.lufthansa.com*

Malaysia Airlines: *www.malaysiaairlines.com*

Mexicana Airlines: *www.mexicana.com.mx*

Olympic Airways: *www.olympic-airways.gr*

Qantas Airways Limited: *www.qantas.com*

Sabena: *www.sabena.com*

Scandinavian Airlines System (SAS): *www.flysas.com*

Saudi Arabian Airlines: *www.saudiairlines.com*

Singapore Airlines: *www.singaporeair.com*

Skyservice: *www.skyserviceairlines.com*

Spanair: *www.spanair.com*

Swissair: *www.swissair.com*

TAM: *www.tam.com.br/*

Thai Airways International: *www.thaiair.com*

Varig Brasil: *www.varig.com.br/*

Virgin Atlantic: *www.virginatlantic.com*

Low-Fare Airlines

This list includes both the transatlantic and the intra-European low-fare airlines.

Air Europa: *www.air-europa.com*

AirEurope: *www.aireurope.it/index_en.html/*

Air Transat: *www.airtransat.com*

buzz: *www.buzzaway.com*

Canada 3000 Airlines: *www.canada3000.com*

City Bird: *www.citybird.com*

Condor: *www.condor.de*

Corsair: *www.corsair-int.com*

easyJet: *www.easyjet.com*

Go: *www.go-fly.com*

LTU International Airways: *www.ltu.com*

Martinair: *www.martinairusa.com*

Royal Aviation: *www.royalair.com*

Ryanair: *www.ryanair.ie*

Virgin Express: *www.virgin-express.com*

WestJet Airlines: *www.westjet.ca*

Multi-Country Visitor Tickets

Many of the big foreign airlines sell special visitor tickets for reduced-fare internal travel in their home area. Only one such program has its own site.

Europe by Air: *www.europebyair.com*

Other Airline Information

These Web sites are sources of miscellaneous airline/aviation information.

AirlineSafety.Com (private site): *www.airlinesafety.com*

AirSafe.com: *www.airsafe.com*

Airwise: *www.airwise.com*

BizTraveler.org: *www.biztraveler.org*

CaptainChris Traveller's Site: *users.otenet.gr/~cpnchris/*

companyTRIP: *www.companytrip.com*

JohnnyJet's Travel News and Tips: *www.johnnyjet.com*

Rules of the Air: *www.rulesoftheair.com*

Vapor Trails: *www.vaportrails.com*

Ticket Agencies

Many online agencies specialize in air tickets, including discounted (consolidator) tickets. While most agencies sell air tickets, many also sell tours, hotel accommodations, and cruises. Consolidators that sell only through other agencies are not included here.

Coupon Brokers

Note: Buying and selling frequent flyer awards violates airline rules. Stay away from these agencies unless you're willing to run a serious risk.

AirAwards: *www.airawards.com*

Award Traveler: *www.awardtraveler.com*

Frequent Flyer Points: *www.frequentflyerpoints.com*

Mileagebrokers.com: *www.mileagebrokers.com*

Travel Enterprises: *www.travelenterprises.com*

Courier/Hitch Agencies

Several of these agencies provide information about low-cost courier travel, and one arranges "hitch" flights.

Adventure1.com: *www.adventure1.com/privy2.htm/*

Air Courier Association: *www.aircourier.org*

Airhitch: *www.airhitch.org*

Cheap Airline Tickets *Fly Courier*: *www.beatthemonkey.com/cheaptickets/*

Global Courier Travel: *www.couriertravel.org*

International Association of Air Travel Couriers: *www.courier.org*

General Ticket Agencies

The following ticket agency sites are not affiliated with a particular airline.

1-800-AIRFARE: *www.800airfare.com*

1st-Air.net (Business and First Class travel): *www.1st-air.net*

4GreatFares.com: *www.4greatfares.com*

Adventure1 (courier and consolidator lists): *www.adventure1.com*

Airdisc.com: *www.airdisc.com*

Airfare From Home: *www.airfare-from-home.com*

Airfare.com: *www.airfare.com*

Airfares.com: *www.airfares.com*

AirFares, Inc.: *www.airfares4.com*

Airline Consolidator.com: *www.airlineconsolidator.com*

Airline Reservations Network: *www.2flynow.com*

Air Travel Center: *www.airtravelcenter.com*

The Airtravel Network, Inc.: *www.airtravel.net*

Air Travel Pro: *www.nationwide.net/~morris/*

AVIA Travel: *www.avia.com*

Bargain Airfares: *www.bargain-airfares.com*

ByeByeNOW: *www.byebyenow.com*

Cheap Tickets: *www.cheaptickets.com*

The Corporate Flyer (First and Business Class travel): *www.flyfirstclass.com*

Discount Air, Inc.: *www.discountairbrokers.com*

ebookers (London): *www.ebookers.com*

Economy Travel: *www.economytravel.com*

FlightsForLess.com: *www.flightsforless.com*

FlyCheap.com: *air.travelco.com*

Internet Air Fares: *www.air-fare.com*

LowAirFare.com: *www.lowairfare.com/customer/*

Lowestfare.com: *www.lowestfare.com*

Only-Travel.com: *www.only-travel.com*

PositiveSpace: *www.positivespace.com/new/*

Travelocity.com: *www.travelocity.com*

Travelscape.com: *www.travelscape.com*

Travelselect.com: *www.travelselect.com*

United States Air Consolidators Association: *www.usaca.com*

Vacationland: *www.vacation-land.com*

Round-The-World Specialists

The following agencies specialize in developing custom RTW itineraries; most also sell more conventional air tickets and other travel services.

Air Brokers International: *www.airbrokers.com*

AirTreks.com: *www.highadv.com*

Odyssey Travel (Canada): *www.odyssey-travel.com*

Ticketplanet.com: *www.ticketplanet.com*

TISS: *www.tiss.com*

Cruises

I define cruising broadly to include most kinds of waterborne trips that include onboard accommodations. In the following list, limited regions of focus are indicated.

Barge and Boat Agencies

The following agencies arrange small-boat trips, including both full-service barge cruises and bare-boat rentals.

B&V Associates (Europe): *www.bvassociates.com*

Barge Broker: *www.bargebroker.com*

Barge Connection (Europe): *www.bargeconnection.com*

Britain Afloat: *www.britain-afloat.com*

Collar City Charters: *www.canalboat.com*

Crown Blue Line: *www.crown-blueline.com*

European Waterways Ltd.: *www.gobarging.com*

Ghiolman Yachts Travel Aviation 2000: *www.yachtstravelgreece.com*

H_2O Barge and Houseboat Vacations: *www.barginginfrance.com*

International Yachting Holidays: *www.yachtingholidays.com*

Locaboat (barge rentals): *www.locaboat.com*

Sunsail: *www.sunsail.com*

YachtWorld.com: *www.yachtworld.com/directories/*

Cruise Agencies

You'll find a large number of online agencies that sell cruises—many of them at significant discounts. The following is a list of several of these agencies.

1Cruise.com: *www.1cruise.com*

American Canadian Caribbean Line, Inc.: *www.accl-smallships.com*

Cruise411.com: *www.savtraveler.com*

Cruise Center: *www.thecruisecenter.com*

Cruise Central: *www.kwik-link.com/kwik-link/database/cruises.html/*

CRUISE.COM: *www.cruise.com*

Cruise Holidays of Seattle Centre: *www.cme2cruise.com*

The Cruiseman: *www.cruiseman.com*

Cruisemates.com: *www.cruisemates.com*

The Cruise Professionals: *www.cruiseprofessionals.com*

Cruise Value Centers: *www.cruisevalue.com*

Cruises-N-More, Inc.: *www.cruises-n-more.com*

Elegant Voyages: *www.elegantvoyages.com*

Freighter World Cruises: *www.freighterworld.com*

Great Lakes Cruise Company: *www.greatlakescruising.com*

Harry's Greek Island Travel Guide: *www.greeceathensaegeaninfo.com /Greek-Island-Travel-GuideX.htm/*

icruise.com: *www.i-cruise.com*

Internet Cruise Travel Network: *www.cruisetravel.com*

Marine Expeditions (MEI) & World Cruise Company: *www.meiworldcruisecompany.com*

Maris Freighter Cruises: *www.freighter-cruises.com*

mytravelco.com: *www.mytravelco.com/cruises/*

Paleologos (ferries in Greece): *www.ferries.gr*

Sail With The Stars (theme cruises): *www.sailwiththestars.com*

SmallShip Cruises: *www.smallshipcruises.com*

SmartCruiser: *www.smartcruiser.com*

TravLtips: *www.travltips.com*

Virtuoso: *www.virtuoso-travelocity.com*

Cruise Lines, Conventional

Most big cruise lines maintain sites, but they don't encourage online buying. Instead, they refer you to local agencies. The following list includes cruise lines that use conventional, powered ships as well as a few large ferry systems that provide overnight accommodations and accept advance bookings.

Alaska Marine Highway System (Alaska Ferry): *www.dot.state.ak.us /external/amhs/*

American Canadian Caribbean Cruise Line: *www.accl-smallships.com*

American Classic Voyages Co. (includes Delta Queen): *www.amcv.com*

American Cruise Lines: *www.americancruiselines.com*

American Hawaii Cruises: *www.cruisehawaii.com*

America West Steamboat Company: *www.columbiarivercruise.com*

Bahamas Fast Ferries: *www.bahamasferries.com*

B.C. Ferries: *www.bcferries.bc.ca*

Bergen Line Services (Norwegian coastal trips): *www.bergenline.com*

Cape Canaveral Cruise Line: *www.capecanaveralcruise.com*

Carnival Cruise Lines: *www.carnival.com*

Celebrity Cruises: *www.celebrity-cruises.com*

Classical Cruises: *www.classicalcruises.com*

Clipper Cruise Line: *www.clippercruise.com*

Commodore Cruise Line: *www.commodorecruise.com*

Costa Cruises: *www.costacruises.com*

Crystal Cruises: *www.crystalcruises.com*

Cunard Line: *www.cunardline.com*

Discovery Cruise Line (Florida-Bahamas day trips): *www.discoverycruise.com*

Disney Cruise Line: *www.disneycruise.com*

Dolphin Cruises (Gulf Coast day trips): *www.dolphincruise.com*

First European Cruises: *www.first-european.com*

Glacier Bay Tours & Cruises: *www.glacierbaytours.com*

Holland America Line: *www.hollandamerica.com*

KD River Cruises of Europe: *www.rivercruises.com*

Lake Michigan Carferry: *www.ssbadger.com*

Lindblad Expeditions: *www.lindblad.com*

Norwegian Cruise Line: *www.ncl.com*

Orient Lines: *www.orientlines.com*

Premier Cruise Lines: *www.premiercruises.com*

Quark Expeditions: *www.quarkexpeditions.com*

Radisson Seven Seas Cruises: *www.rssc.com*

Regal Cruises: *www.regalcruises.com*

Renaissance Cruises: *www.renaissancecruises.com*

Rhine Cruise Lines: *www.rhine-cruise-lines.com*

RiverBarge Excursion Lines: *www.riverbarge.com*

Royal Caribbean International: *www.rccl.com*

Royal Hawaiian Cruises (interisland day trips): *www.royalhawaiiancruises.com*

Royal Olympic Cruises: *www.royalolympiccruises.com*

Seabourn Cruise Line: *www.seabourn.com*

Seajets (Florida-Bahamas day hydrofoils): *www.seajets.com*

Silversea Cruises: *www.silversea.com*

Society Expeditions: *www.societyexpeditions.com*

Swan Hellenic Cruises: *www.swan-hellenic.co.uk*

Temptress Adventure Cruises: *www.temptresscruises.com*

United States Lines (Hawaii): *www.unitedstateslines.com*

Uniworld Cruises (European rivers): *www.uniworldcruises.com*

Victoria Cruises (Yangtze River): *www.victoriacruises.com*

World Explorer Cruises: *www.wecruise.com*

Cruise Lines, Sailing Ships/Yachts

A few lines, listed here, specialize in sailing-ship cruises.

Sea Cloud Cruises: *www.seacloud.com*

Star Clippers: *www.starclippers.com*

Windjammer Barefoot Cruises: *www.windjammer.com*

Windstar Cruises: *www.windstarcruises.com*

Zeus Tours & Yacht Cruises: *www.zeustours.com*

Gateway Sites and General Information

The following sites provide useful links and general information about cruising.

Cruise2.com Cruise Portal: *www.cruise2.com*

Cruise Calendar: *www.cruisecalendar.com*

Cruise Critic: *www.cruisecritic.com*

Cruise Lines International Association (CLIA): *www.cruising.org*

CruiseOpinion.com: *www.cruiseopinion.com*

CruiseReviews.com: *www.cruisereviews.com*

Ferries of the British Isles and Northern Europe: *homepages.enterprise.net /nickw00000/*

shipSTATS.com: *www.shipstats.com*

The Working Vacation Inc.(cruiseship jobs): *www.theworkingvacation.com*

Destinations

Use these destination sites to help you decide where you want to go and to plan your trip once you have your destination in mind.

Activities

You can access a wide variety of activities through one of the excellent gateway sites listed or through a general destination site.

Cultural Activities

The following sites can help you locate information about museums, concerts, and such.

CultureFinder: *www.culturefinder.com*

FestivalFinder: *www.festivalfinder.com*

The International Council of Museums (ICOM): *www.icom.org*

Michael's Opera Links: *www.stairway.org/bjorling/opralink.htm/*

Museums in the USA: *www.museumca.org/usa/*

New York City Museums: *www.go-newyorkcity.com/museums/*

OPERA America: *www.operaam.org*

OperaStuff: *www.operastuff.com*

Time Out: *www.timeout.com*

Recreational Activities

If you are planning a vacation around a particular recreational activity, or you want to include an activity on your trip, check out these sites.

Book4golf.com (including online tee time booking): *www.book4golf.com*

FishSearch.com: *www.fishsearch.com*

Global Gold Guide: *www.globalgolfguide.com*

GolfOnline: *www.golfonline.com*

Golf-Travel Com: *www.golf-travel.com*

GoSki: *www.goski.com*

SkiIn: *www.skiin.com*

SkiNet.com: *www.skinet.com*

Surf Check: *www.surfcheck.com*

SurfLine: *www.surfline.com*

TennisOnline.com: *www.tennisonline.com*

World Wide Angler: *www.worldwideangler.com*

Commercial Attractions

Many people plan their vacations around a visit to a particular theme park or commercial attraction. The following sites will help you make those kinds of travel plans.

General Attractions

The following are some good gateway sites focused on general attractions.

4ThemeParks.com: *www.4themeparks.4anything.com*

The American Midway: *www.americanmidway.com*

Casino City: *www.casinocity.com*

The Casino Net: *www.the-casino-net.com*

FunGuide: *www.funguide.com*

Hawaii Attractions Association: *www.hawaiiattractions.com*

Themeparks.com: *www.themeparks.com*

Tim Melago's Directory of Amusement Park and Roller Coaster Links: *www.users.sgi.net/~rollocst/amuse.html/*

Werner's "Not Disney" Theme Parks, Fairs, & Amusement Parks: *www.yesterland.com/parklinks.html/*

World Waterpark Association: *www.waterparks.org*

Specific Attractions

Many of the best known attractions, such as the ones listed here, maintain their own web sites, as do many others you can access through destination sites, gateways, and search engines.

Anheuser-Busch Adventure Parks: *www.4adventure.com*

Busch Gardens: *www.buschgardens.com*

College Football Hall of Fame: *www.collegefootball.org*

Cypress Gardens: *www.cypressgardens.com*

Disney.com: *Disney.go.com*

Elvis Presley's Graceland: *www.elvis-presley.com*

Hershey Entertainments & Resorts: *www.hersheypa.com*

Hooptown, USA: *www.hooptown.com*

Knott's Berry Farm: *www.knotts.com*

National Baseball Hall of Fame and Museum: *www.baseballhalloffame.org*

Pro Football Hall of Fame: *www.profootballhof.com*

Queen Mary: *www.queenmary.com*

SeaWorld Adventure Parks: *www.seaworld.com*

Six Flags Theme Parks: *www.sixflags.com*

Universal Studios: *www.universalstudios.com*

Destinations Outside the United States

This list includes most of the world's countries, plus a few representative major tourist cities. You can easily locate other cities through the national sites or through a search engine.

Algeria: *www.algeria-tourism.org*

Anguilla: *www.net.ai*

Antigua & Barbuda: *www.antigua-barbuda.org*

Argentina: *wam.com.ar/tourism/*

Aruba: *www.aruba.com*

Australia: *www.australia.com, www.austtravel.com.au*

    Great Barrier Reef: *www.great-barrier-reef.com*

    Melbourne: *melbourne.8m.com*

    Sydney: *www.travelsydney.com*

Austria: *www.austria-tourism.at, www.anto.com*

Bahamas: *www.bahamas.com*

Barbados: *www.barbados.org*

Belize: *www.travelbelize.org*

Belgium: *www.visitbelgium.com*

Bermuda: *www.bermudatourism.com*

Bonaire: *www.infobonaire.com*

Brazil: *www.embratur.gov.br*

Britain (*see* United Kingdom)

British Virgin Islands: *www.britishvirginislands.com*

Cambodia: *www.cambodia-web.net*

Canada: *www.travelcanada.ca, gocanada.about.com*

    Alberta: *www.explorealberta.com*

    British Columbia: *www.travel.bc.ca, www.hellobc.com*

    Manitoba: *www.travelmanitoba.com*

    New Brunswick: *www.tourismnbcanada.com*

    Newfoundland & Labrador: *www.gov.nf.ca/tourism/*

    Northwest Territories: *www.nwttravel.nt.ca*

    Nova Scotia: *www.explore.gov.ns.ca*

    Nunavut: *www.nunatour.nt.ca*

    Ontario: *www.travelinx.com*

    Prince Edward Island: *www.peiplay.com*

    Quebec: *www.bonjourquebec.com*

    Saskatchewan: *www.sasktourism.com*

    Yukon: *www.touryukon.com*

Cayman Islands: *www.caymanislands.ky*

Chile: *www.sernatur.cl*

China: *www.cnto.org*

Costa Rica: *www.tourism-costarica.com*

Croatia: *www.htz.hr*

Curacao: *www.curacao-tourism.com*

Cyprus: *www.cyprustourism.org*

Czech Republic: *www.czechcenter.com*

Denmark: *www.visitdenmark.com*

Dominican Republic: *www.dominicana.com.do*

Dubai: *dubaitourism.co.ae*

Egypt: *touregypt.net*

Ethiopa: *www.ethiopianembassy.org*

Falkland Islands: *www.tourism.org.fk/*

Fiji: *www.BulaFiji.com, www.internetfiji.com*

Finland: *www.thekingsroad.com, www.mek.fi*

France: *www.francetourism.com, www.franceguide.com, www.france.com /francescape/*

    Burgundy: *www.burgundy-tourism.com*

    Cote d'Azur: *www.crt-riviera.fr*

    Paris: *www.paris.org, www.parisfrance.com*

    Provence: *www.provence.guideweb.com*

Germany: *www.germany-tourism.de*

Great Britain (*see* United Kingdom)

Greece: *www.gnto.gr*

Grenada: *www.grenada.org*

Guam: *www.visitguam.org*

Guatemala: *www.inguat.net*

Honduras: *www.in-honduras.com*

Hong Kong: *www.hkta.org*

Hungary: *www.hungarytourism.hu*

Iceland: *www.goiceland.org*

India: *www.tourindia.com, www.allindiaguide.com, www.destinationindia.com, www.inetindia.com/travel/index.php3/*

Indonesia and Bali: *www.indonesia-tourism.com*

Ireland: *www.ireland.travel.ie, www.shamrock.org*

    Northern Ireland: *www.ni-tourism.com*

Israel: *www.goisrael.com, www.israel.com*

Italy: *www.enit.it, www.italian-connection.co.uk/*

    Milan: *www.CityLightsNews.com/ztmimp1.htm/*

    Rome: *www.romeguide.it, www.twenj.com/romevisit.htm/*

    Venice: *www.writing.org/venice.htm/*

Jamaica: *www.jamaicatravel.com*

Japan: *www.jnto.go.jp*

Jordan: *www.seejordan.org*

Kenya: *www.kenyatourism.org*

Korea: *www.knto.or.kr, www.korea.com*

Lithuania: *www.tourism.lt*

Luxembourg: *www.visitluxembourg.com, www.ont.lu*

Macau: *www.macautourism.gov.mo*

Malaysia: *tourism.gov.my*

Malta: *www.visitmalta.com*

Martinique: *www.martinique.org*

Mexico: *www.mexico-travel.com*

   Access Mexico: *www.mexconnect.com*

   Mexico Ministry of Tourism: *www.safemexico.com*

   Mexico Online (1): *www.mexonline.com*

   Mexico Online (2): *www.mexicool.com*

   Mexico Travel: *www.mexico-travel.com*

Monaco: *www.monaco.mc*

Morocco: *www.tourism-in-morocco.com*

Nepal: *www.welcomenepal.com*

Netherlands: *www.visitholland.com, www.holland.com*

New Zealand: *www.tourisminfo.govt.nz, www.purenz.com*

Nicaragua: *www.intur.gob.ni*

Norway: *www.tourist.no, www.norway.org*

Peru: *www.peruonline.net*

Philippines: *www.filipino.com*

Poland: *www.polandtour.org*

Portugal: *www.portugal.org*

Romania: *www.rotravel.com*

Russia: *www.russia-travel.com*

St. Kitts-Nevis: *www.interknowledge.com/stkitts-nevis/*

St. Lucia: *www.st-lucia.com*

St. Maarten: *www.st-maarten.com*

St. Vincent & The Grenadines: *www.svgtourism.com*

Samoa: *www.samoa.co.nz*

Scotland: *www.holiday.scotland.net*

Seychelles: *www.sey.net*

Singapore: *www.newasia-singapore.com*

Slovenia: *www.slovenia-tourism.si*

South Africa: *www.southafrica.com, www.tradepage.co.za/seesa/main.htm/*

Spain: *www.tourspain.es, tuspain.com, www.okspain.org*

Sri Lanka: *www.lanka.net/ctb*

Sweden: *www.visit-sweden.com, www.gosweden.org*

    Stockholm: *www.stoinfo.se*

Switzerland: *www.myswitzerland.com*

Tahiti: *www.gotahiti.com*

Taiwan: *www.tbroc.gov.tw*

Thailand: *www.tourismthailand.org*

    Bangkok: *www.bangkokpost.net*

Trinidad & Tobago: *www.discovertrinidad.com*

Tunisia: *www.tourismtunisia.com*

Turkey: *www.turkey.org*

Turks & Caicos: *www.turksandcaicostourism.com*

United Kingdom: *www.visitbritain.com, www.britannia.com, www.knowhere.co.uk, www.limitless.co.uk/dine/*

    Late Night London: *www.latenightlondon.co.uk*

    London: *www.londontown.com,www.londontraveller.com /londontraveller/gateway4_flash.html/*

Uganda: *www.utbsite.com*

Uruguay: *www.turismo.gub.uy*

Wales: *www.ceredigion.gov.uk*

Destinations Within the United States

This list includes all states, plus a few representative major tourist areas. You can easily locate other cities through the state sites or through a search engine.

Alabama: *www.state.al.us*

Alaska: *www.alcanseek.com, www.travelalaska.com, www.vacationalaska.com*

    Anchorage: *www.anchorage.net*

Arizona: *www.arizona.com, www.azcentral.com, www.webcreationsetc.com /Azguide/*

    Flagstaff: *www.flagstaff.az.us*

    Phoenix: *www.ci.phoenix.az.us*

    Tucson: *www.desert.net/tw/bot/*

Arkansas: *www.arkansas.com*

    Little Rock: *www.littlerock.com*

California: *gocalif.ca.gov*

    Los Angeles: *www.lacvb.com, www.latimes.com*

    Palm Springs: *www.palm-springs.org*

    San Diego: *www.sandiego.org, www.sandiegoinsider.com, www.sandiego-online.com*

    San Francisco: *www.sfvisitor.org, www.bayinsider.com, www.bestofthebay.com, www.sfgate.com/travel/*

Colorado: *www.colorado.com*

    Aspen: *www.aspen.com*

    Denver: *www.denver.org, www.westword.com*

    Vail: *web.vail.net*

Connecticut: *www.tourism.state.ct.us, www.visitconnecticut.com*

Delaware: *www.visitdelaware.com, www.delawaredirect.com, www.state.de.us*

District of Columbia: *www.washington.org*

Florida: *www.flausa.com, www.florida.com*

    Daytona Beach: *www.daytonabeach.com*

    Kissimmee: *www.floridakiss.com*

Miami: *www.miamiandbeaches.com, www.Miami.com*

    Orlando: *www.go2orlando.com*

    St. Petersburg: *www.stpete-clearwater.com*

Georgia: *www.georgia.org*

    Atlanta: *www.accessatlanta.com*

    Savannah: *www.savannah-visit.com*

Hawaii: *www.visit.hawaii.org*, *www.gohawaii.com*, *www.hawaii101.com*, *www.hshawaii.com*, *www.starbulletin.com/doit/*

    Kauai: *www.kauai-hawaii.com*

    Lanai: *www.lanai-resorts.com*

    Maui: *www.maui.net*, *www.visitmaui.com*

    Molokai: *www.molokai-hawaii.com*

    Oahu: *www.visit-oahu.com*

Idaho: *www.visitid.org*

    Sun Valley: *www.visitsunvalley.com*

Illinois: *www.enjoyillinois.com*

    Chicago: *www.ci.chi.il.us/Tourism/*, *www.chicagotribune.com*, *www.chicago-guide.com*, *www.nitescape.com/chicago/blues/*

Indiana: *www.state.in.us/tourism/*, *www.enjoyindiana.com*

    Indianapolis: *www.indianapolis.com*

Iowa: *www.state.ia.us/tourism/*

    Des Moines: *www.ci.des-moines.ia.us*

Kansas: *www.kansascommerce.com*

Kentucky: *www.kentuckytourism.com*

    Louisville: *www.louisville-visitors.com*

Louisiana: *www.louisianatravel.com*

    Baton Rouge: *www.batonrougetour.com*

    New Orleans: *www.bestofneworleans.com*, *www.gumbopages.com*, *www.nolalive.com*, *www.yatcom.com/neworl/vno.html/*

Maine: *www.visitmaine.com*

    Bangor: *www.bangorcvb.org*

Maryland: *www.mdisfun.org*

Massachusetts: *www.mass-vacation.com*, *www.masstourist.com*, *www.visit-massachusetts.com*

    Boston: *www.boston.com*, *www.bostonmagazine.com*, *www.bostonusa.com*

    Cape Cod: *www.capecodchamber.org*

Michigan: *www.michigan.org*, *www.michigan-online.com/tourist.htm*

    Detroit: *www.visitdetroit.com*

    Mackinaw City: *www.mackinawcity.com*

Minnesota: *www.exploreminnesota.com*

>Minneapolis: *www.minneapolis.org*

>St. Paul: *www.stpaulcvb.org*

Mississippi: *www.visitmississippi.org*, *www.mstourism.com*

>Gulf Coast: *www.gulf-coast.com*

>Vicksburg: *www.vicksburg.org*

Missouri: *www.missouritourism.com*

>Branson: *www.bransoncourier.com/city/*, *www.travelnow.com/branson/*

>St. Louis: *www.st-louis.mo.us*

Montana: *www.visitmt.com*, *www.montana.com*, *www.travel.state.mt.us*

Nebraska: *www.visitnebraska.org*

Nevada: *www.travelnevada.com*

>LasVegas.com: *www.lasvegas.com*

>Las Vegas Convention and Visitors Authority: *www.lasvegas24hours.com*

>Reno/Lake Tahoe: *www.playreno.com*

>Vegas.com: *www.vegas.com*

New Hampshire: *www.visitnh.gov*

New Jersey: *www.state.nj.us/travel*, *www.nj.com*, *www.inthegardenstate.com*

>Atlantic City: *www.atlantic-city.net*, *www.atlantic-city-online.com*, *www.atlanticcitynj.com*

New Mexico: *www.newmexico.com*

>Albuquerque: *www.abqcvb.org*

>Santa Fe: *www.santafe.org*

New York: *iloveny.state.ny.us*

>New York City: *www.nycvisit.com*, *www.nytoday.com*

>Niagara Falls: *www.niagara.falls.net*, *www.tourismniagara.com*

North Carolina: *www.visitnc.com*

>Outer Banks: *www.outerbanks.org*

North Dakota: *www.ndtourism.com*

Ohio: *www.ohiotourism.com*

>Cincinnati: *www.cincyusa.com*

>Cleveland: *www.travelcleveland.com*

Oklahoma: *www.otrd.state.ok.us, www.travelok.com*

Oregon: *www.traveloregon.com, www.state.or.us*

Pennsylvania: *www.experiencepa.com, www.state.pa.us*

  Philadelphia: *www.pcvb.org, www.gophila.com*

  Pittsburgh: *www.pittsburgh-cvb.org*

Puerto Rico: *www.prtourism.com*

Rhode Island: *www.visitrhodeisland.com*

South Carolina: *www.southcarolina.com*

  Charleston: *www.charlestoncvb.com*

  Myrtle Beach: *www.myrtlebeachlive.com*

South Dakota: *www.travelsd.com, www.state.sd.us*

Tennessee: *www.tourism.state.tn.us*

  Memphis: *www.ci.memphis.tn.us*

  Nashville: *www.nashscene.com, nashville.citysearch.com*

  Smoky Mountains Tourism: *www.smokymountains.org*

Texas: *www.traveltex.com*

  Dallas: *www.dallas.com, www.dallascvb.com*

  Houston: *www.houston-guide.com*

  San Antonio: *www.sanantoniocvb.com*

U.S. Virgin Islands: *www.usvi.net, www.americasparadise.com*

Utah: *www.utah.com*

  Salt Lake City: *www.visitsaltlake.com*

Vermont: *www.travel-vermont.com*

Virginia: *www.virginia.org*

  Richmond: *www.richmondva.org*

  Williamsburg: *www.williamsburg.com*

Washington: *www.tourism.wa.gov*

  Seattle: *www.seattledining.com, www.seeseattle.org,
  seattle.citysearch.com*

West Virginia: *www.state.wv.us/tourism/*

Wisconsin: *www.travelwisconsin.com*

  Madison: *www.visitmadison.com*

  Milwaukee: *www.milwaukee.org*

Wyoming: *www.wyomingtourism.org*

Events

Many destination sites list event information directly on their Web sites, but you can find information on event-specific Web sites.

Gateway Sites

Through the following sites you can learn about lots of different kinds of events all over the world.

About.com: *home.about.com/local/*

EventsWorldWide: *www.eventsworldwide.com*

Ticket Agencies

The following sites provide ticketing information, and some allow for online purchase.

Applause (NYC): *www.applause-tickets.com*

Attractions Plus: *www.attractionsplus.com*

CityPass: *www.citypass.net*

Golden Tickets (sports): *www.goldentickets.com*

GoTickets.com (motor sports): *www.gotickets.com*

London Theatre Land: *web.onramp.ca/theatreland/*

Nevada Ticket Services (Las Vegas shows): *www.lasvegastickets.com*

Respond.com: *www.respond.com*

SOLDOUT.com (major events): *www.soldout.com*

SportsTickets.net: *www.sportstickets.net*

Telecharge.com: *www.telecharge.com*

Theatre Direct International: *www.theatredirect.com*

Ticketmaster.com: *www.ticketmaster.com*

Tickets.com: *www.tickets.com*

Tickets To...: *www.ticketsto.com*

TicketWeb: *www.ticketweb.com*

WebTickets.com: *www.webtickets.com*

WebTix (postings from individual sellers): *www.tixs.com*

YouTicket.com (Las Vegas shows): *www.youticket.com*

Gateway Sites

In addition to using specific destination sites, you can research destination information through the following gateway sites.

CitySearch: *www.citysearch.com*

CyberWonders Global Travel: *www.cyberwonders.com/global.html/*

Lynx2Travel (New England): *www.lynx2travel.com*

National Scenic Byways: *www.byways.org*

Rec.Travel Library: *www.travel-library.com*

Roadside America: *www.roadsideamerica.com*

RoadTrip America: *www.roadtripamerica.com*

seektravel.com: *www.seektravel.com*

TIA Discover America: *www.seeamerica.org*

Top Travel Sites: *www.toptravelsites.com*

Tourism Offices Worldwide Directory: *www.towd.com*

wcities.com: *www.wcities.com*

Other Destination Information

The following sections detail sites relevant to destinations.

Climate and Weather

It's easy to get someone's guess about the weather just about anywhere in the world. Most home pages also have weather links.

AccuWeather: *www.accuweather.com*

Intellicast: *www.intellicast.com*

Live Weather Images: *www.weatherimages.org*

The National Oceanic and Atmospheric Administration Weather Page: *www.esdim.noaa.gov/weather_page.html/*

The Weather Channel: *www.weather.com*

Food and Restaurants

Here are some sites for the gourmet readers.

4 Kosher (United States): *www.4kosher.com*

CuisineNet (United States): *www.cuisinenet.com*

Dine.com (United States): *www.dine.com*

FoodWeb: *www.foodweb.com*

Restaurant Row: *www.restaurantrow.com*

Savvy Diner (United States): *www.savvydiner.com*

Shamash Kosher Restaurant Database (United States): *www.shamash.org /kosher/*

The Vegetarian Pages: *www.veg.org*

Zagat Survey (United States): *www.zagat.com*

Medical Services

These sites are maintained by organizations that provide medical aid to travelers overseas. Most are membership organizations; arrange membership before you leave.

Global Emergency Medical Services: *www.globalems.com*

HotelDocs (on-call service, United States): *www.hoteldocs.com*

International Society of Travel Medicine: *www.istm.org*

International SOS: *www.intsos.com*

MEDEX: *www.medexassist.com*

MEDJET Assistance: *www.medjetassistance.com*

PersonalMD.com: *www.personalmd.com*

Traveler's Emergency Network (TEN): *www.tenweb.com*

Parks and Natural Resources

Here's a sampling of gateway sites to natural-resource sites. You'll find lots more links through state and national sites.

American Park Network: *www.americanparknetwork.com*

Great Outdoor Recreation Pages: *www.gorp.com*

The National Park Service: *www.nps.gov*

New Zealand Outside: *webnz.com/outside/*

Parks Canada: *www.parkscanada.pch.gc.ca*

U.S. Army Corps of Engineers Recreation Services: *www.usace.army.mil /recreation/*

USDA Forest Service: *www.fs.fed.us/links/forests.shtml/*

Financial Information

Here you'll find sites with all the financial information—banking, currency, charge card information, and insurance—you should need on your trip.

Banking

ATM Locators

There are two sites on which you can locate ATMs, worldwide.

MasterCard/Maestro/Cirrus ATM Locator: *www.mastercard.com/atm/*

Visa/Plus: *www.visa.com/pd/atm/*

Currency Exchange

Most home pages also easily link you to a currency converter.

The Chase Manhattan Corporation: *www.chase.com*

International Currency Express: *www.foreignmoney.com*

OANDA Currency Converter: *www.oanda.com*

The Universal Currency Converter: *www.xe.net/ucc/*

Charge Card Information

Several of these sites provide detailed comparisons of the costs and benefits of different charge cards.

bankrate.com: *www.bankrate.com*

BankWeb: *www.bankweb.com*

bCard: *www.bcard.net*

CardWeb: *www.cardweb.com*

FrequentFlier.com (mileage-earning card comparisons): *www.frequentflier.com/card-intro.htm/*

TRAVEL.com: *www.travel.com*

Major Card Issuers

These are the sites of the institutions that issue a majority of charge cards used in the United States.

American Express: *www.americanexpress.com*

Bank of America: *www.bankofamerica.com*

Capital One: *www.capitalone.com*

Diners Club International: *www.citibank.com/dinersus/*

First USA: *www.firstusa.com*

Household International: *www.household.com*

MBNA: *www.mbna.com*

Security First Network Bank: *www.sfnb.com*

Unicard Travel Association: *www.unicard.com*

Travel Insurance

Increasingly, travel agencies and tour operators automatically add insurance to your trip bill. Online prices, however, might be better.

1travelinsurance.com: *www.1travelinsurance.com*

Access America: *www.accessamerica.com*

AIGAssist: *www.aigtravel.com*

Assist America: *www.assistamerica.com*

The Berkely Group: *www.berkely.com*

CSA Travel Protection: *www.csatravelprotection.com*

Independent Insurance Agents of America, Inc.: *www.independentagent.com*

Insurance Consultants International: *www.globalhealthinsurance.com*

MEDEX Assistance: *www.medexassist.com*

Nolo on Travel Insurance: *www.nolo.com/encyclopedia/ctim_ency.html/*

Travel Guard: *www.travel-guard.com*

Travel Insured: *www.travelinsured.com*

Travelex Insurance Services: *www.travelex-insurance.com*

TravelMed Assistance Group: *www.tmassist.com*

Travel Protection Services (CNA policies): *www.travelprotect.com*

Unicard Travel Association (UTA): *www.unicard.com*

Universal Travel Protection Insurance: *www.utravelpro.com*

Worldwide Assistance Services: *www.worldwideassistance.com*

General Travel Information

Some sites provide a wide range of travel information. The following sites are primarily informational, although they might incidentally sell something. For other sources of general information, also see listings for guidebooks and publications.

CIA World Factbook: *www.odci.gov/cia/publications/factbook/*

Columbus World Travel Guide: *www.wtg-online.com*

Global Sources: *www.go-global.com*

Tapped Into Travel: *www.tappedintotravel.com*

Travelbyus.com: *www.travelbyus.com*

TRAVEL.com: *www.travel.com*

TravelFacts: *www.travelfacts.com*

Travel-Finder: *www.travel-finder.com*

Travelfinders: *www.travelfinders.com*

TravNet! International World Forum Index: *www.comdinet.com/tn /tni0000.htm/*

TripSpot: *www.tripspot.com*

Help and Support

You'll find many Web sites that can provide you with health and safety information before you travel, offer you support during your trip, and help you solve any problems that might arise when you're on vacation.

Consumer Gripe Sites

To let off some steam about a particular travel frustration, visit the following sites.

NorthWorst Air: *www.northworstair.org*

Passenger Rights for Airline Passengers: *www.airlinessuck.com*

PassengerRights.com: *www.passengerrights.com*

The Ticked-Off Traveler: *www.ticked.com*

Untied Airlines: *www.untied.com*

Yahoo Air Rage Headlines: *headlines.yahoo.com/full_coverage/us /air_rage_and_passenger_rights/*

Government and Public Organizations

For the latest on safety in the travel industry, plus international security issues, check out the following sites.

Air Transport Action Group: *www.atag.org*

Attorney General Guide to Travel Scams: *www.cslnet.ctstateu.edu /ATTYGENL/travinfo.htm/*

Centers for Disease Control and Prevention Vessel Sanitation Program (cruise ship sanitation scores): *www.cdc.gov/nceh/vsp/vsp.htm/*

FAA International Aviation Safety Assessment: *www.faa.gov/avr/iasa/*

Federal Trade Commission (scam investigations): *www.ftc.gov*

National Consumers League National Fraud Information Center & Internet Fraud Watch: *www.fraud.org*

U.S. State Department (travel warnings): *www.travel.state.gov /travel_warnings.html/*

Publications

Several publishers of guidebooks and travel publications maintain Web sites, many of which provide extensive coverage from the original printed sources.

Arthur Frommer's Budget Travel: *www.frommers.com*

Concierge (Condé Nast Traveler): *www.concierge.com*

Fodor's: *www.fodors.com*

Let's Go: *www.letsgo.com*

Lonely Planet: *www.lonelyplanet.com*

National Geographic Traveler: *www.nationalgeographic.com*

Rough Guides: *travel.roughguides.com*

Travel and Leisure: *www.pathfinder.com/travel/*

Travel Holiday: *www.travelholiday.com*

Travelterrific.com (online magazine): *www.travelterrific.com*

Web Surfer Travel Journal (online magazine): *www.go.to/wstj/*

Telephones—Long Distance Rates and Cell Phone Rental

Here is a listing of sites where you can compare long-distance charges and rent a cell phone for an overseas trip.

AT&T: *www.att.com*

CallNOW.com: *www.callnow.com*

Cellhire: *www.cellhire.com*

Decide.com (phone comparisons): *www.decide.com*

EZTEL (international long distance: *www.eztel.com*

InTouch USA: *www.intouchusa.com*

Omnipoint: *www.omnipoint-pcs.com*

Planetfone: *www.planetfone.com*

RentCell: *www.rentcell.com*

Roberts Rent-a-Phone: *www.robertsworldwide.com*

Smartcoms by Parker: *www.smartcoms.com*

Sprint: *www.sprint.com*

WorldCell: *www.worldcell.com*

WorldCom: *www.wcom.com*

Tour Packages

You'll find a ton of tour package information on the Internet. The following sections offer a sampling to get you started.

Gateway Sites and General Information

These sites can lead you to hundreds of specialized tour operators. The Specialty Travel Index is especially useful.

National Tour Association (NTA): *www.ntaonline.com*

Specialty Travel Index: *www.spectrav.com*

Travelroads Adventure Travel Directory: *www.travelroads.com*

United States Tour Operators Association: *www.ustoa.com*

Specialized Tour Packages

I've broken down the various kinds of specialized tour packages you can find on the Web into several categories; the category headings should be self-explanatory. The listing is fragmentary and illustrative; you can find hundreds more special interest tours by searching on one of the large travel gateway sites.

Adventure Travel

Above the Clouds: *www.aboveclouds.com*

Adventure Center: *www.adventurecenter.com*

Adventureplanet/Adventurebus: *www.adventureplanet.com*

Adventureseek: *www.adventureseek.com*

Destination Wilderness: *www.wildernesstrips.com*

Extraordinary Places: *www.eplaces.com*

Gorp: *www.gorp.com*

JOURNEYS International: *www.journeys-intl.com*

Mountain Travel Sobek: *www.mtsobek.com*

Wild Adventures: *www.wildadventures.com*

Wilderness Travel: *www.wildernesstravel.com*

African-American Travelers

Soul of America: *www.soulofamerica.com*

Archaeological Travel

ArchaeoExpeditions: *www.interimpact.com/expeditions/*

Far Horizons Archaeological and Cultural Trips: *www.farhorizon.com*

Arts and Cultural Travel

Art Research Tours and International Studios: *www.artis-tours.org*

IST Cultural Tours: *www.ist-tours.com*

Opera Tours to Europe: *www.operatours.com*

Eco-Tourism

Classic Journeys: *www.classicjourneys.com*
Eco Travel Center: *www.ecotour.org*
Forum Travel Ventures: *www.forumtravel.com*
Wildland Adventures: *www.wildland.com*

European Travel

EUROPEonsale.com: *www.europeonsale.com*

Family Travel

About.com Travel with Kids: *www.travelwithkids.about.com*
Baby Center: *www.babycenter.com/travel/*
Family.com: *www.family.go.com*

Food/Wine Travel

Cuisine International: *cuisineinternational.com*
Rhode School of Cuisine: *www.to-gastronomy.com*

Garden Travel

Coopersmith's England: *www.coopersmiths.com*
Expo Garden Tours: *www.expogardentours.com*

Gay and Lesbian Travelers

Above and Beyond Tours: *www.abovebeyondtours.com*
David Tours: *www.davidtours.com*
Footprints Travel: *www.footprintstravel.com*

Historical Travel

History America Tours: *www.historyamerica.com*
History Channel Tours: *www.historychanneltours.com*

Physically Challenged Travelers

Access-Able Travel Source: *www.access-able.com*
Accessible Journeys: *www.disabilitytravel.com*
Accessible Vans of America: *www.accessiblevans.com*

Disabledtravel.com: *www.disabledtravel.com*

JourneyQuest.com: *www.journeyquest.com/handicapped.htm/*

Medically Escorted Cruises & Tours: *www.assistedtravel.com*

Wheelchair Getaways: *www.wheelchair-getaways.com*

Religious Travelers

All Star Travel Pilgrimages: *www.allstartours.com*

Christian Travel and Study Programs: *www.ctsp.co.il*

Trans World Travel: *www.transworldtravel.com*

Unitours: *www.unitours.com*

Safaris

Africa Safari Company: *www.africansafarico.com*

Association of Professional Safari Guides: *wwwsafariguides.com*

Safaricentre: *www.safaricentre.com*

Senior Travelers

AARP: *www.aarp.org*

CTE (United Kingdom): *www.cte.uk.com*

Elderhostel: *www.elderhostel.org*

ElderTreks: *www.eldertreks.com*

Grand Times: *www.grandtimes.com*

Hofer Tours: *www.hofertours.com*

SeniorCom, Inc.: *www.senior.com/travel/*

Seniors at Sea: *www.seniorsatsea.com*

SeniorsSearch: *www.seniorssearch.com*

Senior Women's Travel: *www.poshnosh.com*

ThirdAge: *www.thirdage.com*

Vantage Deluxe World Travel: *www.vantagetravel.com*

Vavo: *www.vavo.com*

Walking the World: *www.walkingtheworld.com*

The World Outside: *www.theworldoutside.com*

Single Travelers

Club Solo Vacations: *www.solovacations.com*

Connecting: solo travel network: *www.cstn.org*

Cruise Planners Single Adventure Tours: *www.singles-cruises.com*

O Solo Mio Singles Tours (some for seniors): *www.osolomio.com*

Sports Events Travel

Golden Sports Tours: *www.goldenint.com*

Spectacular Sports Specials: *www.spectacularsport.com*

Sportours: *www.sportours.com*

Student/Youth Travelers

Academic Travel Services: *www.academictravel.com*

American Student Travel: *www.astravel.com*

Ameritours: *www.ameritours.com*

Contiki: *www.contiki.com*

Educational Travel Tours, Inc.: *www.educationaltraveltours.com*

Leisure Tours International: *www.leisuretours.com*

People to People Student Ambassador Program: *www.studentambassadors.org*

Spring Break Travel: *www.springbreaktravel.com*

STA Travel: *www.sta-travel.com*

Sunchase Ski & Beach Breaks: *www.sunchase.com*

Travel Adventures: *www.traveladv.com*

TripHub.com: *www.triphub.com*

usit Campus: *www.usitcampus.co.uk*

World Class Vacations: *www.wcv.com*

Volunteer Travel

Earthwatch: *www.earthwatch.org*

Global Volunteers: *www.globalvolunteers.org*

Women Travelers

Wild Women Adventures: *www.wildwomenadv.com*

Women Traveling Together: *www.women-traveling.com*

Tour Operators

Here are a few of the country's larger tour operators. Some of them sell directly to the public; others don't. I've listed the tour-package sites for the giant U.S. lines, but the smaller lines and many international lines also operate vacation programs with sites; check through the airline home sites. Listings are mainly as examples; there are literally thousands of other tour operators.

Abercrombie & Kent: *www.abercrombiekent.com*

American Vacations: *www.aavacations.com*

Apple Vacations: *www.applevacations.com*

California Parlor Car Tours: *www.calpartours.com*

Collette Tours: *www.collettetours.com*

Continental Airlines Vacations & Specials: *www.continental.com/vs/*

Delta Vacations: *www.deltavacations.com*

Eurocentres: *www.eurocentres.com*

Funjet Vacations: *www.funjet.com*

Funjet Vacations Pleasure Break: *www.pleasurebreak.com*

Globus & Cosmos: *www.globusandcosmos.com*

GOGO Worldwide Vacations: *www.gogowwv.com*

HistoryAmerica TOURS: *www.historyamerica.com*

Homeric Tours, Inc.: *www.homerictours.com*

INTRAV: *www.intrav.com*

LastMinuteTravel.com: *www.lastminutetravel.com*

Maupintour: *www.maupintour.com*

MLT Vacations: *www.mltvacations.com*

Northwest Airlines WorldVacations: *www.nwaworldvacations.com*

Online Vacation Mall: *www.onlinevacationmall.com*

Perillo Tours: *www.perillotours.com*

Pleasant Holidays: *www.pleasantholidays.com*

Signature Vacations: *www.signature.ca*

Tauck Tours: *www.tauck.com*

Trafalgar Tours: *www.trafalgartours.com*

Travcoa: *www.travcoa.com*

Travelscape: *www.travelscape.com*

United Vacations: *www.unitedvacations.com*

Vacation.com: *www.vacation.com*

Vacationland: *www.vacation-land.com*

Value Holidays: *www.valhol.com*

WeddingTrips.com: *www.weddingtrips.com*

Transportation (Ground)

Here's the best the Web has to offer in terms of transportation, whether you prefer to travel by car, bus, or train.

Bus Travel

Sometimes the best way to see an area, or the most economical way to get from one place to another, is by taking a bus. The following sites will help you with bus travel.

Busabout: *www.busabout.com*

Greyhound Lines: *www.greyhound.com*

International Motor Coach Group: *www.imncoach.com*

Driving

Whether you rent a car or drive your own, most of you will at some point take a trip that takes you on the open road.

Information and Assistance

For help with the details of road travel, check out the following sites.

AAA: *www.aaa.com*

Etak (traffic information for 65 metro areas): *www.etak.com*

Free Trip (routing plus accommodations booking): *www.freetrip.com*

Hidden America (touring ideas): *www.hiddenamerica.com*

Moto Europa: *www.ideamerge.com/motoeuropa/*

National Motorists Association: *www.motorists.com*

National Scenic Byways Program: *www.byways.org*

U.S. Roads (safety and other information): *www.usroads.com*

Rental Car Agencies

A few online agencies claim to provide discounted car-rental rates.

Auto Europe: *www.autoeurope.com*

Autorentnet: *www.autorentnet.com*

bnm.com Guide to Airport Rental Cars: *www.bnm.com*

Cars-Rentals-Discounts.com: *www.cars-rentals-discounts.com*

Cruise America (RV rentals): *www.cruiseamerica.com*

Drive4U.com: *www.drive4u.com*

El Monte RV (RV rentals): *www.elmonterv.com*

kemwel holiday autos: *www.kemwel.com*

WheelsForRent.com: *www.affinityrentacar.com*

Rental Car Companies

All of the following sites permit online reservations.

Alamo Rent-A-Car: *www.go-value.com*

Avis: *www.avis.com*

Budget Rent A Car: *www.budgetrentacar.com/index1.html/*

Discount Car and Truck Rentals (Canada): *www.discountcar.com*

Dollar Rent A Car: *www.dollar.com*

easyRentacar.com (United Kingdom): *www.easyrentacar.com*

Enterprise Rent-A-Car: *www.pickenterprise.com*

Europcar: *www.europcar.com*

Hertz: *www.hertz.com*

National Car Rental: *www.nationalcar.com*

Renault Eurodrive: *www.eurodrive.renault.com*

Rent-A-Wreck Rent-A-Car: *www.rent-a-wreck.com*

Thrifty Car Rental: *www.thrifty.com*

Local Ground Transport

You can arrange other types of transportation from the following sites.

AlaskaPass: *www.alaskapass.com*

Gray Line: *www.grayline.com*

MetroPlanet: *www.metropla.net*

RideBoard.com (ride sharing): *www.rideboard.com*

SuperShuttle: *www.supershuttle.com*

Rail Travel

The Internet can provide plenty of information on rail travel in North America, Western Europe, Japan, and Australasia, but useful information is scarce for other regions of the world.

Agencies

The following agency sites can help you with schedules, tickets, and such.

Australia Rail Maps and Timetable Index: *people.enternet.com.au/~cbrnbill /maps/austrail.htm/*

BritRail: *www.britrail.net*

Rail Connection: *www.railconnection.com*

Rail Europe: *www.raileurope.com/us/*

General Information and Gateway Sites

All too much of the Internet's rail content is about rail (real and model) as a hobby rather than as a mode of transport. These sites should point you in the right direction for travel.

Cyberspace World Railroad: *www.cwrr.com*

National Model Railroad Association's Directory of World Wide Rail Sites: *www.ribbonrail.com/nmra/*

Railroad Webring: *webring.rrdepot.com*

RailServe: *www.railserve.com*

Railway Technology: *www.railway-technology.com*

TFM Mexico: *www.gtfm.com.mx*

TrainWeb: *www.trainweb.com*

Transit Maps: *www.nycsubway.org/transitmaps/*

UK Railways on the Net: *www.rail.co.uk*

The Webville & Hypertext Railroad Company's Interchange Yard: *www.spikesys.com/interchg.html/*

Railway Systems

Here are sites operated by (or in behalf of) some of the world's more important passenger rail systems:

Alaska Railroad: *www.akrr.com*

Amtrak: *www.amtrak.com*

Amtrak Unlimited (an unofficial but useful information site): *www.amtraktrains.com*

BC Rail: *www.bcrail.com/bcr*

BritRail: *www.britrail.com*

Japan National Tourist Information San Francisco Office: *www.sfjnto.org*

Railtrack: *www.railtrack.co.uk*

VIA Rail Canada: *www.viarail.ca*

Late-Breaking News

Two radical new Web sites—of considerable importance to both consumers and the industry—were proposed just as I was completing my draft of this book:

- *Orbitz* (*www.orbitz.com*) is planned as an outlet for off-price airline tickets. It's fundamentally different from existing sites such as Expedia and Travelocity in that it will be jointly owned by several major airlines and that supposedly it will offer discount deals that the airlines will not offer anywhere else.

- *HotWire* (*www.hotwire.com*) is another airline-based venue for selling off airline seats that are still available at the last minute.

Because both sites involve joint ownership by airlines that are supposed to be competitors, the proposals have raised significant antitrust questions. I can't even begin to predict how the various regulatory agencies will ultimately view these sites. If they are approved in anything like their present forms, however, both could become extremely significant sites within a year or so. Stay tuned.

Index

H

H$_2$O, 127
half-price programs
  accommodations, sites, 216
  hotels and, 100
health, emergencies, 238
help sites, 242
Hertz, 165
hidden extras, 180
Hilton, senior club, 89
hitching flights, 79
Holiday Inn Express, 105
Holland America, 118
HomeExchange.com, 108
home exchanges. *See also*
  accommodations
  agency sites, 208
Homeric Tours, 146
Hong Kong, 23
Hooptown, USA, the Basketball Hall of
  Fame, 24
host families, 109
Hostelling International, 111
hostels, 111, 211
Hotel Reservations Network (HRN), 98
hotel-car vacation packages. *See*
  vacation packages, hotel-car
hotels. *See also* accommodations
  AARP and, 89
  agencies, sites, 211
  airfares and, vs. vacation
    packages, 134
  airline tie-ins and, 102
  bargain-hunting, problems, 112
  brokers, 95, 97
  chains, sites, 213
  cities/resort areas and, 94
  corporate rates and, 91
  discount booking agencies and, 95
  discount prices and, 10
  discounters, 87
  discounting systems, 94
  Entertainment rate and, 100
  First Class and, 90
  frequent stay programs and, 102
  half-price programs and, 100
  Internet access and, 176

hotels (*continued*)
  long-distance calls and, 175
  packages, 93
  peak/off-peak prices, 103
  per-person pricing, 112
  prices, comparing, 90
  promotions, 91
  rating systems, 90
  ratings, standards, 112
  reverse auctions and, 99–100
  room rates, 90, 93–94, 99
  sales, 90
  senior discounts, 89
  sites, 90, 215
  wholesalers, 97
Houseboating Page, 128
houses. *See also* vacation rentals
  retreat, 111

I

I want sites, 124
icruise, 122
independent sites, 12
information
  gaps, online travel and, 106
  overload, 201
  sites, 8
insurance
  medical, 171
  rental cars and, 170
  travel, 170–71
  travel, sites, 241
  trip-cancellation, 108, 171
  trip-interruption, 56
international
  calling, 175–76
  car rentals, 167
  driving, 168–69
  Internet access, 176
  security, travel and, 188
  travel, CDW/LDW and, 177
  travel, cellular phones and, 177
  travel, vacation rentals, 107
International Association of Air Travel
  Couriers, 79
International Currency Express, 6
International Driving Permits, 168

R

S

safety, 188, 220
safety nets, 149
sailing ships, sites, 225
San Francisco, 16
Saturday-night-stay restrictions, 40, 62, 63
save, as deceptive description, 182
scam artists, 1
scams, 180, 187
scenic railroads, Internet and, 157
schedules, rail, 162
search engines, 11
searches, narrowing, 20
seat maps, airlines, 83
security, international, 188
senior discounts, 89, 163–64
Senior HHonors, 89
senior travelers
    car rentals and, 168
    discounts, for European travel, 163
    Medicare and, 171
    senior ID, Internet and, 163
    vacation packages, sites, 245
Servas, 109
services
    medical, sites, 239
    travel (see travel services)
Ship Stats, 119
ships, cruise, 116–18
Shoestring Travel, 60
shop-your-request sites, 62
shopping online, charge card protections, 189
shore excursions, 129
Short Let Company, 110
short trips, 62
short-notice travel, 69
Shuttle by United, 51
Siberia, 23
sightseeing
    barges and, 126
    cruises and, 114, 129
    vacation packages and, 134
Singapore Airlines, RTW and, 77
single-supplier sites, 6

singles
    cruises and, 121
    vacation packages, sites, 248
sites, 245. See also Web sites
    accommodations, 205
    activities, 226
    agencies (see agency sites)
    air travel, 216, 220
    airlines (see airline sites)
    attractions, 24
    auctions, 123, 207
    B&Bs, 105–6
    baggage delivery, 216
    banking, 240
    barge and boat agencies, 222, 224
    B&Bs, 207
    bus travel, 250
    camping, 210
    car rental, 250–51
    charge cards, 240
    cities, 16–17
    classifying, 1
    commercial attractions, 227
    consolidators (see consolidator sites)
    consumer, 9
    courier/hitch agencies, 220
    cruise 118–19, 222–25
    cultural activities, 226
    currency exchange, 240
    destinations (see destination sites)
    driving support, 250
    dude ranches, 211
    event, 237
    financial, 240
    freighter, 124
    frequent flyer, 81, 217
    gateway (see gateway sites)
    government, 8
    government, travel support, 243
    gripe, 242
    guidebook, cruises and, 117
    half-price programs, 216
    home exchange agencies, 208
    hostels, 211
    hotels, 90, 209
    hotel agencies, 211
    I want, 124
    information, 8
    low-fare airlines, 53–54, 216, 219

The manuscript for this book was prepared using Microsoft Word 2000. Pages were composed by Online Training Solutions, Inc. (OTSI) using Adobe PageMaker 6.52 for Windows, with text in Stone Serif and display type in Univers. Composed pages were delivered to the printer as electronic prepress files.

Cover Graphic Designer

Patrick Lanfear

Production Artist

Tom Draper Design

Interior Designer

James D. Kramer

Interior Artist

Rob Nance

OTSI Editorial Team

Joyce Cox
Nancy Depper
Gabrielle Nonast
Joan Preppernau

OTSI Production Team

R.J. Cadranell
Leslie Eliel

Contact OTSI at:

E-mail: joanp@otsiweb.com
Web site: *www.otsiweb.com*

Proof of Purchase

Do not send this card with your registration.
Use this card as proof of purchase if participating in a promotion or
rebate offer on *Online Travel*. Card must be used in conjunction with
other proof(s) of payment such as your dated sales receipt—see offer details.

Online Travel

WHERE DID YOU PURCHASE THIS PRODUCT?

CUSTOMER NAME

Microsoft®
mspress.microsoft.com

Microsoft Press, PO Box 97017, Redmond, WA 98073-9830

OWNER REGISTRATION CARD

Register Today!

0-7356-0111-6

Return the bottom portion of this card to register today.

Online Travel

FIRST NAME   MIDDLE INITIAL   LAST NAME

INSTITUTION OR COMPANY NAME

ADDRESS

CITY   STATE   ZIP

(   )

E-MAIL ADDRESS   PHONE NUMBER

U.S. and Canada addresses only. Fill in information above and mail postage-free.
Please mail only the bottom half of this page.

For information about Microsoft Press®
products, visit our Web site at
mspress.microsoft.com

Microsoft®